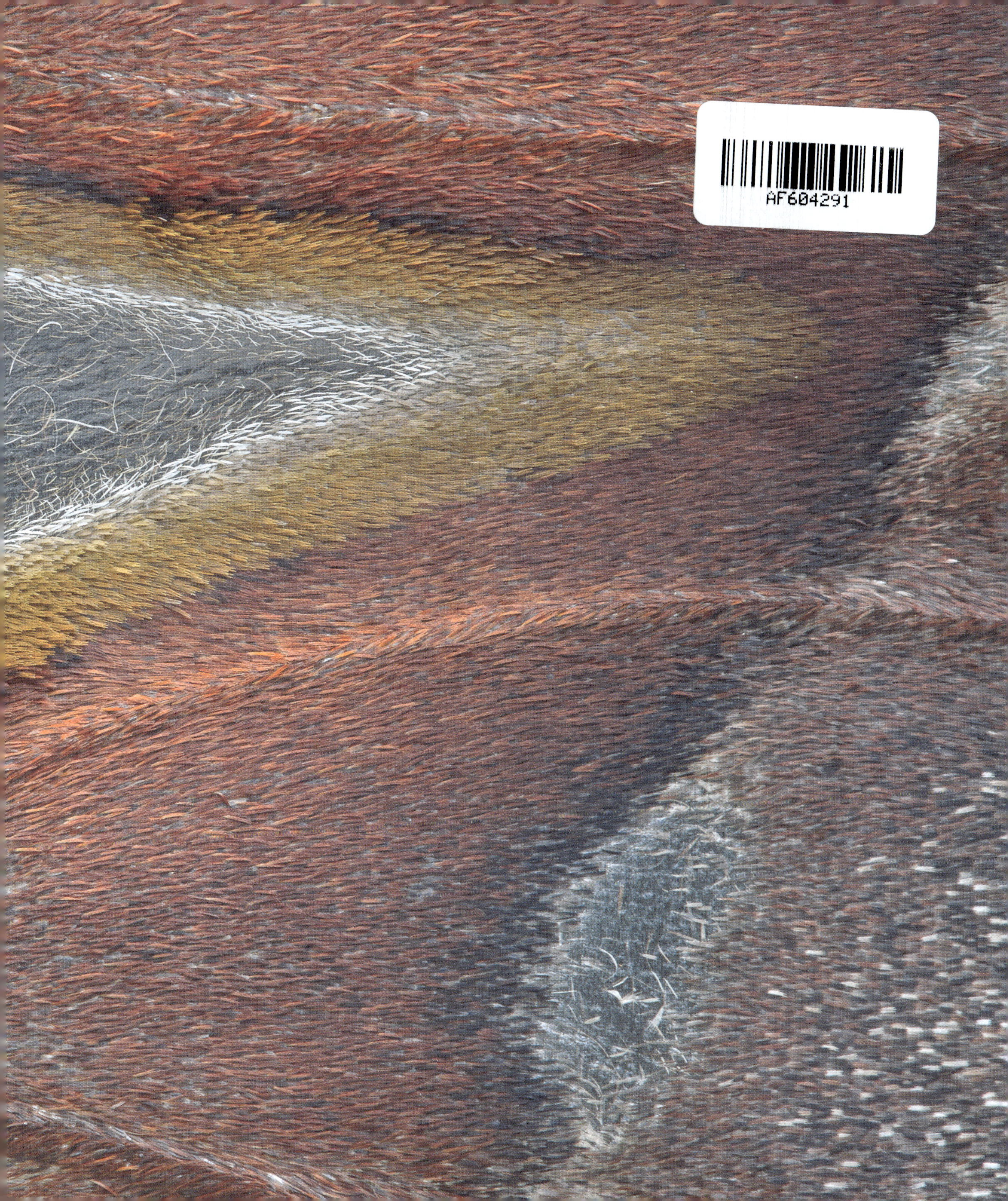

Small Wonders

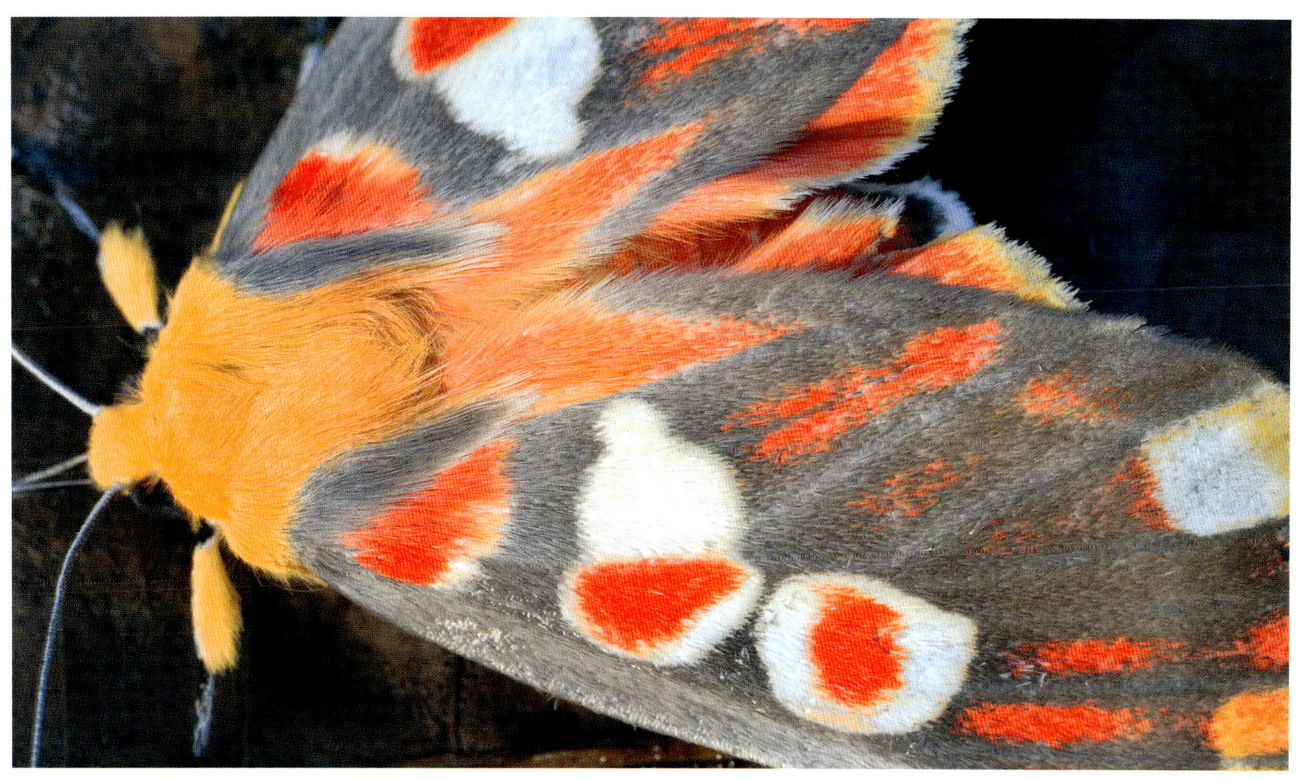

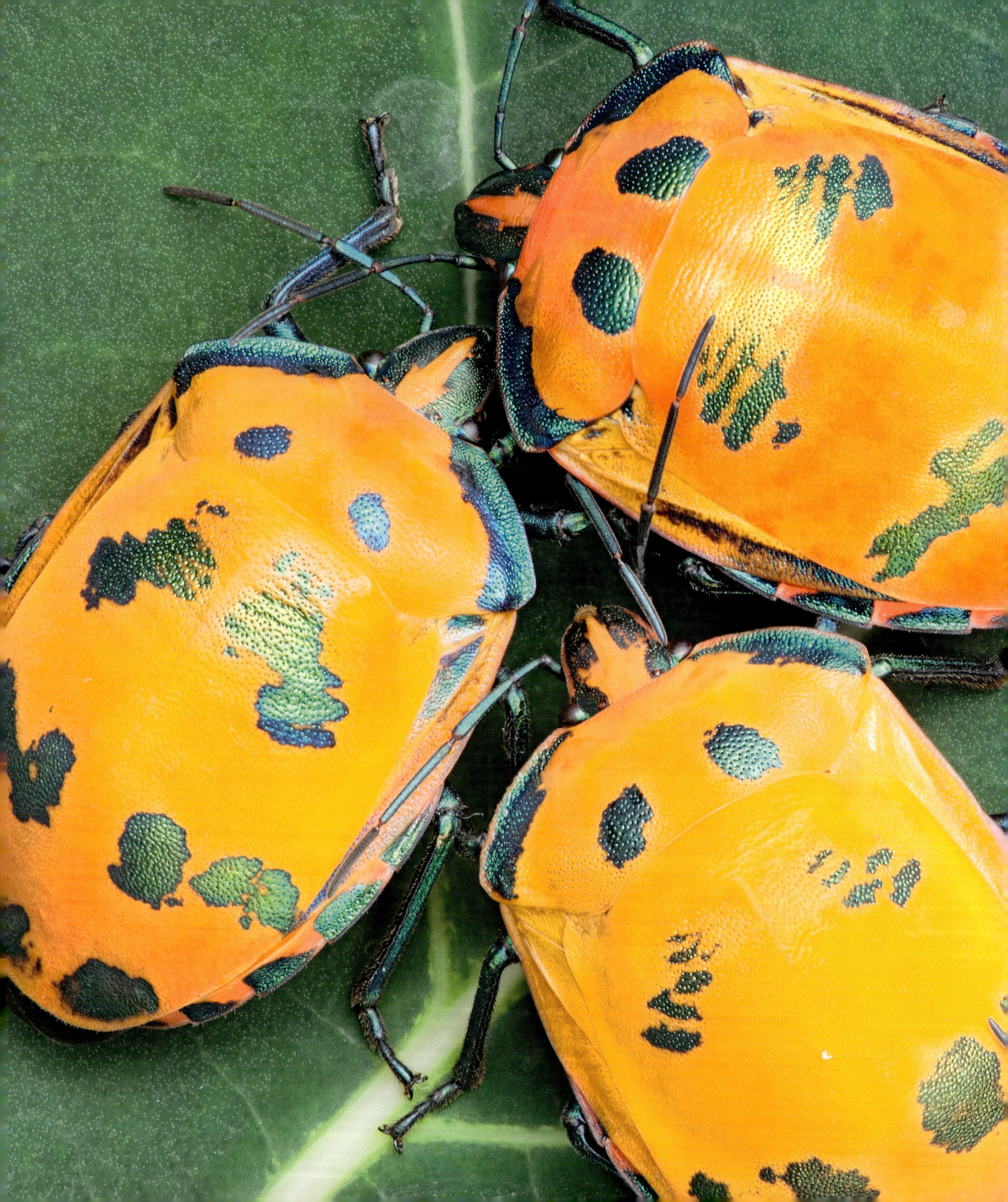

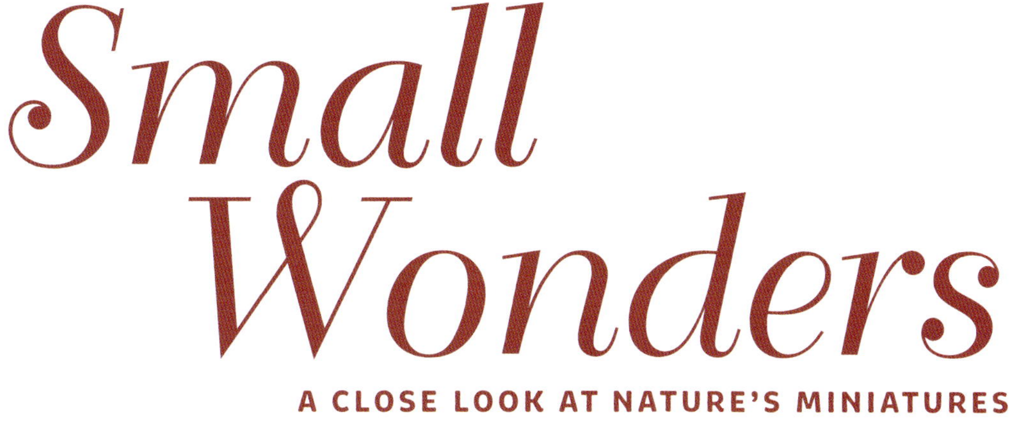

Small Wonders

A CLOSE LOOK AT NATURE'S MINIATURES

STANLEY *and* KAISA BREEDEN

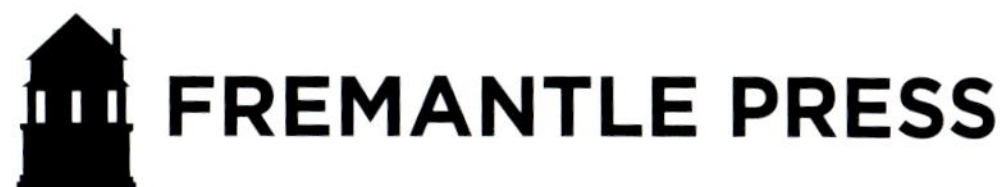

Endpapers

The clear window in the forewing of a male Hercules Moth, *Coscinocera hercules*, the largest moth in the world (see also pages 10–11).

Half-title

The rarely seen Redspot Hypsidia moth, *Hypsidia erythropsalis*, hides its brilliance in the green vastness of the rainforests of northeastern Australia.

Frontispiece

Harlequin Bugs, *Tectocoris diophthalmus*, cluster together on the upper sides of leaves. Their bright colours are a warning to predators that they taste bad and are poisonous.

Opposite

Common Jezebel, *Delias nigrina*. In Old Testament times the Phoenician princess Jezebel (also spelled Jezabel) greatly annoyed the prophet Elijah with her forthrightness. In seventeenth-century England the Puritans condemned makeup for its association with the biblical Jezebel. Her name came to stand for a bold and shameless woman. But how did she become associated with a group of beautiful butterflies? We like to think that the insects' strokes of colour resemble her makeup.

To give an idea of the scale of the miniatures, subjects marked with this dinkus ☙ are shown life-size on pages 110–111.

First published 2014 by
FREMANTLE PRESS
25 Quarry Street, Fremantle 6160
(PO Box 158, North Fremantle 6159)
Western Australia
www.fremantlepress.com.au

Printed by Everbest Printing Company, China.
Colour management by Kaisa Breeden.

National Library of Australia
Cataloguing-in-Publication entry

Author: Breeden, Stanley, 1938– author.
Title: Small wonders : a close look at nature's miniatures / Stanley and Kaisa Breeden.
ISBN: 9781925160147 (hardback)
Notes: Includes index.
Subjects: Animals–Size–Australia–Pictorial works.
Wildlife photography–Australia.
Nature photography–Australia.
Other Authors/Contributors: Breeden, Kaisa, author.
Dewey Number: 778.932

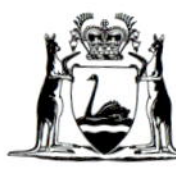

Government of **Western Australia**
Department of **Culture and the Arts**

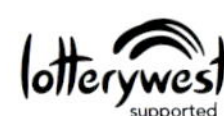

Fremantle Press is supported by the State Government through the Department of Culture and the Arts.

Acknowledgements

We are blessed to know many kind people who have gone above and beyond the call of friendship to thrash around in the bush looking for subjects for us to photograph – an extra hearty (and anonymous) soul even resorting to cavorting naked in a frog pond by the light of the moon brandishing a net. These include Kylie Freebody and Larry Crook and their intrepid staff at the Eacham Revegetation Unit, Helen McConnell, Cliff and Dawn Frith, Ashley Field, Bruce Gray, Margit Cianelli and our sharp-eyed daughters Maya and Tara.

Other friends have generously let us pester them for identifications of mysterious subjects – David Rentz, Buck Richardson, Geoff Thompson, Max Moulds and Kevin Thiele.

It has been terrific to work with all the wonderful team at Fremantle Press again, particularly our publisher, Jane Fraser, and our editor, Naama Amram.

Thanks everyone!

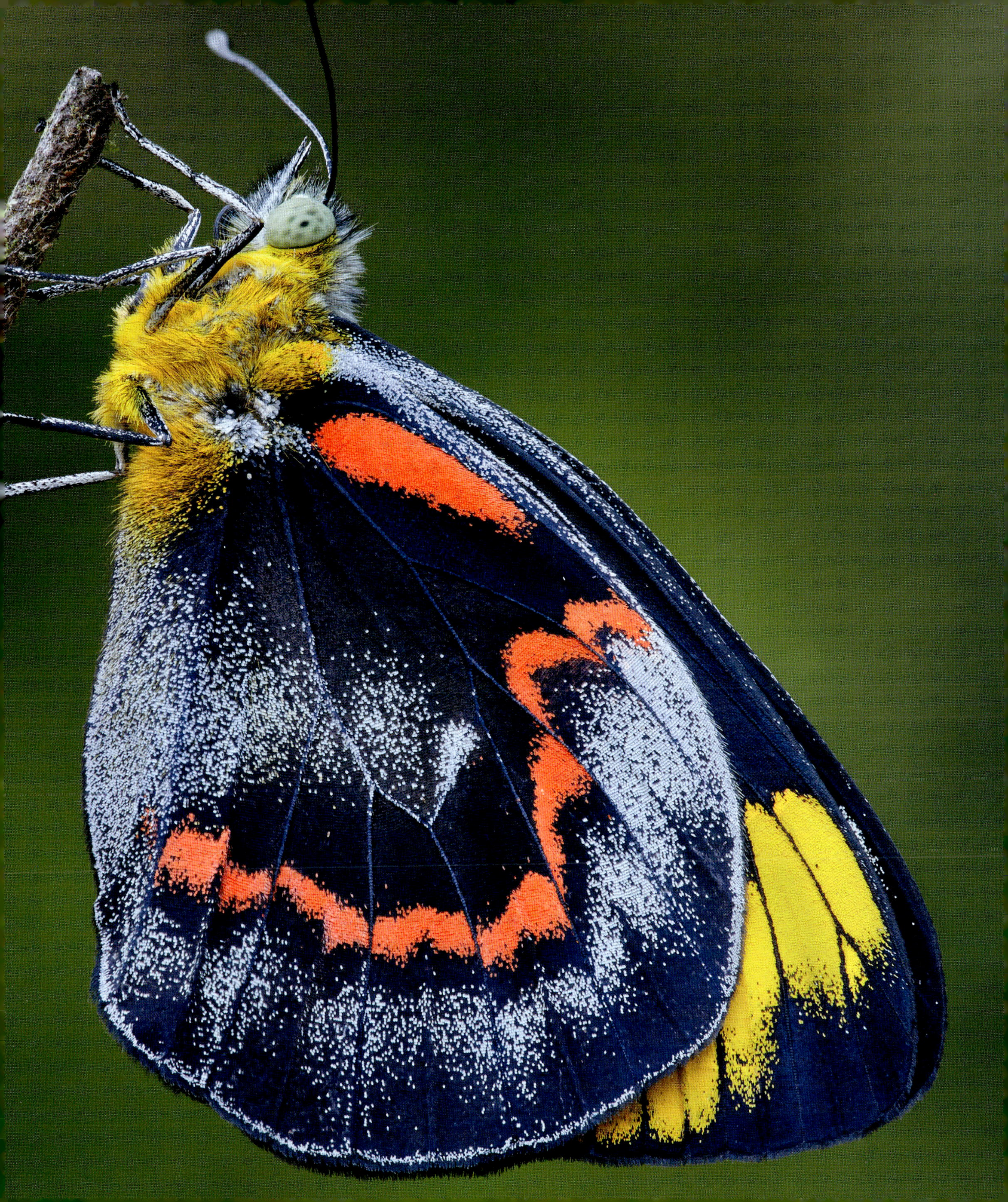

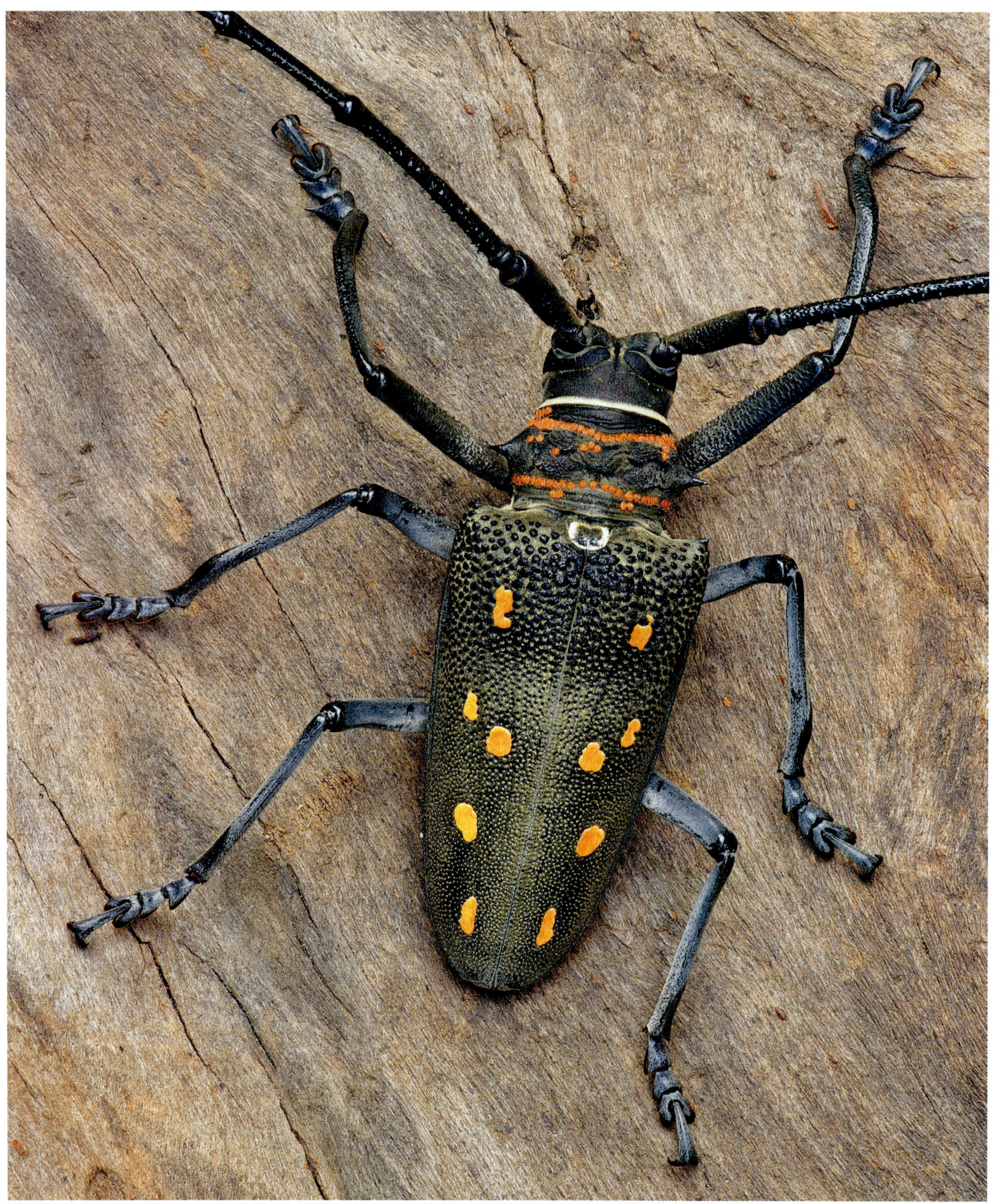

Opposite

The orange necklaces on this Fig Borer, *Batocera frenchii*, are made up of biting mites. This large (50 mm) beetle's larvae feed on the dead or decaying wood of fig trees for two or three years before pupating.

Below

Sometimes a scientific name has a charm all of its own. This small (33 mm) katydid has been named *Lichenagraecia cataphracta*, which means 'spiny lichen mimic'. So closely does it resemble lichen that it has only rarely been found. Only a dozen or so individuals have been recorded.

Following pages

This close-up of the back of a Giant Shield Bug, *Oncomeris flavicornis*, encapsulates the beauty and magnificence of nature's miniatures. The beauty is in the colours, patterns and textures. This photograph was taken by natural light, which illuminates with greater subtlety than artificial sources. A wash of sunlight coaxed iridescence from its wings. ☙

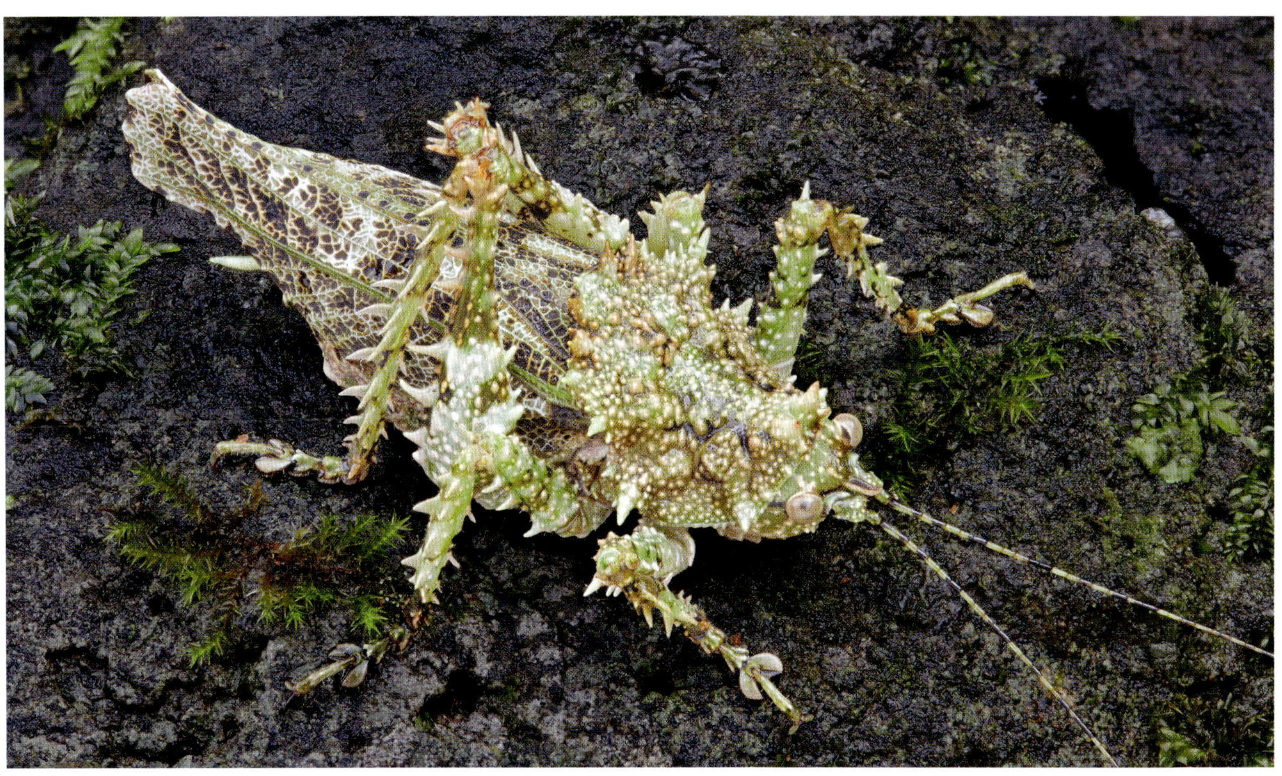

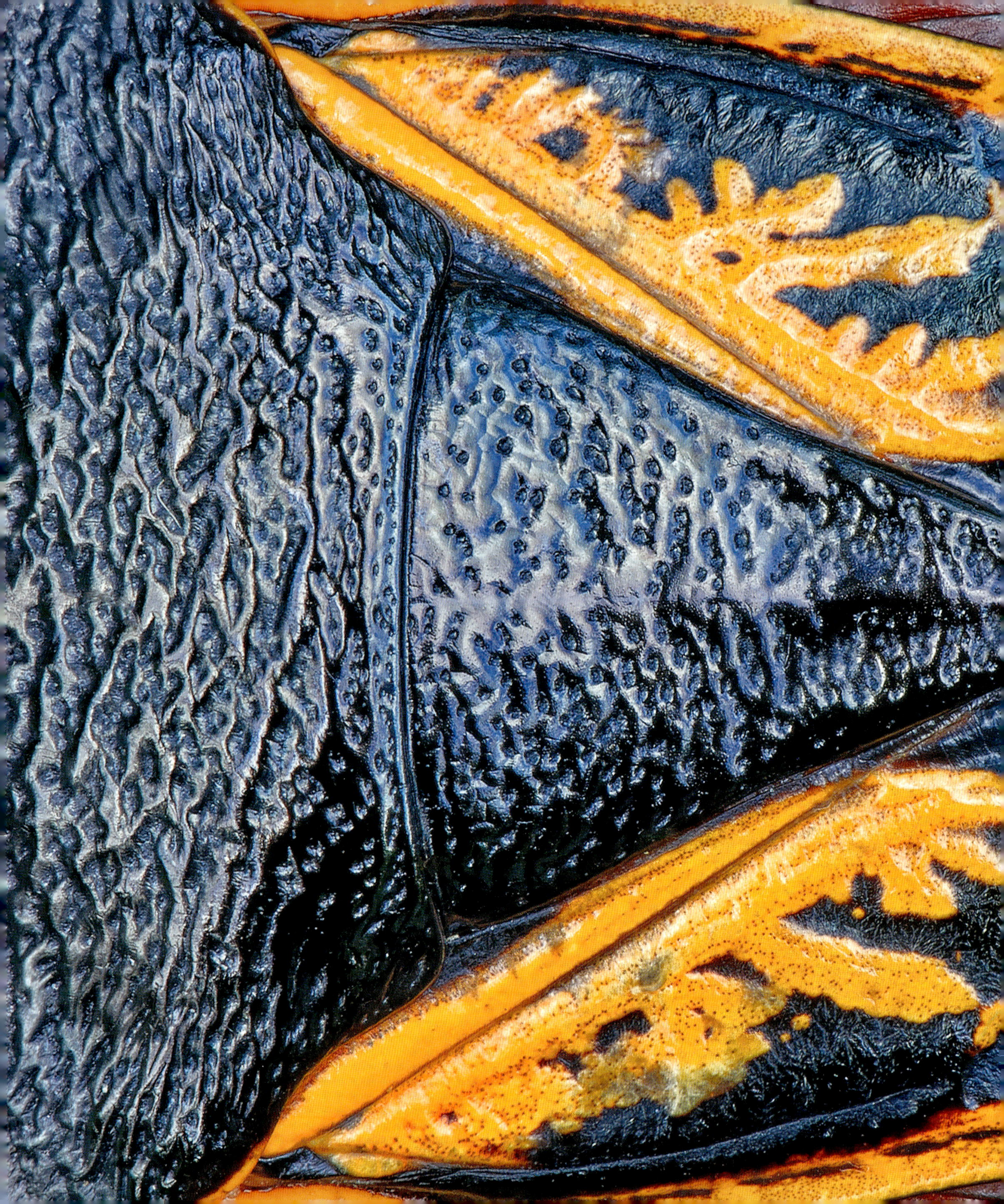

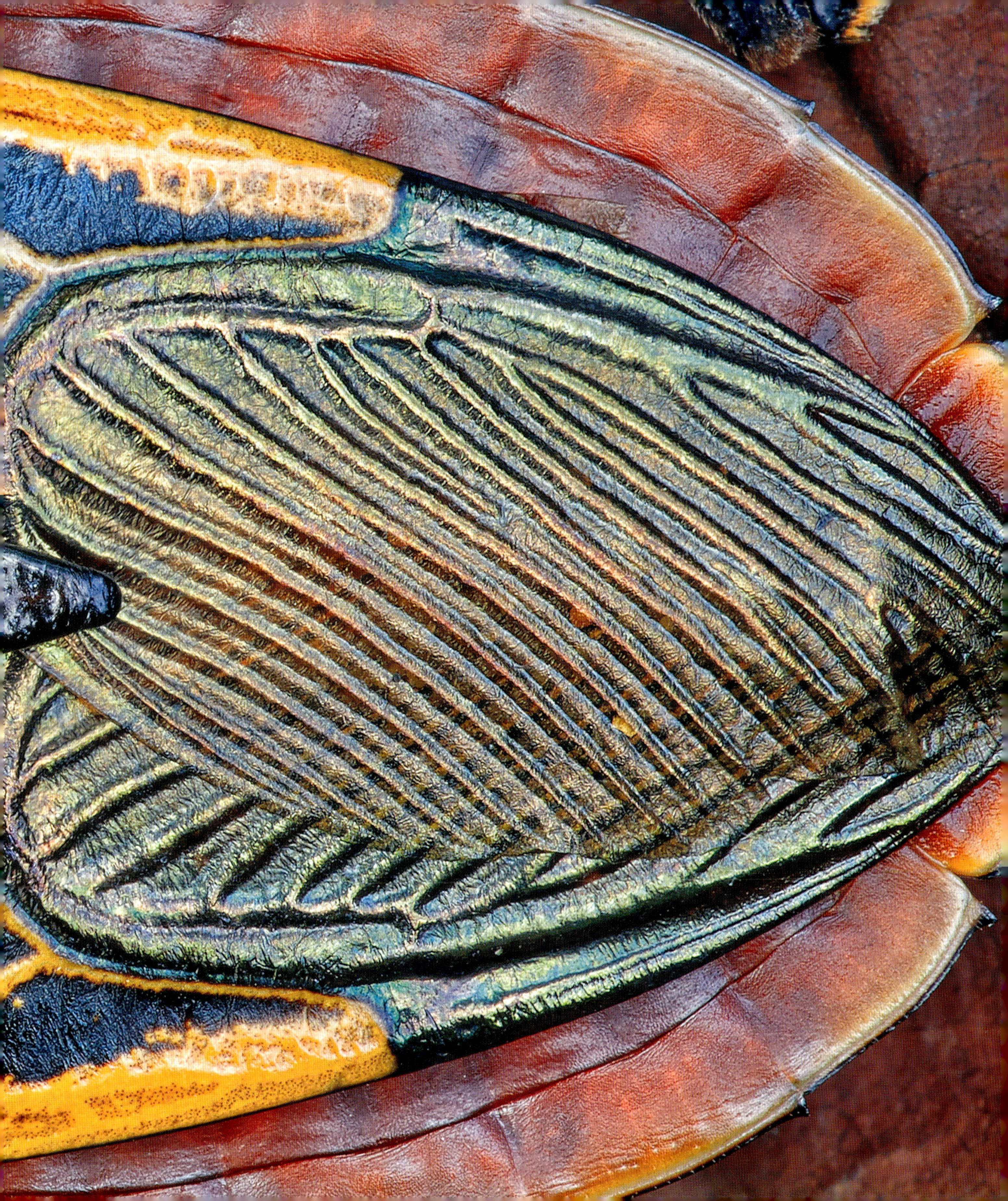

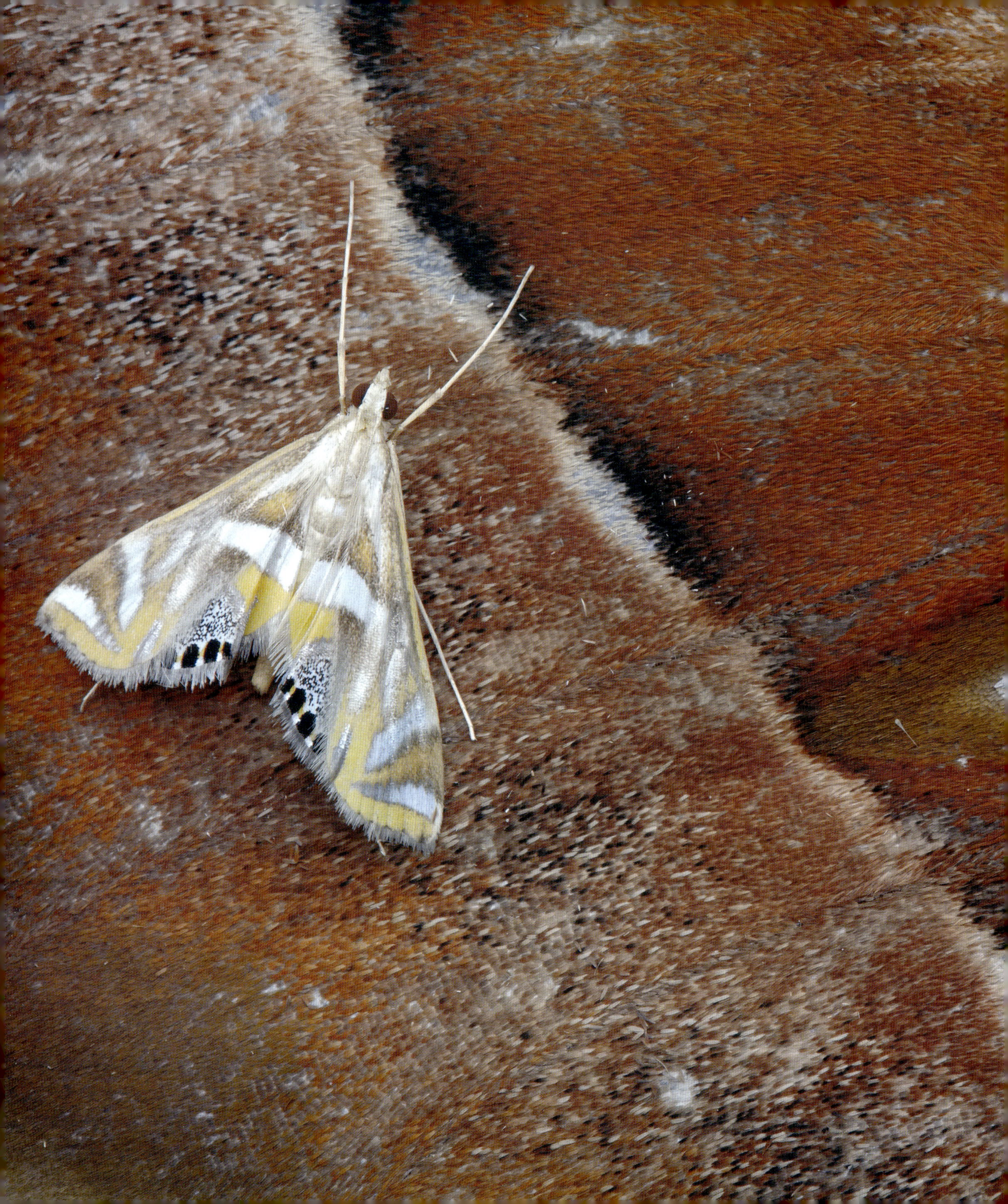

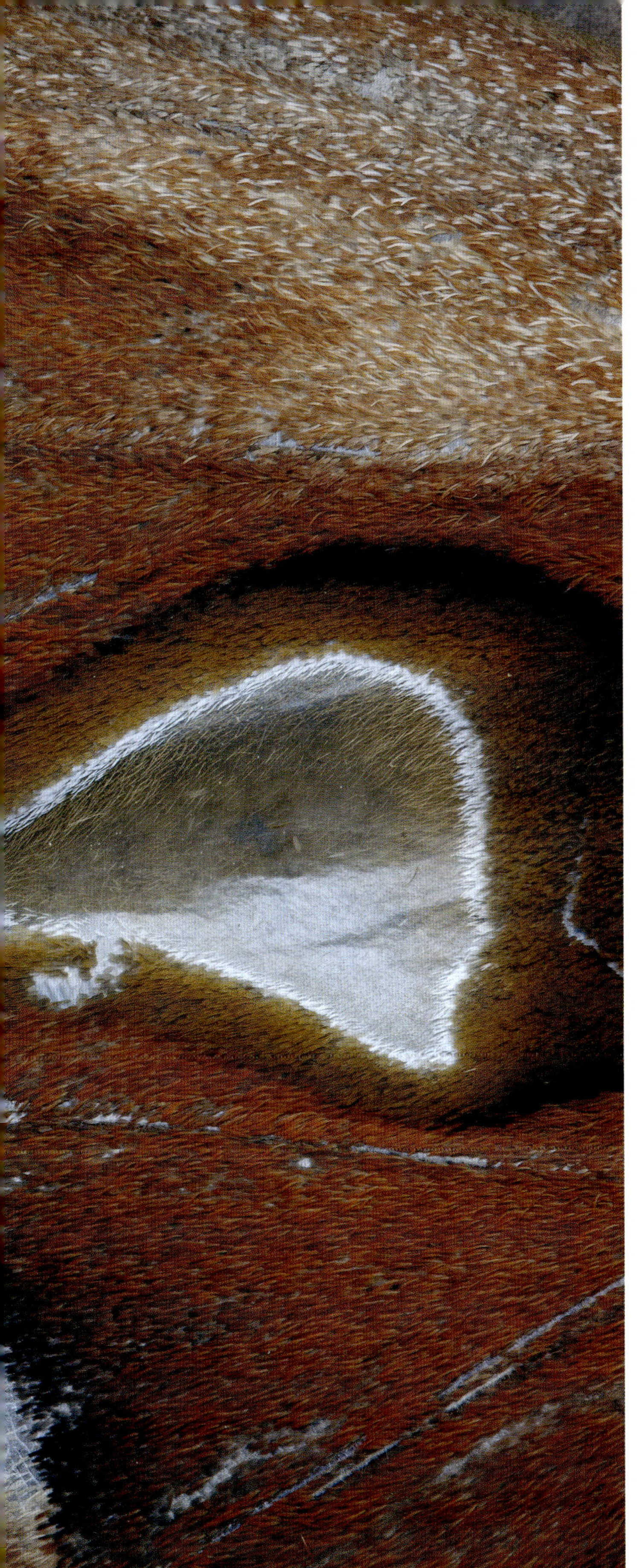

Left

This tiny moth, *Margarosticha australis*, measures 14 mm across. It has come to rest on the outspread wings of a male Hercules Moth, *Coscinocera hercules*. While there are a great many moths smaller than *Margarosticha*, there is none larger than the Hercules. It is the largest moth in the world. The female's wingspan can measure up to 270 mm.

Following page

The Cuckoo Wasp, *Stilbum cyanurum*, asleep. It is only 16 mm long. Moments after we took the last photograph, it lifted its head, wiped its eyes with its front feet and its wings with its hind feet, and flew off. Cuckoo Wasps were given their name because they lay their eggs in the nests of other wasps. ଓ

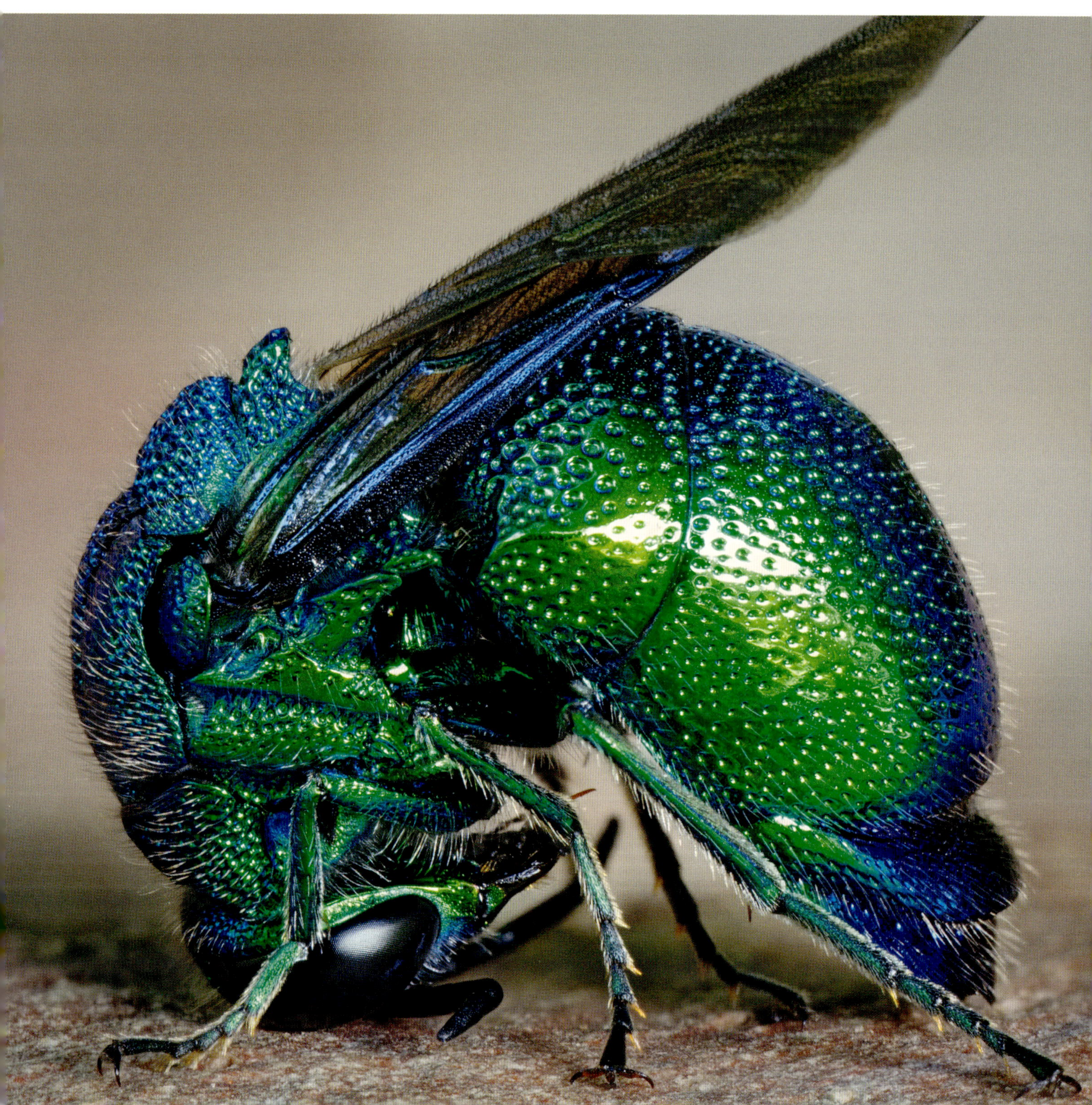

Introduction

When you enter an unspoilt piece of bush, you breathe deeply. The fresh air may be scented with the perfume of wildflowers and eucalyptus leaves. You take in the cries and songs of birds. Sunshine warms your skin and gives form to the trees and rock formations. Distant hills and plains have a blue haze. This harmonious whole gives you a feeling of wellbeing. You are in touch with the primordial world. Your source.

You could call the wide scene that soothes your spirit the First Kingdom. But wherever you might be, you are within two other kingdoms – the Middle Kingdom and the Micro Kingdom.

This book is a journey into the Middle Kingdom – the realm of nature's miniatures. When you look closely at tree trunks, clusters of flowers, among rocks – you soon become aware of a world inhabited by cicadas, beetles, spiders, dragonflies, small lizards, frogs and hordes of others. Among them you will see the faces of slightly larger animals – pink nose of a possum, eye of a gecko, scale-covered head of a python. For the purposes of this book all are miniatures. These are not beautiful objects for you to discover in a treasure hunt. They are alive. They leap, run, fly, dig, sing, climb, eat, mate, hunt, fight, sting. Many undergo profound changes of form during their lifetime through metamorphosis. Looking ever more closely you discover a whole new world of indescribable beauty – beauty of colours, shapes, patterns and textures.

Beyond this Middle Kingdom lies the Micro Kingdom, a world you cannot easily enter for the organisms that live there are too small for you to see. They are microscopic, and we will not enter the micro-world in this volume.

To get to know the inhabitants of the Middle Kingdom can be a bit of a fiddle. Often it is not wholly satisfactory. When you lean forward to get an intimate view of, say, a butterfly drinking nectar from a flower, the insect will fly away. If you've come prepared with a butterfly net, managed to catch one, fumbled your 10X magnifying glass out of your pocket and brought magnifier and butterfly right up to one eye while squinting with the other, you might be able to have a better look. At last you focus on a wing and marvel at the bright colours of overlapping scales that cover its surface, the dark compound eyes, the coiled tongue. You have glimpses and impressions of such beauty that it takes your breath away, but the lens has limited depth of field – only patches here and there are in sharp focus. Your field of view is limited. You can see a part of a wing but not the whole of it. Something steady and clear that shows the entire butterfly remains elusive. A certain fuzziness remains. The clarity seen at close quarters is limited. Until now.

Through high-end digital photography you can see the denizens of the Middle Kingdom with a clarity not before possible. You can contemplate the beauty and variety of nature's miniatures without fuzziness and see intriguing details you may never have suspected were there.

The most important quality that makes digital photography such a powerful instrument for looking closely into nature is clarity. This clarity is made up of several elements. Compared to the old, chemical photography, digital technology delivers greater tonal range, better definition, unparalleled colour fidelity and much reduced noise (grain in film). However, there is no button marked 'clarity' on even the most sophisticated camera, and the 'Clarity' tool in Photoshop can sacrifice important detail. It takes thoughtful processing to get the most out of your camera's files. When you do, truly luminous and authentic photographs are possible.

Another, non-technical, component of clarity is the light. We always take our photographs with natural light. It brings out all the fine nuances and subtleties of a subject's colour and shape – a quality of light difficult, if not impossible, to replicate in a studio. Natural light can make a picture sing.

All the above elements result in photographs similar to those taken on film, only much better. There is another that makes close-ups *different*, a leap forward in how we see and relate to nature. It is the ultimate factor that banishes fuzziness when looking closely into nature, and that is focus stacking. This technique, where we take a number of exposures at different focal points and then blend these into a single picture, allows for virtually unlimited depth of field. Shallow depth of field, where only a small slice of the subject is in sharp focus, was always a limiting factor. But not anymore. It is as if a veil has been lifted. A beetle or a frog now appears as if in three dimensions. Today digital pictures can be greatly enlarged without loss of detail giving an ever clearer view into nature.

Luminosity, 3D-effect, natural light, getting the most out of all the possibilities that digital photography offers – these amount to nothing less than a new vision of the natural world. Lizards look more scaly, snakes more sinuous. The frogginess of frogs leaps out at you. Butterflies are more elegant and moths more mysterious. The structures of the inhabitants of the Middle Kingdom – wings of cicadas, eyes of geckos, jaws of beetles – are revealed so clearly you can sense their purpose.

In some quarters digital photography is treated with great suspicion. There is a perception that if you take digital photographs you must use Photoshop, and if you use Photoshop you can alter, distort and falsify. And because you can, the cynics say, you will. The more out of the ordinary the photograph, the greater the suspicion. It is easy enough to intensify colour, to alter shapes and change backgrounds. But we have not. To the contrary. As well as clarity, our driving force is authenticity. Just as Photoshop and other software can falsify, it can authenticate. We have striven to get colours, even the most intense colours, just right. We use multiple focus stacking to clarify, never to falsify.

Opposite

The Long-tailed Pygmy Possum, *Cercartetus caudatus*, sips nectar and hunts insects among flowers in Australia's tropical rainforest.

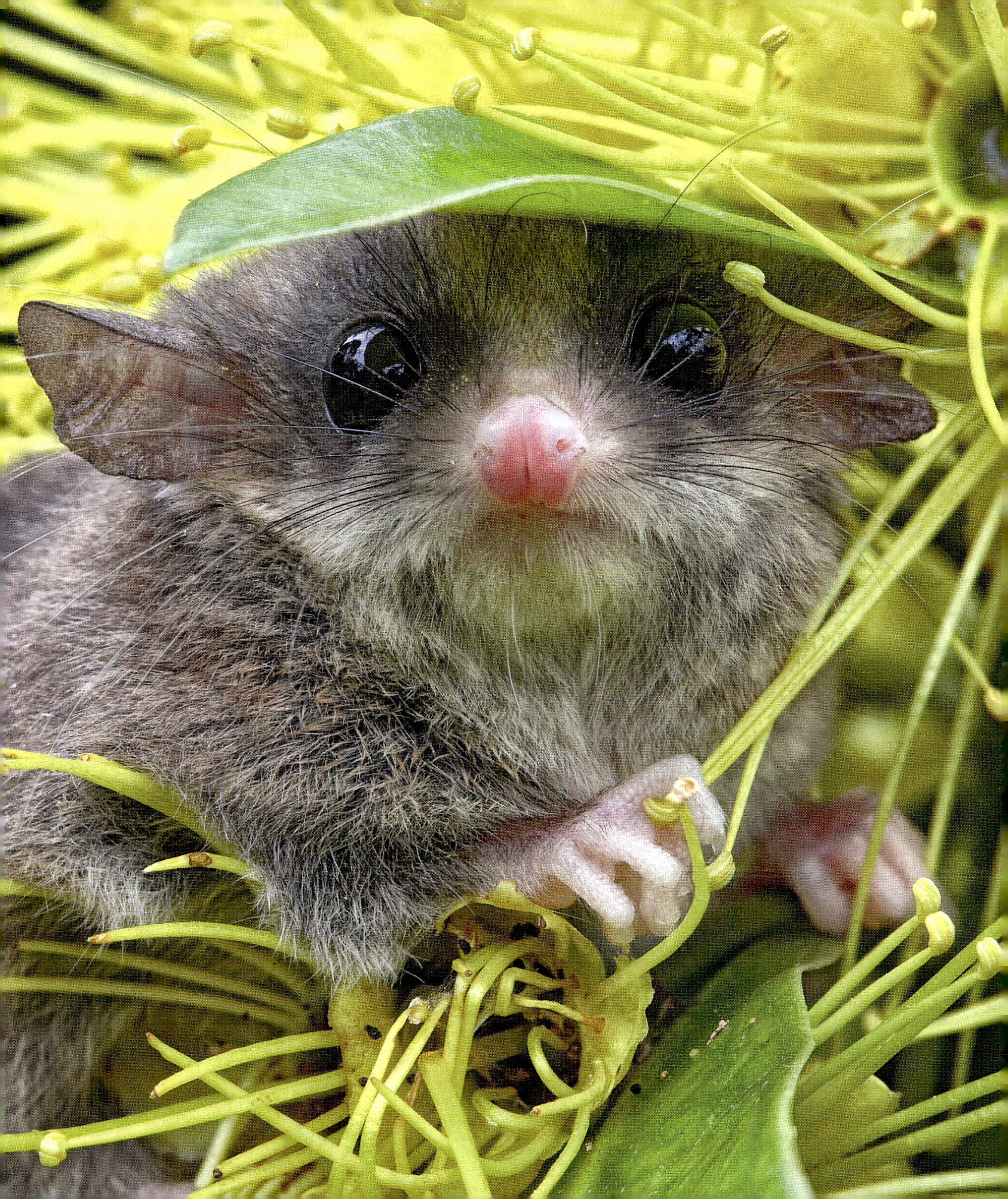

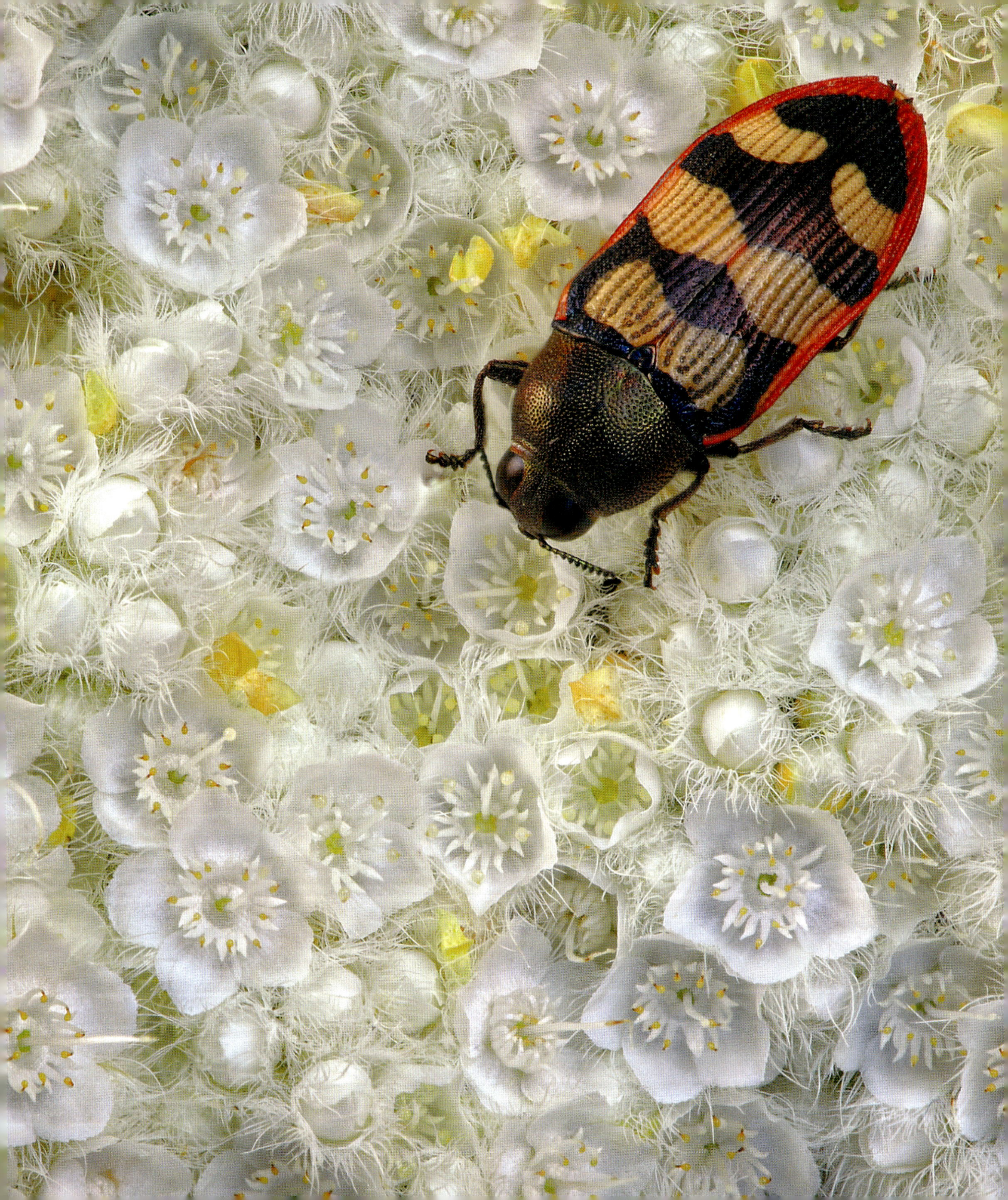

We have tried to give an impression of the vast variety of Australia's small animal life. Many of the photographs in this volume were taken in the tropical rainforest of northeast Queensland, including our backyard. Some of the animals we photographed here are found nowhere else and are quite rare. This includes the Lichen-mimicking Katydid (page 7). Others, such as the Tailed Emperor (page 36), are common right across the north and east. The Tawny Frogmouth (pages 28–29) is found in every corner of the continent, while the Pilbara Barking Gecko (pages 76–77) has so far only been found in the Hamersley Range of Western Australia. The Pine-cone Lizard (pages 58–59) is common right across the dry south.

In some ways this book is an invitation. An invitation to explore the Middle Kingdom and so to experience the sense of wonder summoned up by looking closely into nature. Just about every natural place on earth is brimming with miniatures – with beauty and enchantment that enrich our lives.

Focus stacking: capturing a contemplation

Focus stacking in the wild is almost cinematic, like many frames of video or film condensed into a single photograph. You see things that take time to observe, that cannot be captured with a single click of the shutter – a breeze moving a leaf, shifting light, a frog's throat pulsing, and a depth of focus as your eye would study a subject from the foreground to the background.

This records not just a moment but a duration of time – capturing a contemplation.

We all move so fast through our lives that we don't have time to stop and really look. But stopping to observe nature is stopping to look and think about our source. It is something we need, and something to learn from. It re-calibrates us and puts us in perspective with the natural world.

Opposite

The jewel beetle *Castiarina sagittaria* on the flowers of *Verticordia eriocephala*, a species of featherflower known as Lambswool in the wildflower country of Australia's southwest.

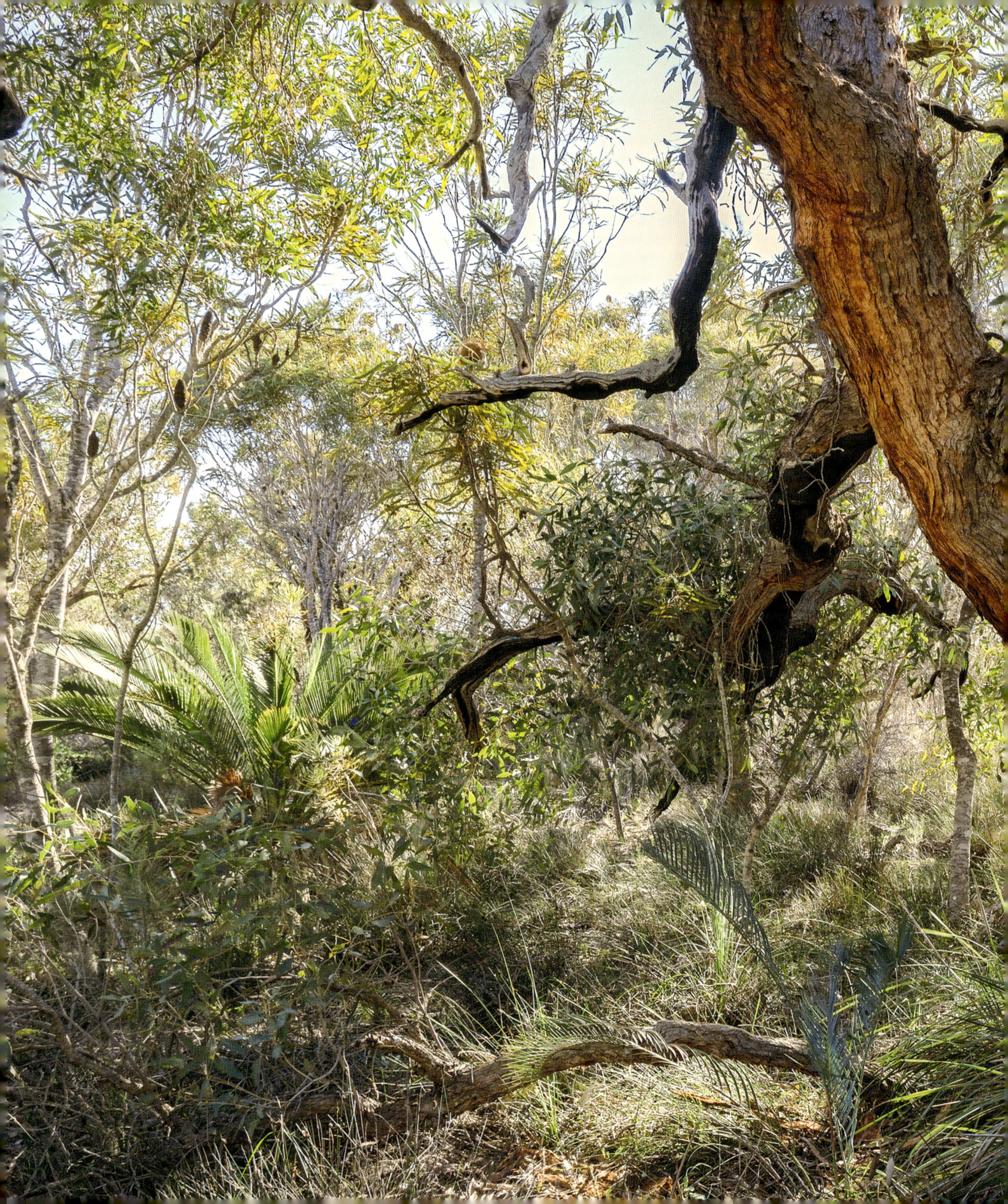

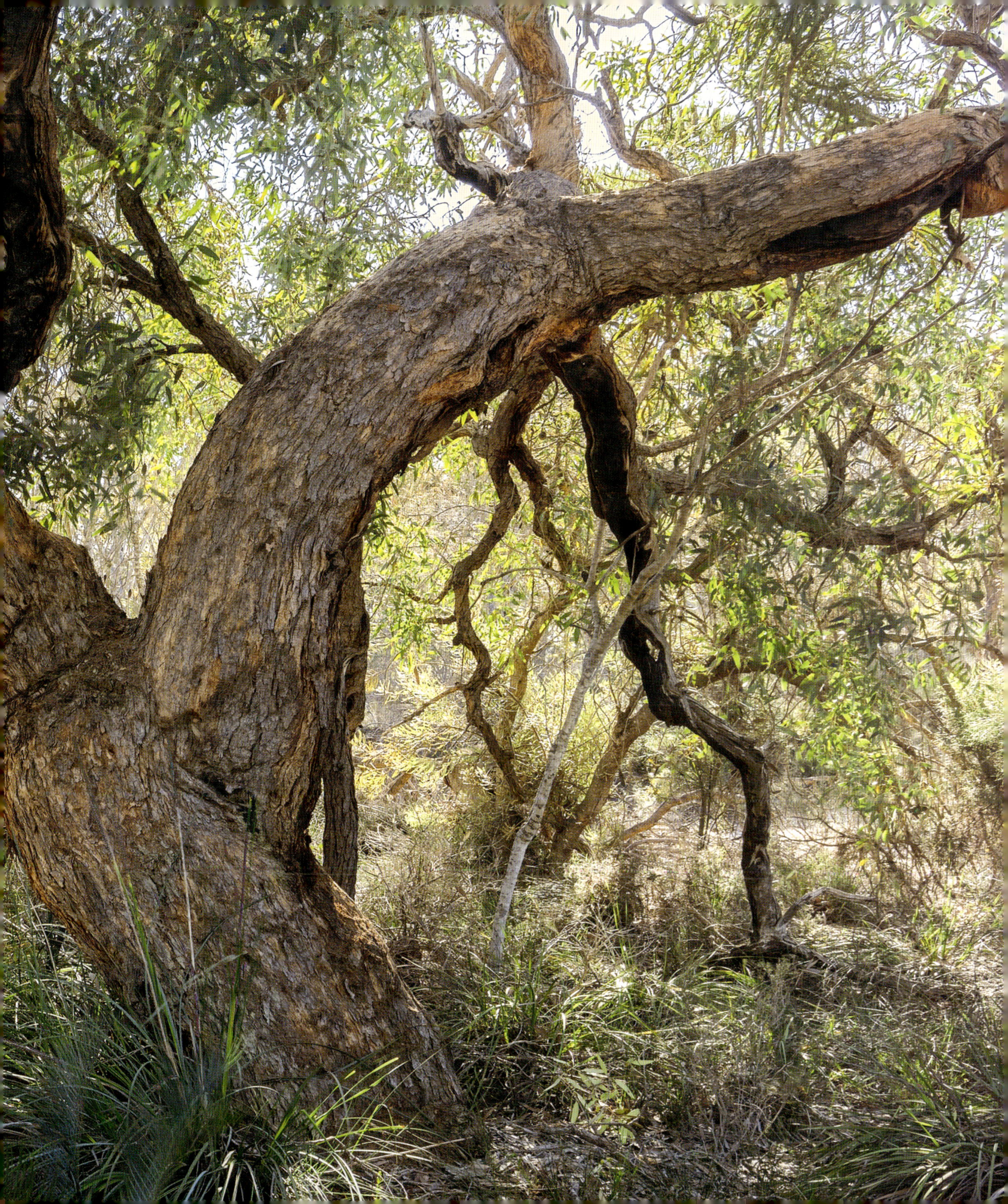

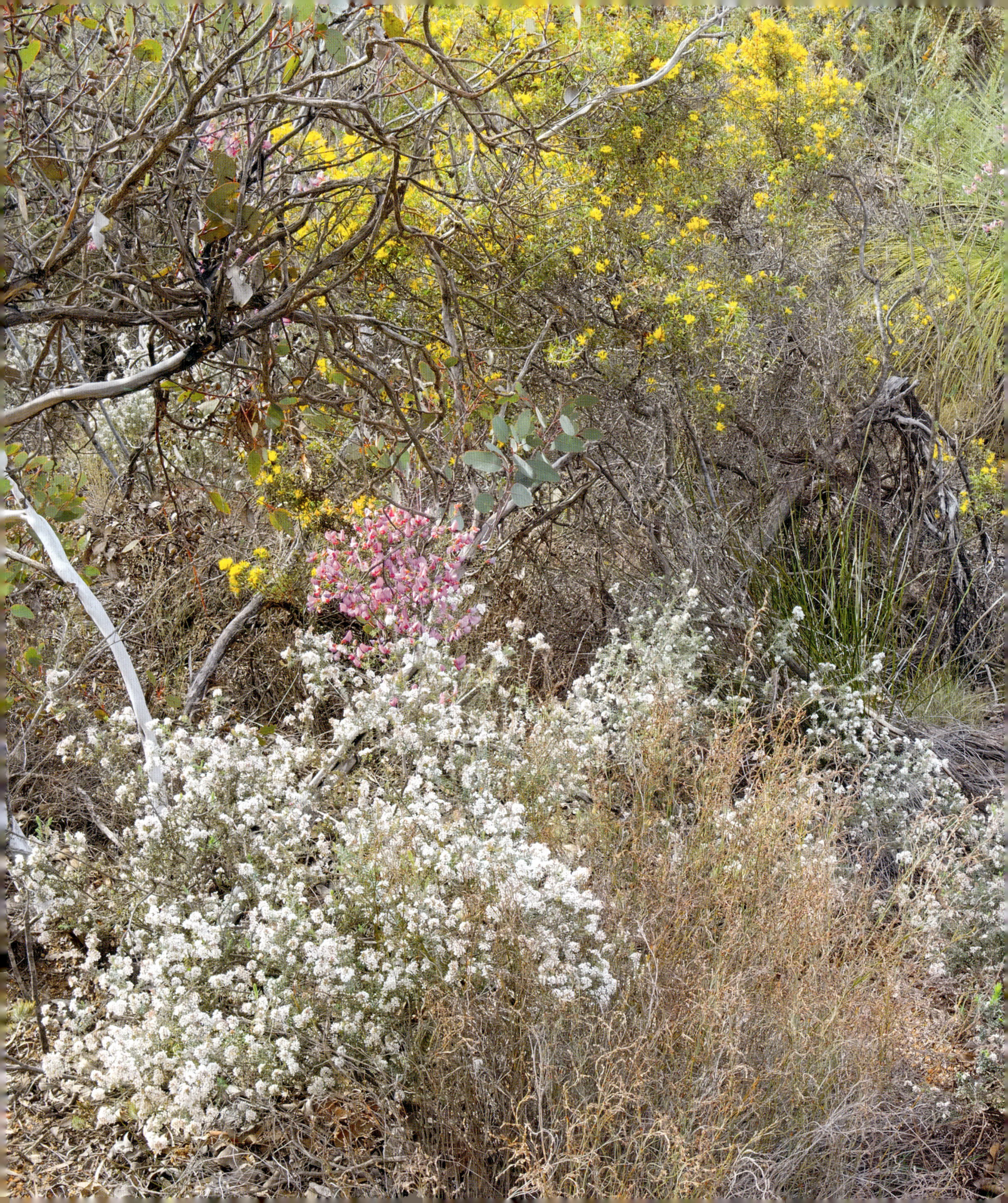

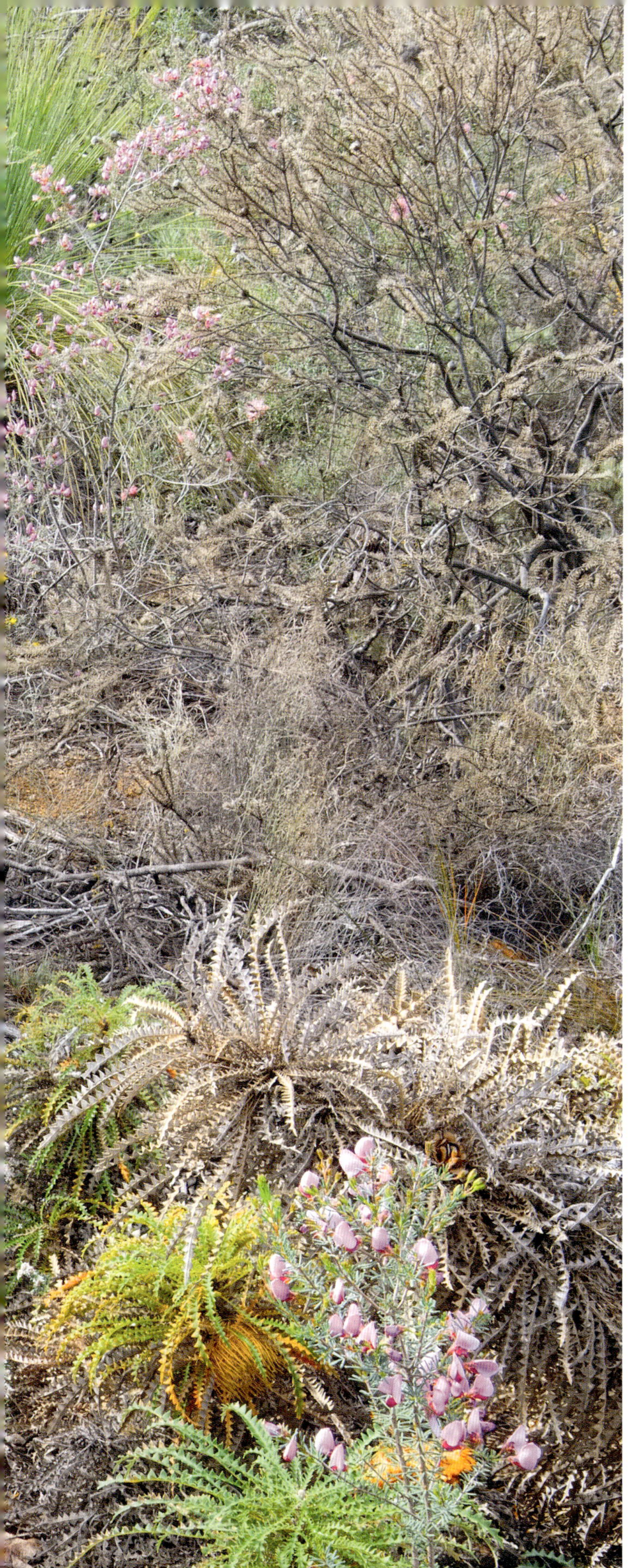

Preceding pages

A Coastal Blackbutt, *Eucalyptus todtiana*, in a banksia-eucalypt woodland in the continent's southwest corner. Like most natural habitats, it is brimming with exquisite miniatures. All you have to do to find them is look closer, and closer, and closer ...

Left

In spring the southwest's heathlands are transformed by wildflowers.

Following pages

By looking closely at flowers we enter the realm of the miniatures. Ants inspect the bud and flower of a Mottlecah, *Eucalyptus macrocarpa*, looking for nectar, pollen and other insects to eat.

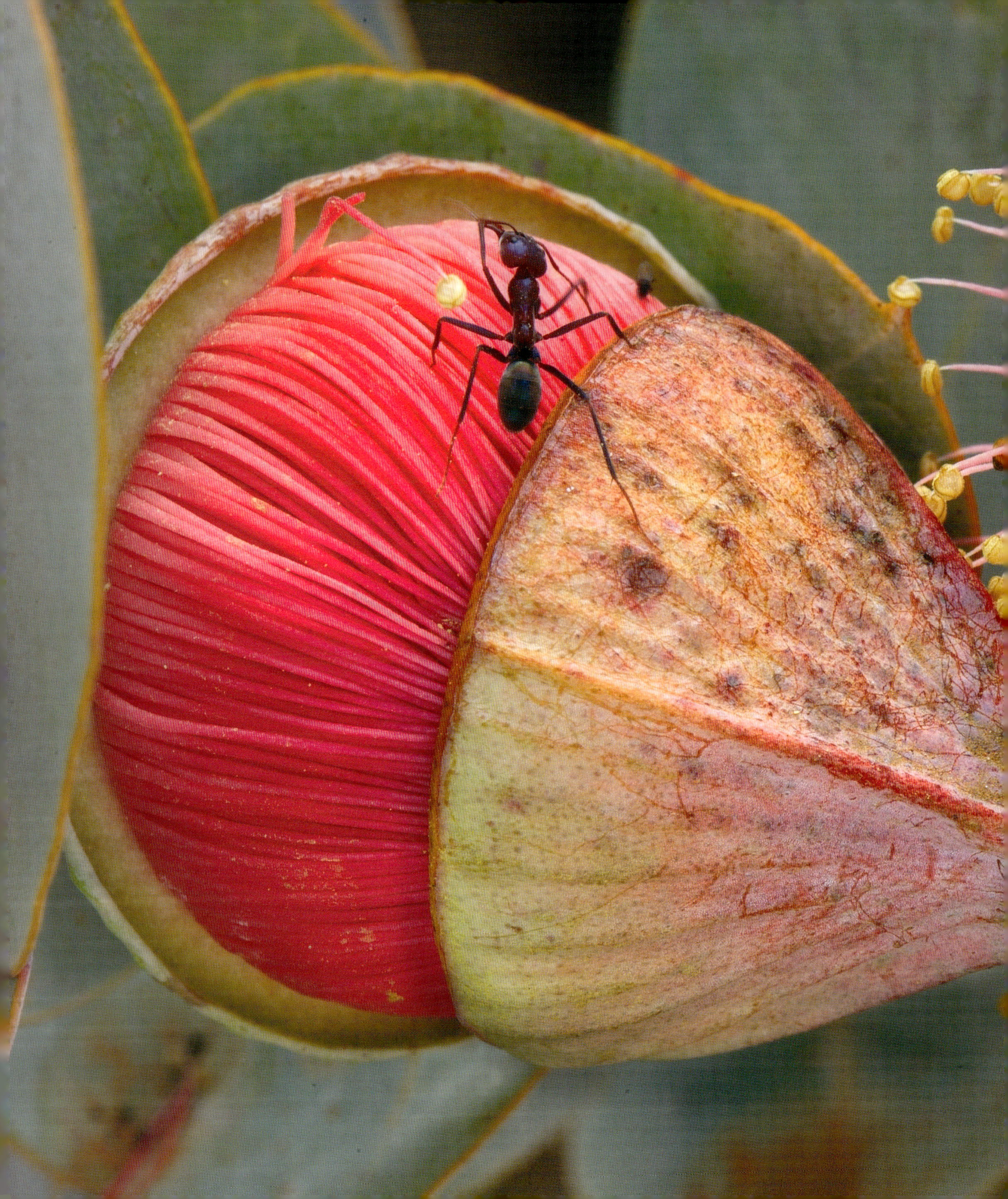

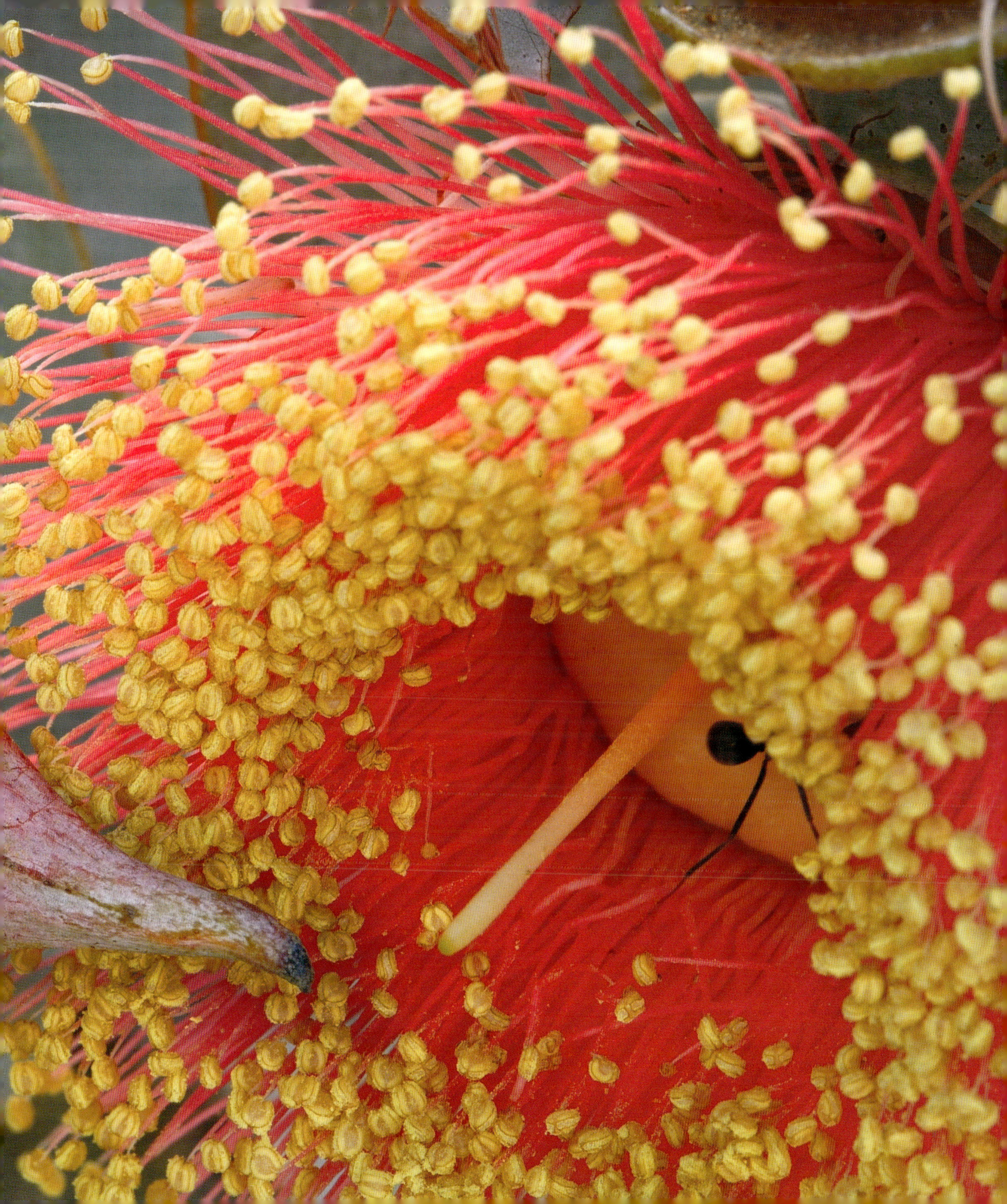

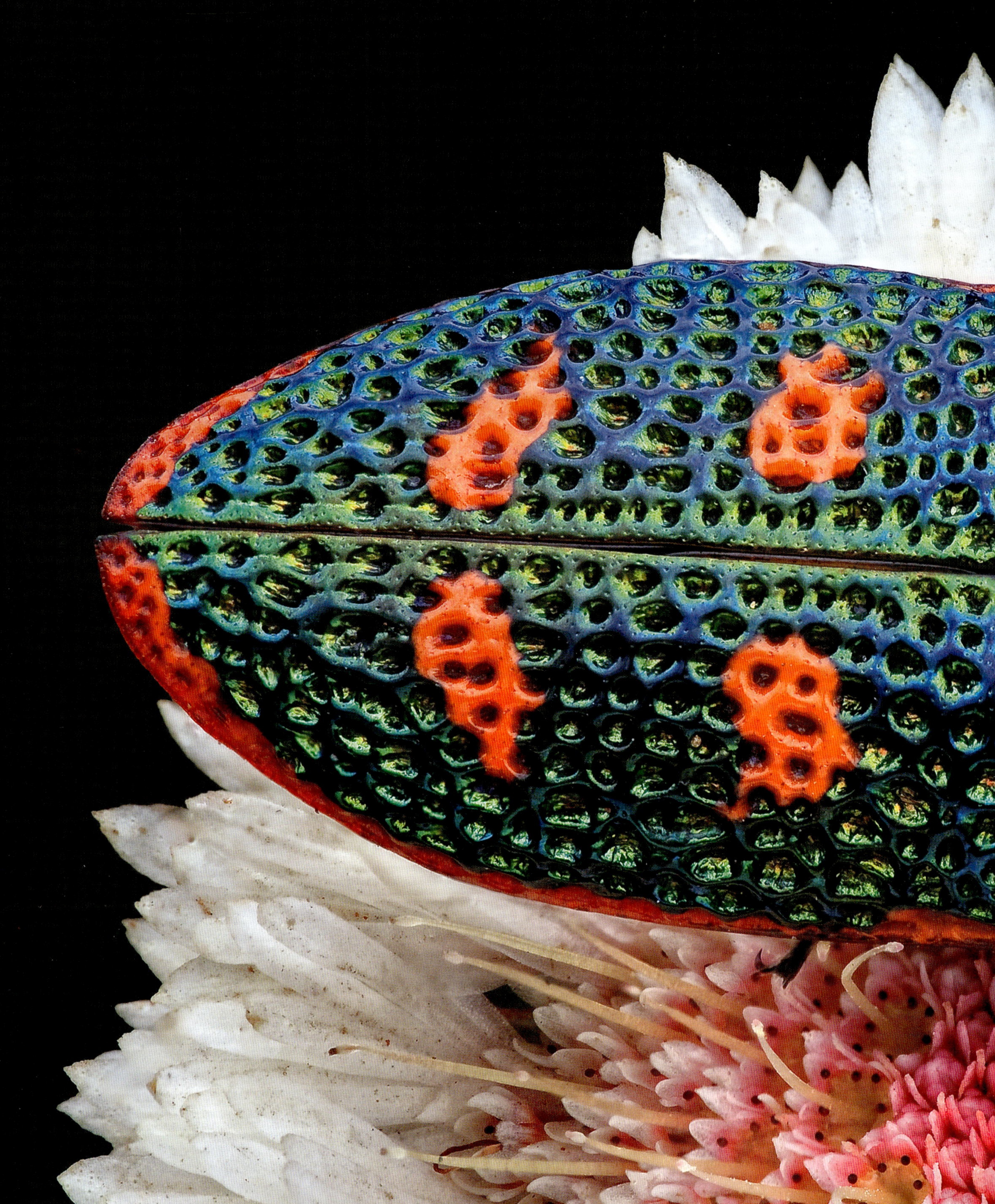

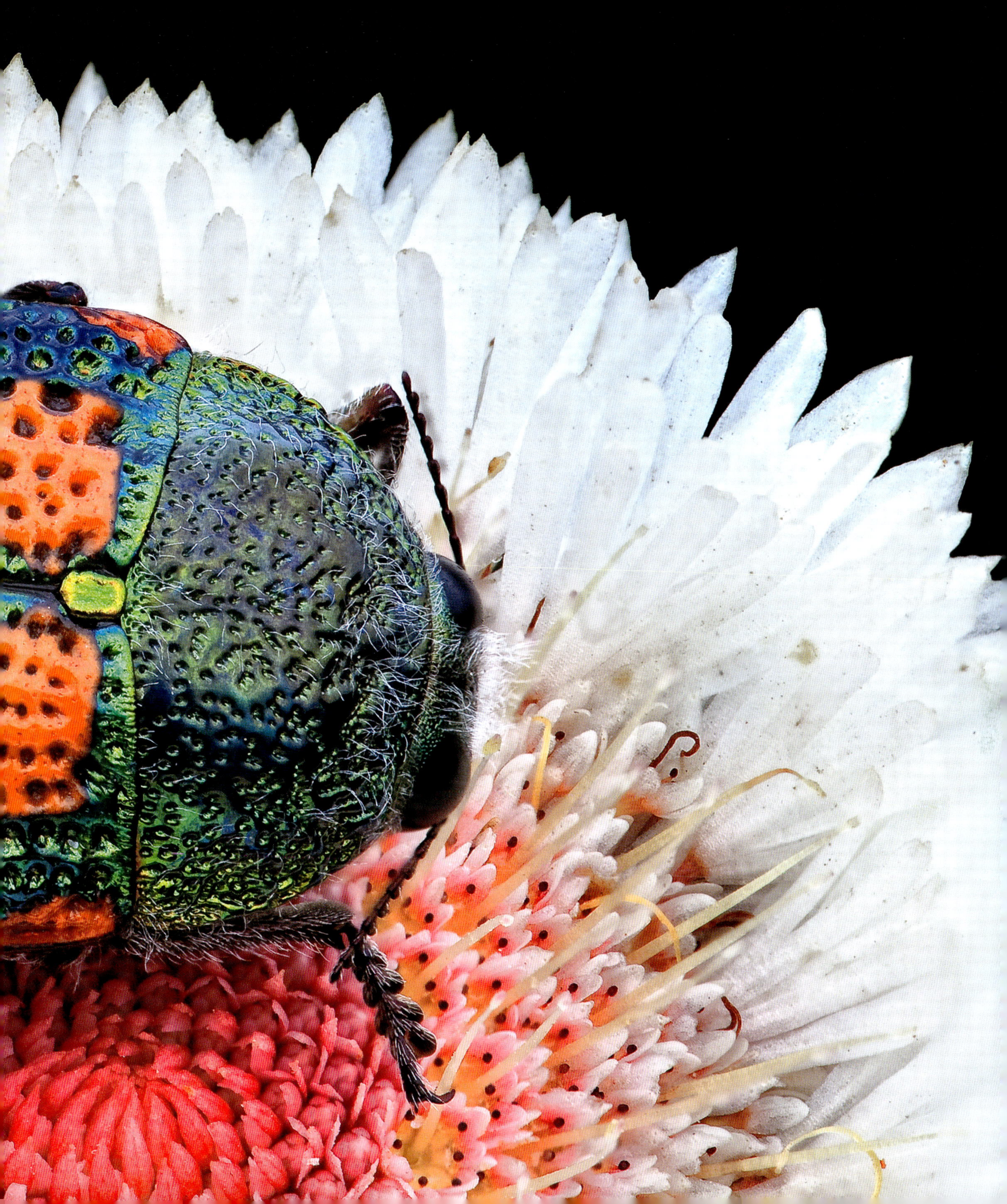

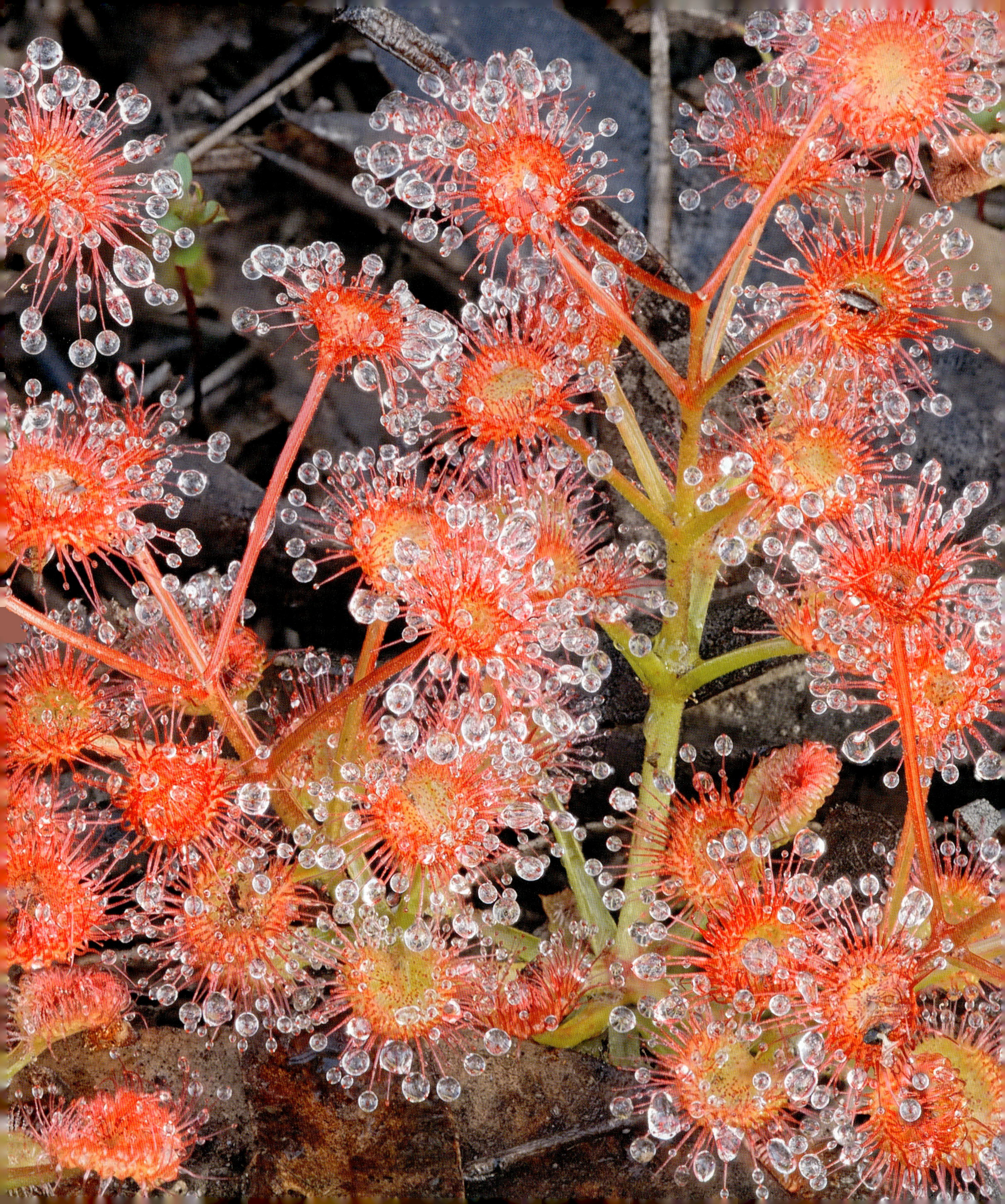

Preceding pages

Looking closer still you might find the sculptured *Stigmodera roei*, a species of jewel beetle.

Opposite

In a swampy hollow among wildflowers a Leafy Sundew, *Drosera stolonifera*, has set its traps of sticky drops. Insects attracted to the sparkle become fatally entrapped. Once caught the plant will digest the tiny animals. The minute insects ensnared are in yet another realm – that of the microscopic.

Below

A small ant, seemingly dazed, wanders among the tightly packed flowers of a Cut-leaf Banksia, *Banksia praemorsa*.

Following pages

In a few cases we have stretched the definition of miniature so that we could include small parts of larger animals, such as this attentive frogmouth. As you search for miniatures a Tawny Frogmouth, *Podargus strigoides*, may be looking over your shoulder, probably unnoticed because of its camouflage. This bird occurs throughout Australia, in just about any habitat – dry or wet, cold or hot. So wherever your search for miniatures leads you, a Tawny Frogmouth may be watching.

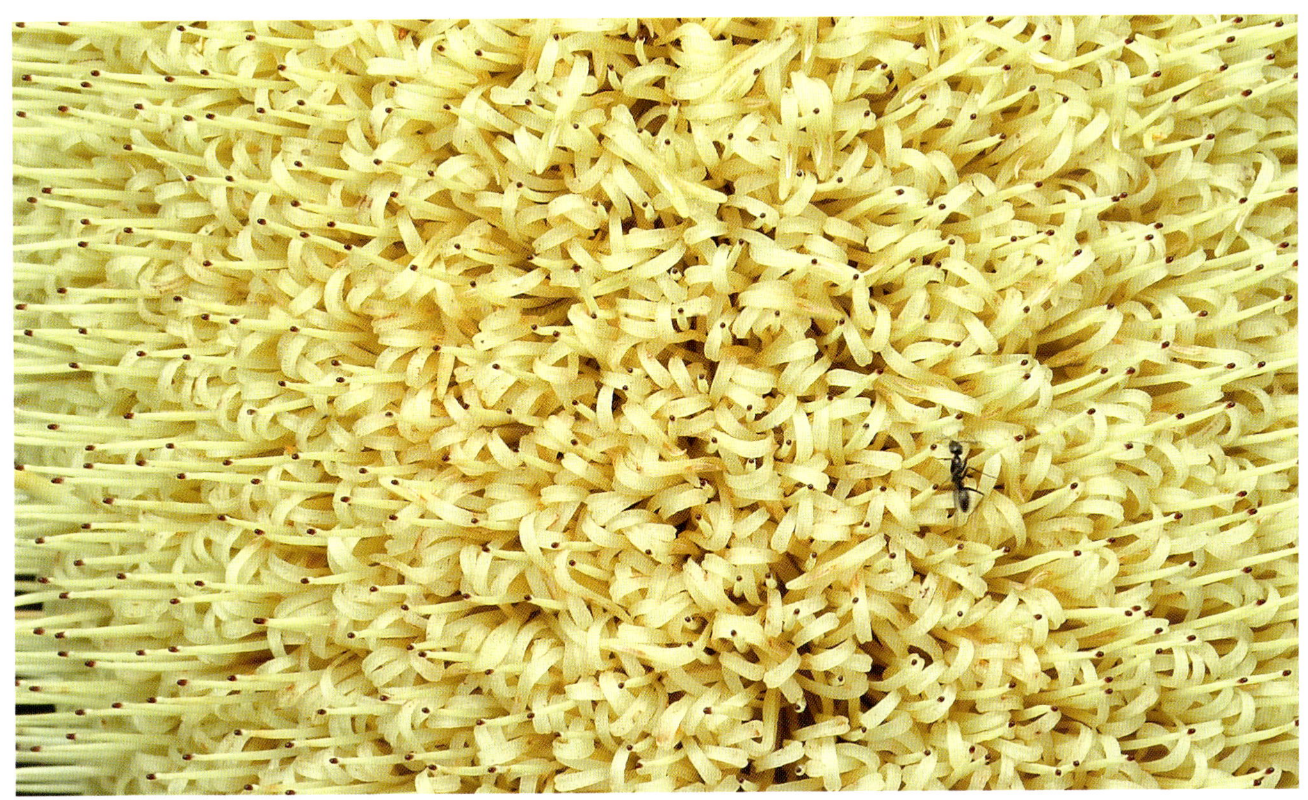

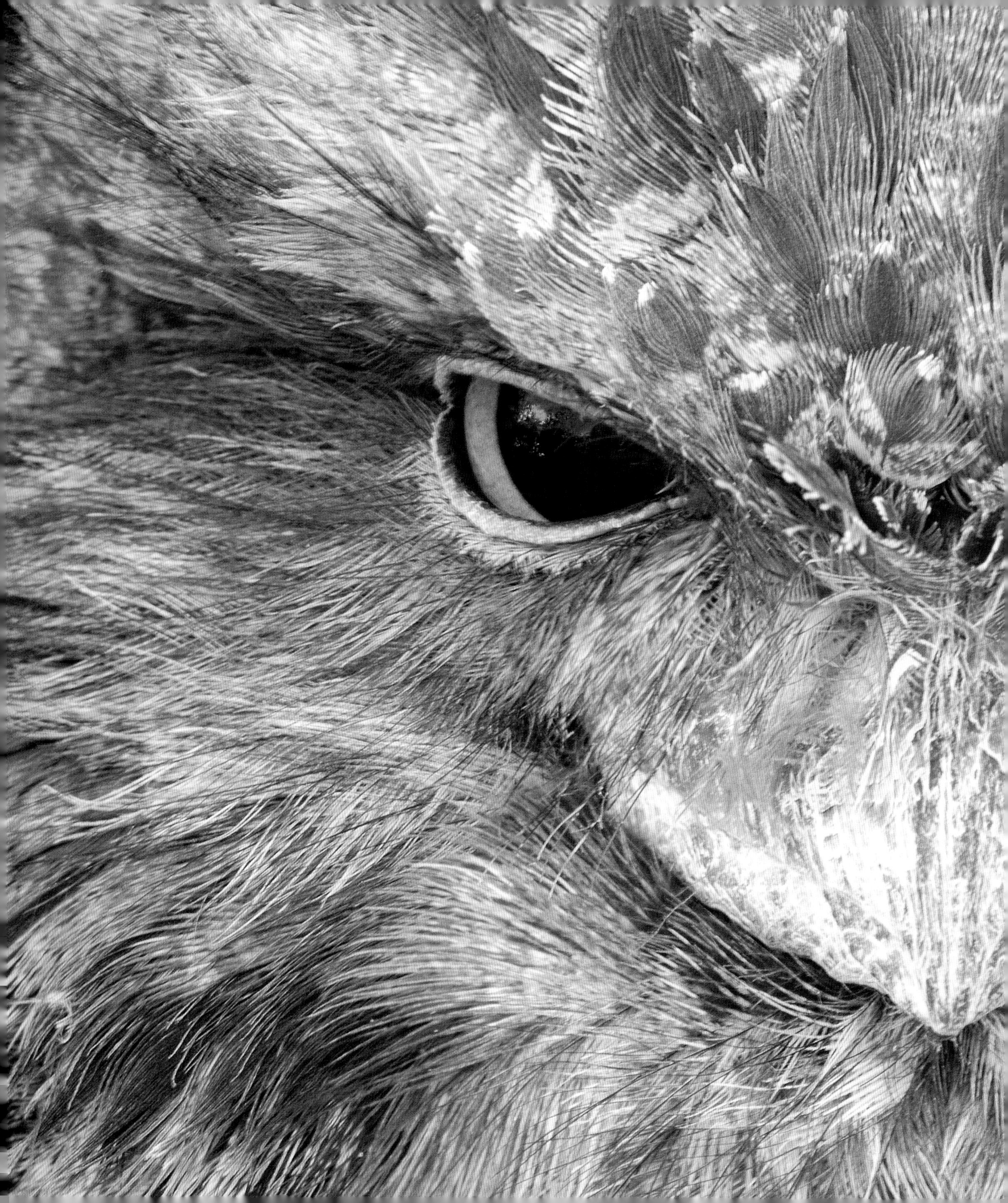

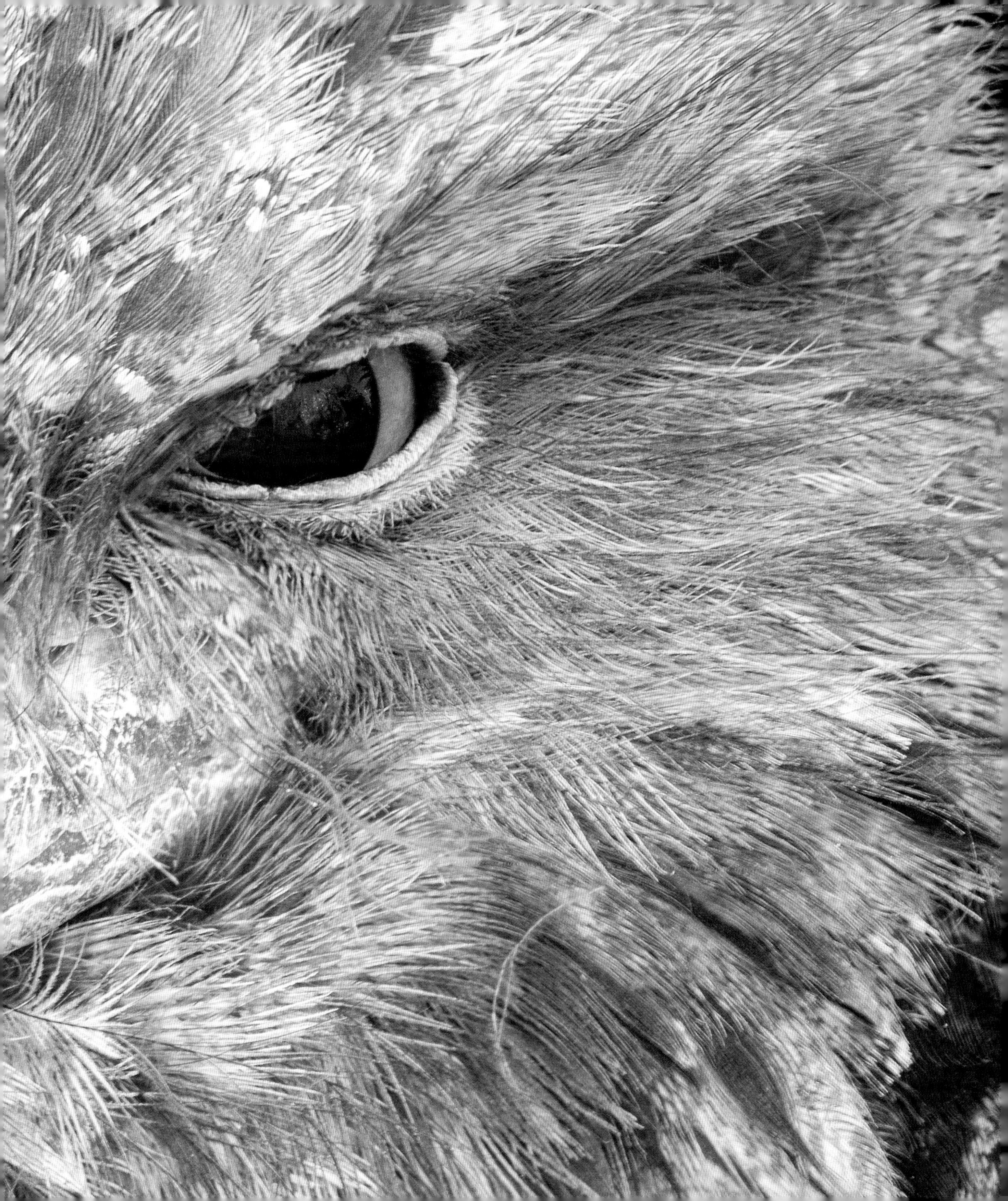

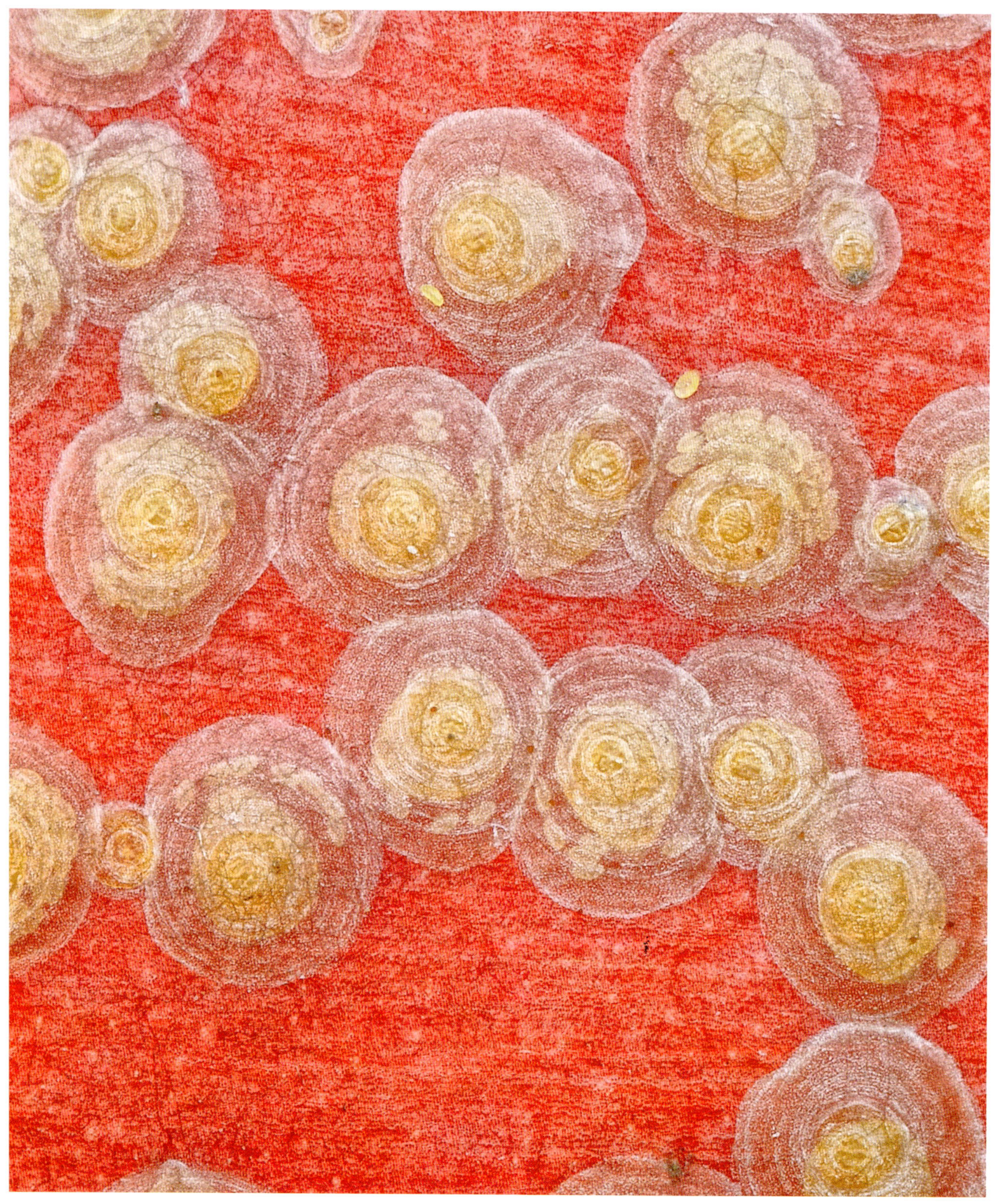

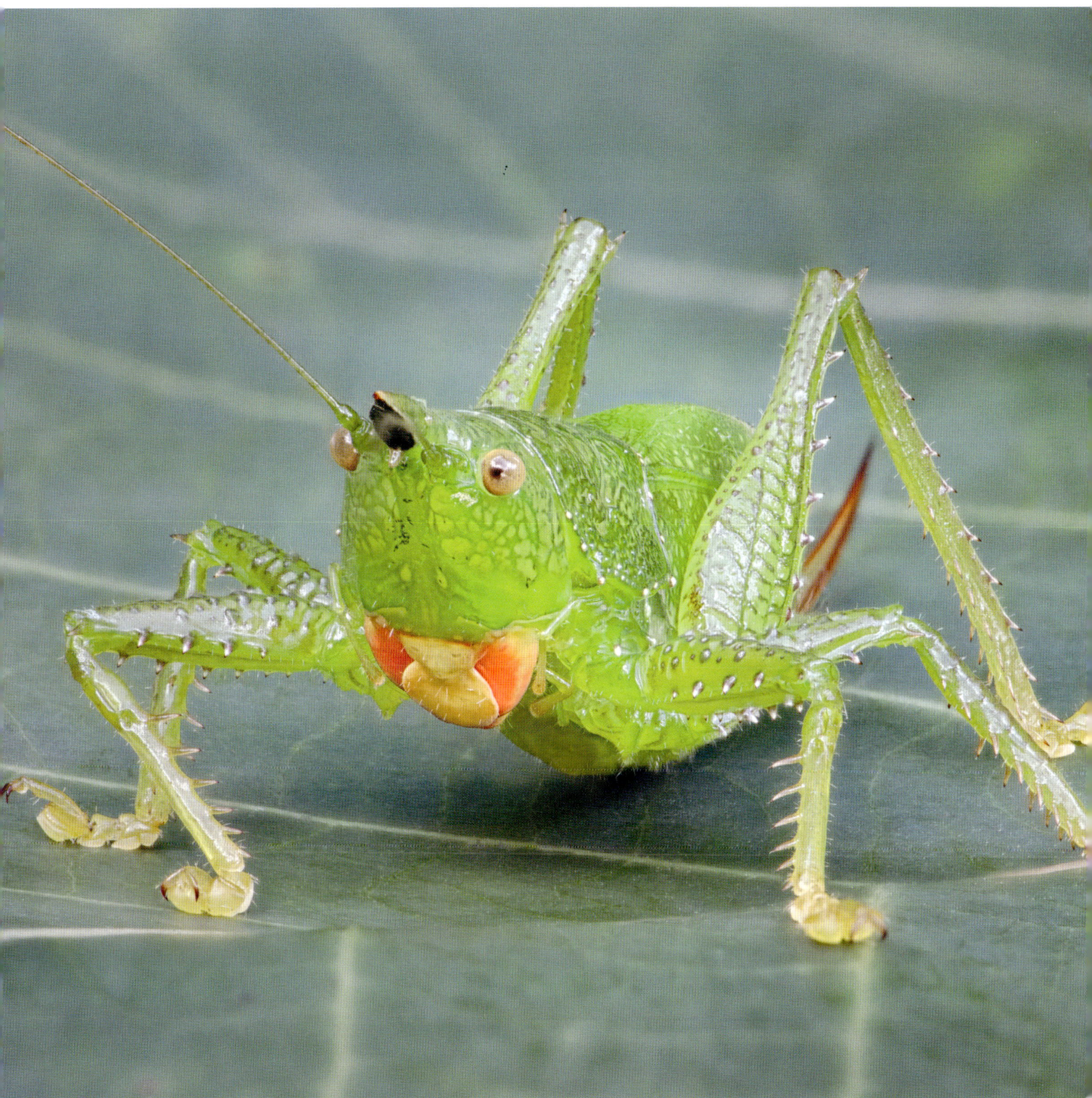

Page 30

Tiny plant lice have built these circular structures on the fruit of a Black Palm, *Normanbya normanbyi*. The structures, called lerps, shelter the animals as they suck the fruit's juices.

Page 31

The Pink-faced Emerald, *Emeraldagraecia munggarifrons*, is a newly described small (22 mm) katydid from the tropical rainforest. Its formidable jaws mark it as a hunter of even smaller insects. ☙

Below

Brown Stag Beetle, *Prosopocoilus torrensis*. Stag beetles do not have 'antlers', but immensely strong pincer-like jaws. These are used in male-to-male combat, subduing females and defence against predators (see also pages 72–73).

Opposite

This tiny unnamed moth, when standing upright, is 14 mm 'tall'. We call it Proud Moth, because of its stance. When fluttering about in the light, it appears as a tiny animated brown flake. Only when enlarged does it show its colours and the structure of its scales. ☙

Following pages

To show the colours and engineering of its wings, we had to get very close to this Northern Cherrynose Cicada, *Macrotristria sylvara*.

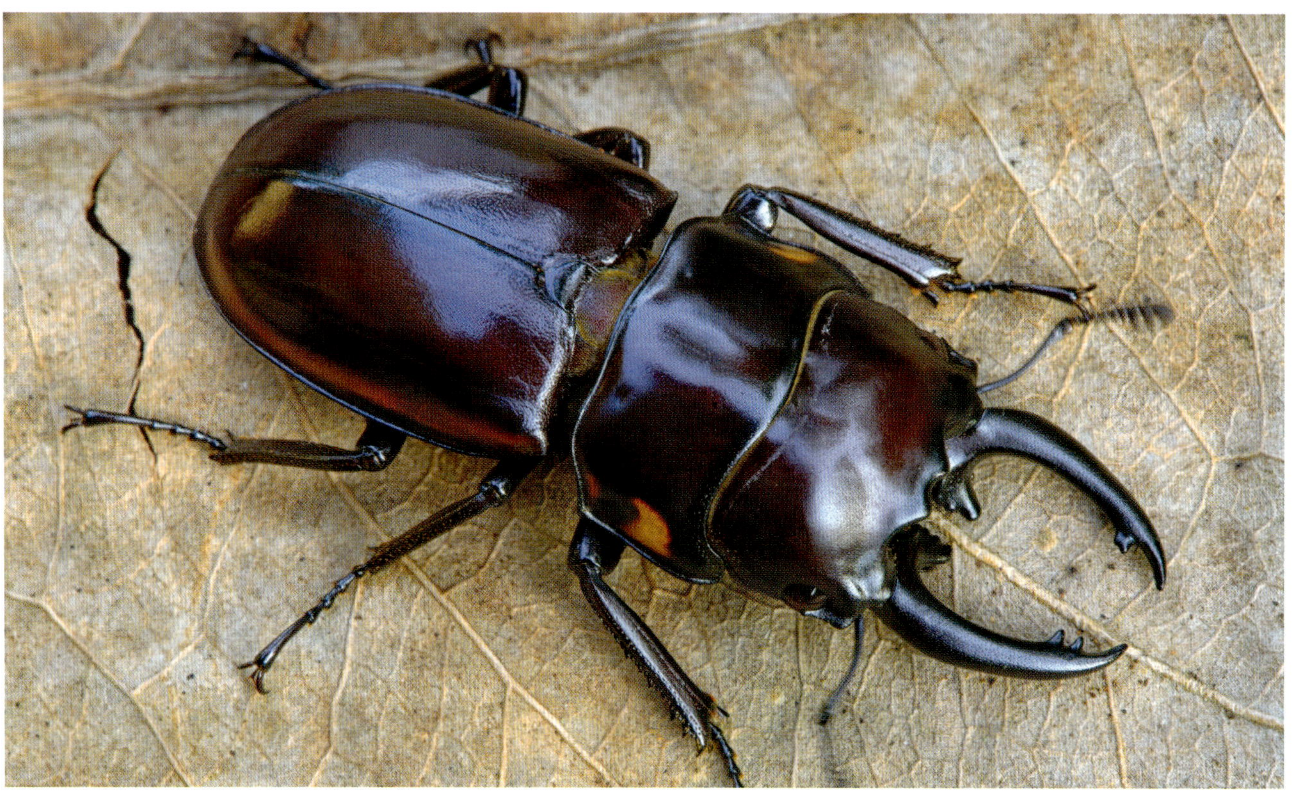

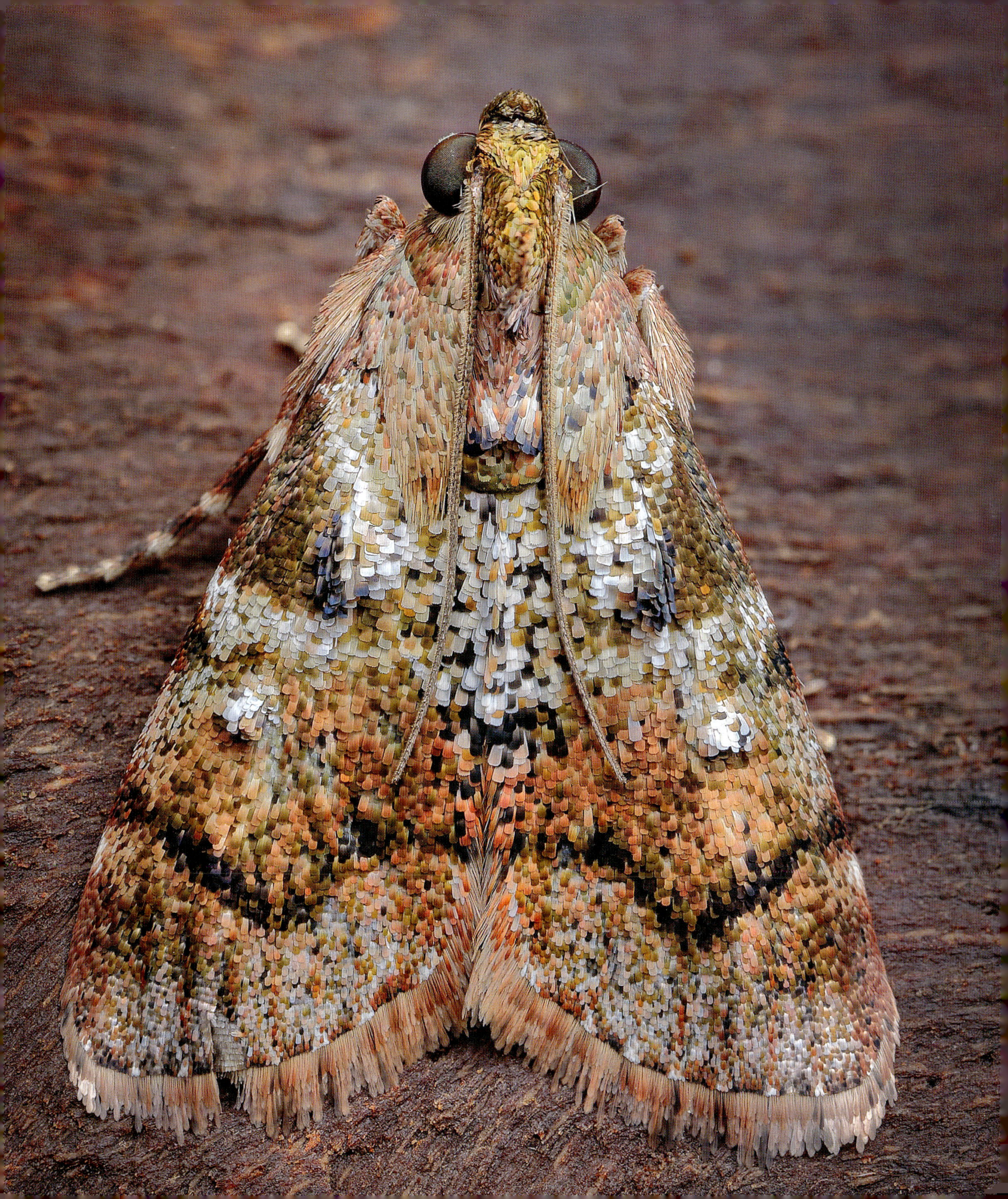

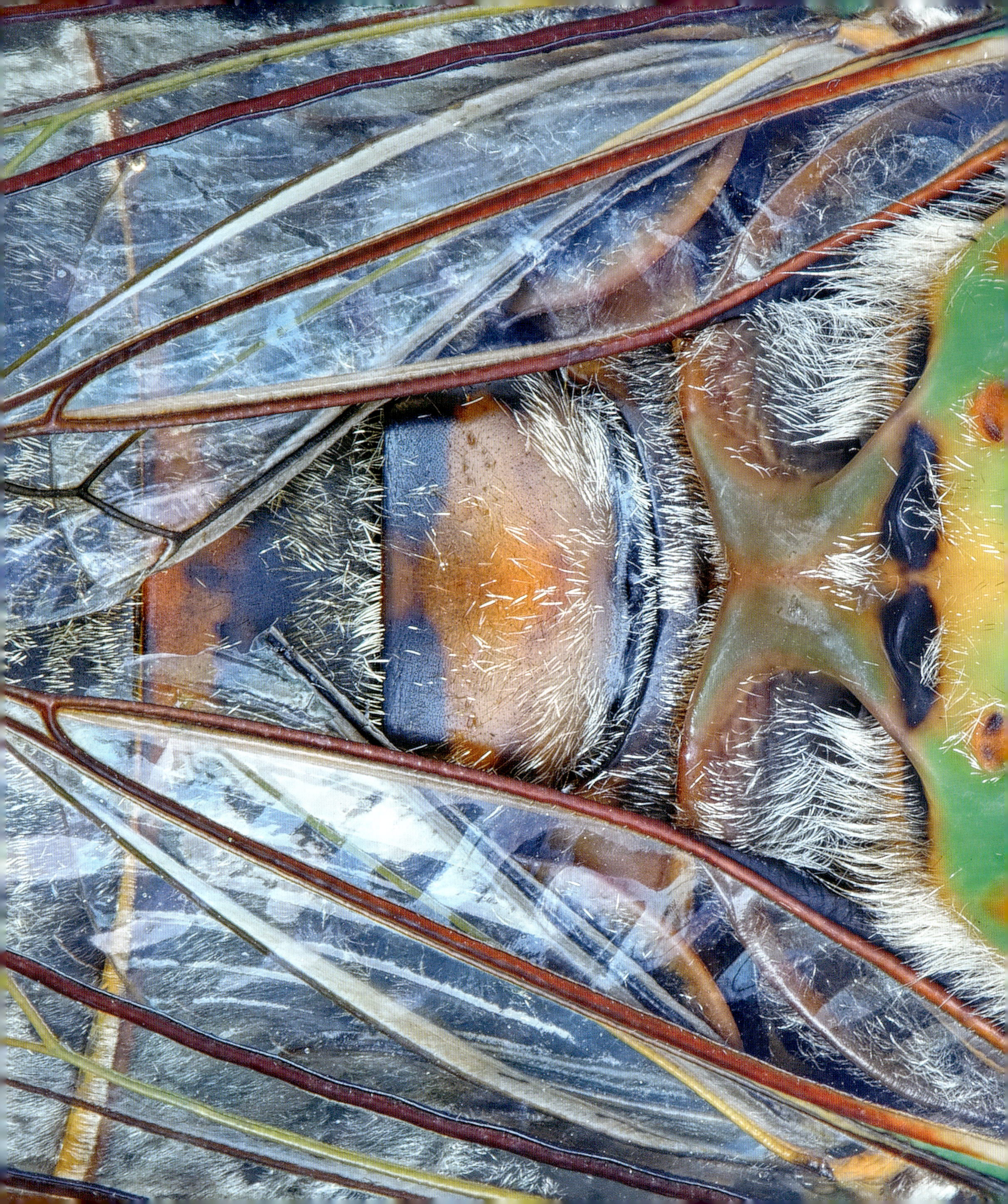

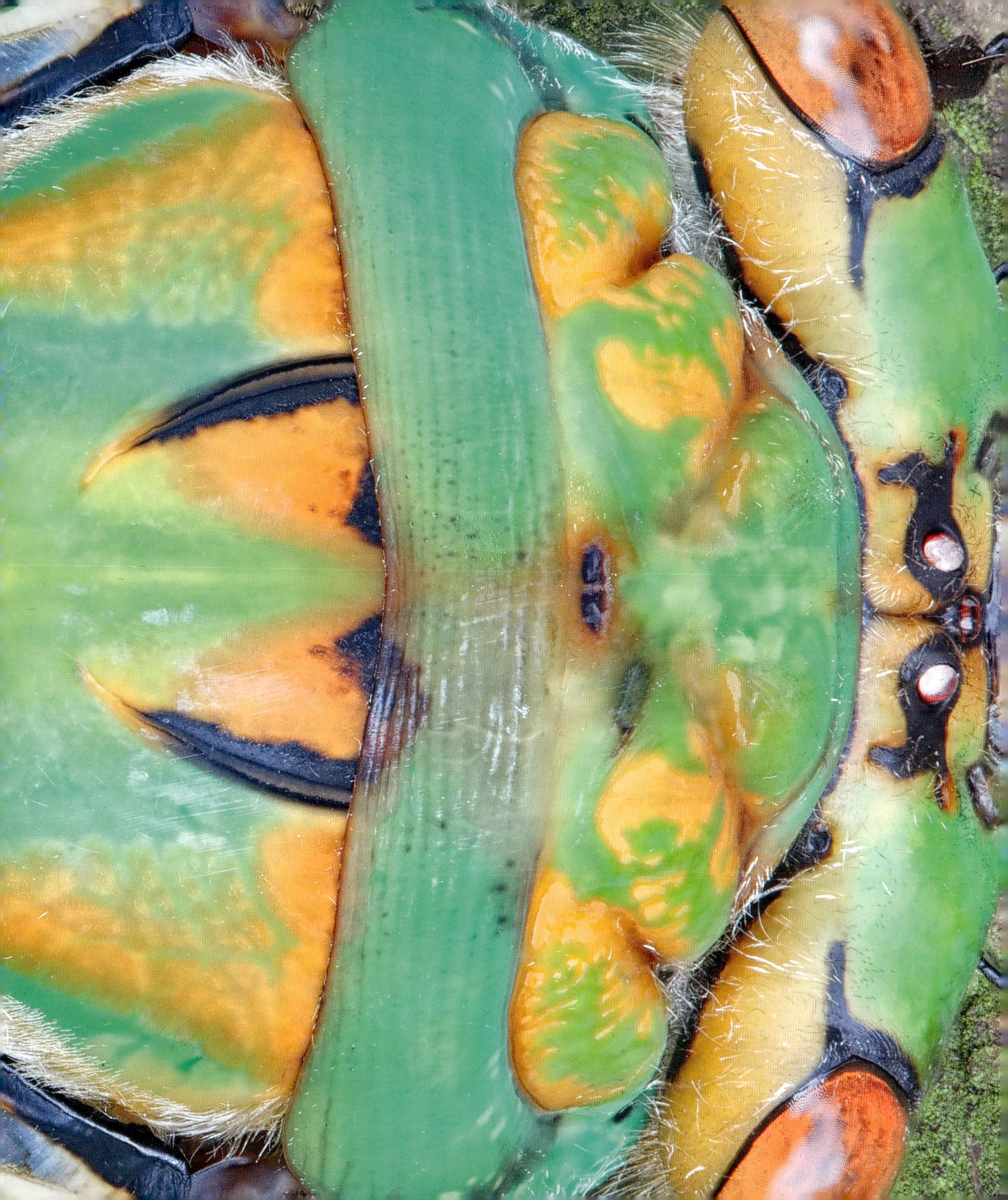

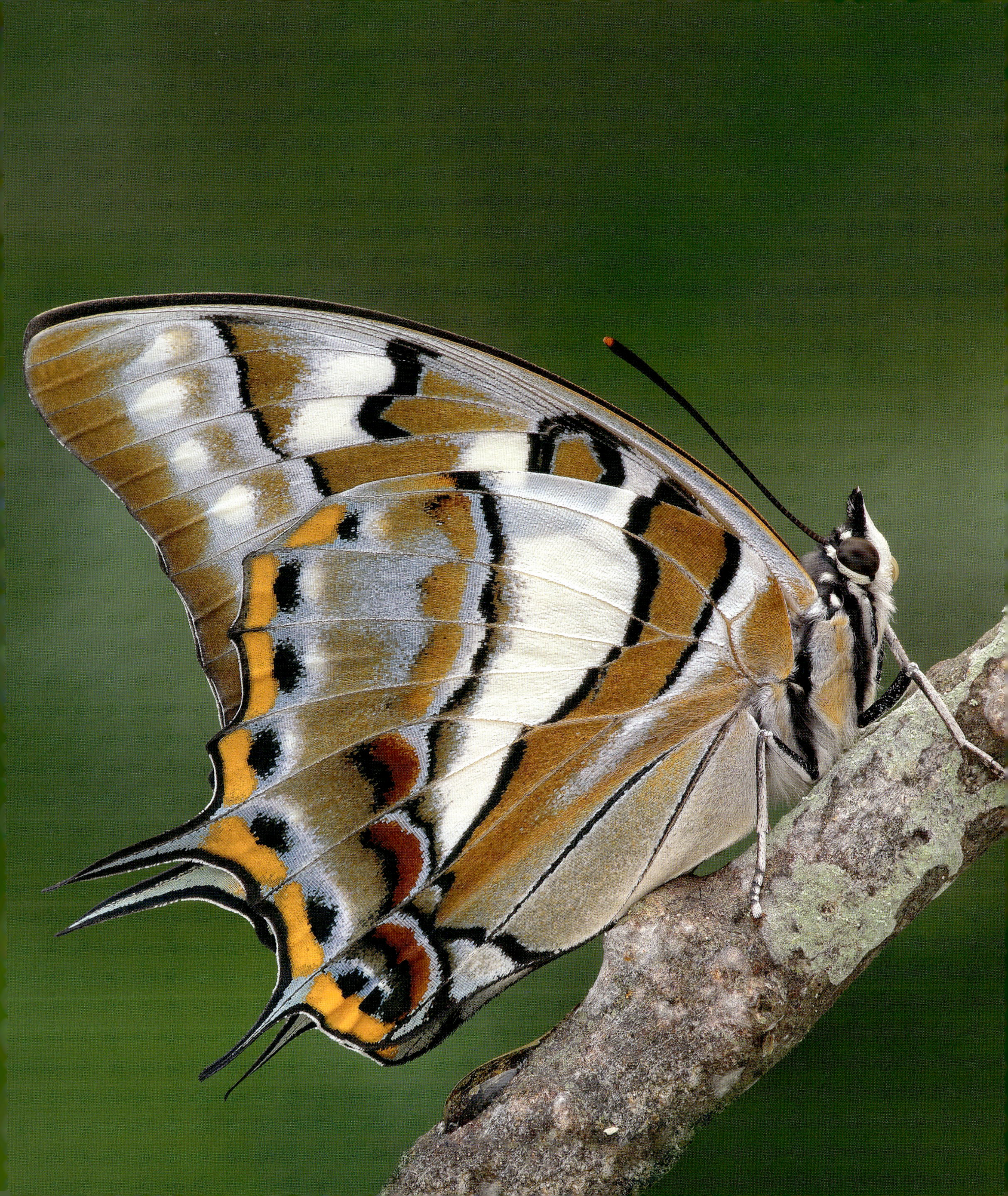

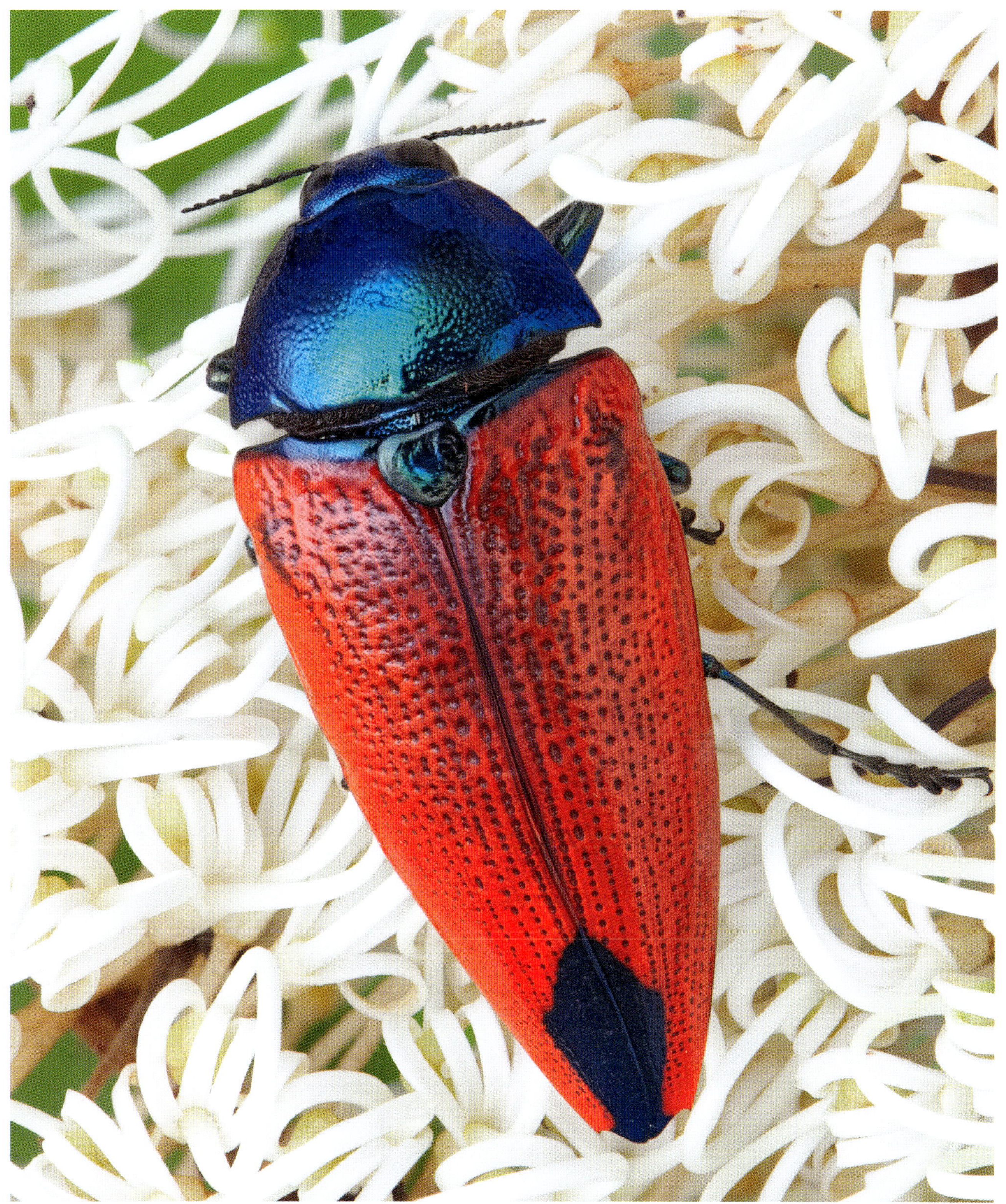

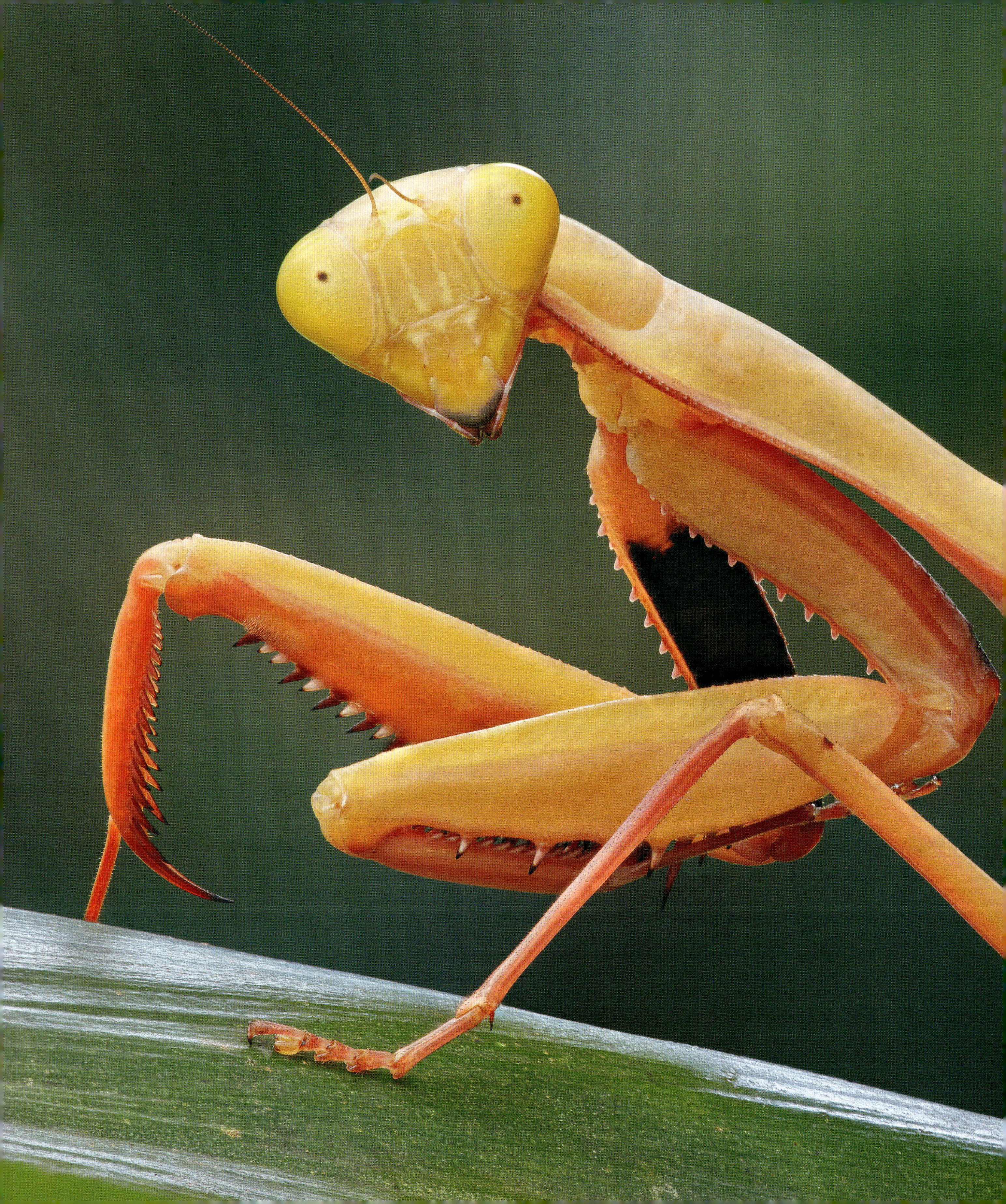

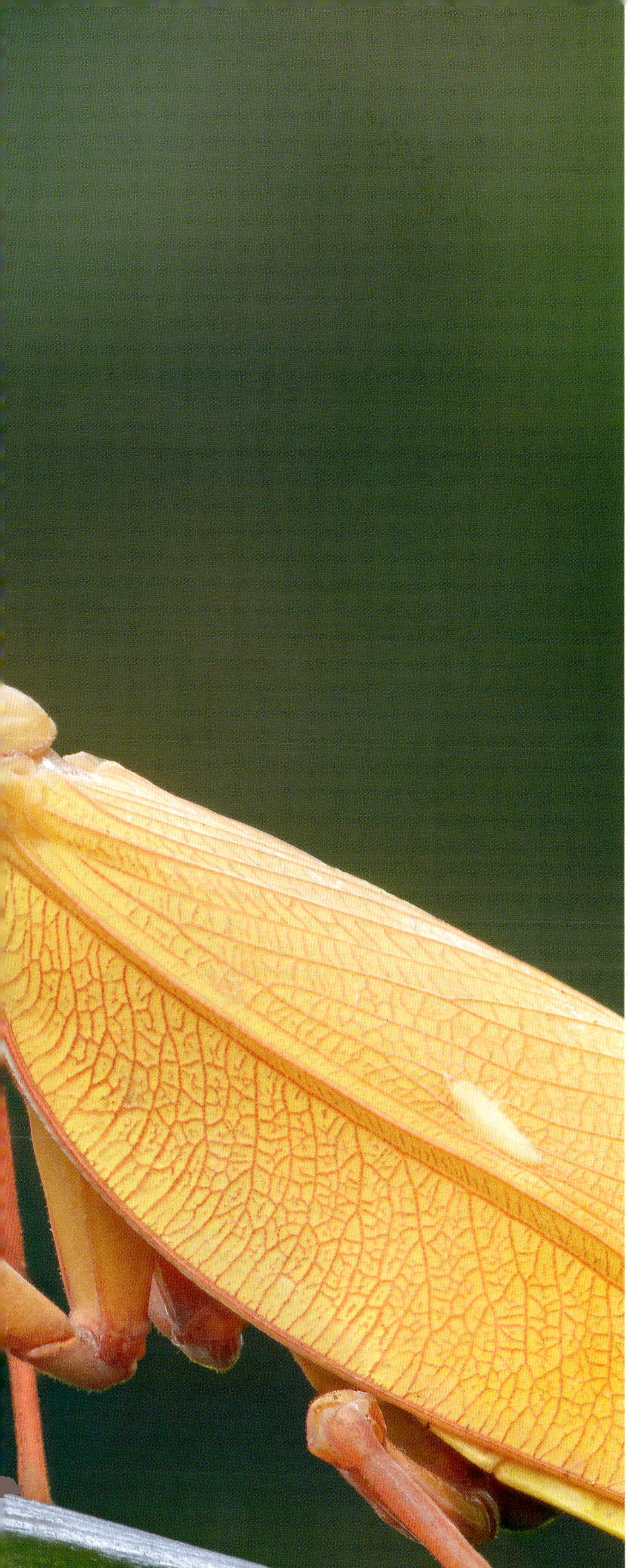

Page 36

With a wingspan of 75 mm the Tailed Emperor, *Polyura sempronius*, is one of Australia's larger butterflies. It can be seen flying with speed and grace right across northern and eastern Australia including the big cities.

Page 37

Nearly all of Australia's 1,200 or so kinds of jewel beetles live up to their name with bright colours and flashing iridescence. Even so some stand out, such as the Red and Purple Jewel Beetle, *Metaxymorpha hauseri*. ❦

Left

Hierodula majuscula is a regal praying mantis. She is large (72 mm) and looks you straight in the eye. She stalks not just other insects but also small frogs and lizards. Usually a camouflaging green, this golden variety is quite rare.

Page 40

With its muscular legs this White-kneed Cricket, *Penalva flavocalceatus*, can make prodigious leaps – chest-high on a tall person. It feeds at night on decaying leaves on the forest floor.

Page 41

Head-down on a tree trunk the Leaf-tailed Gecko, *Saltuarius cornutus*, lies in ambush for insects and other prey.

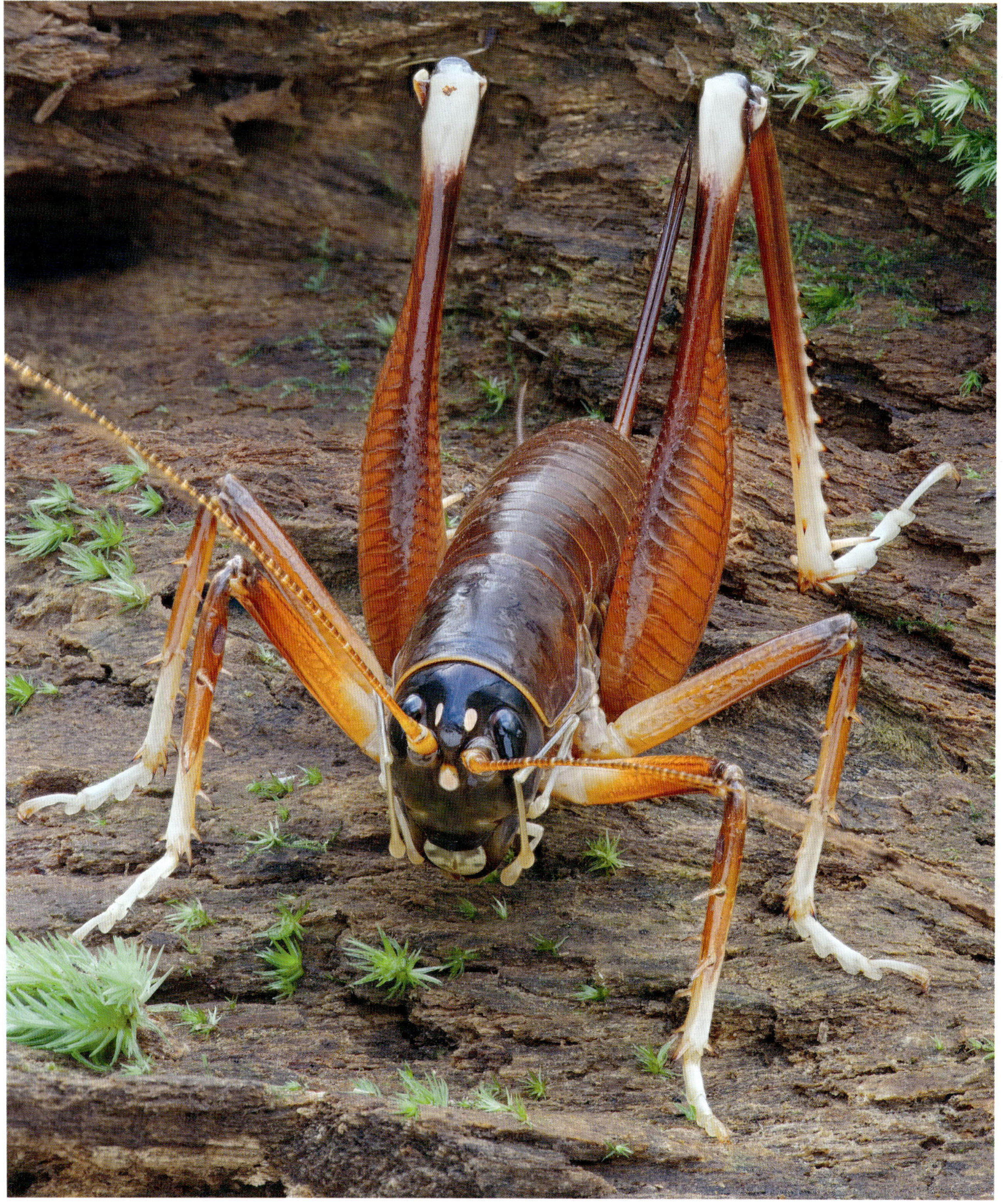

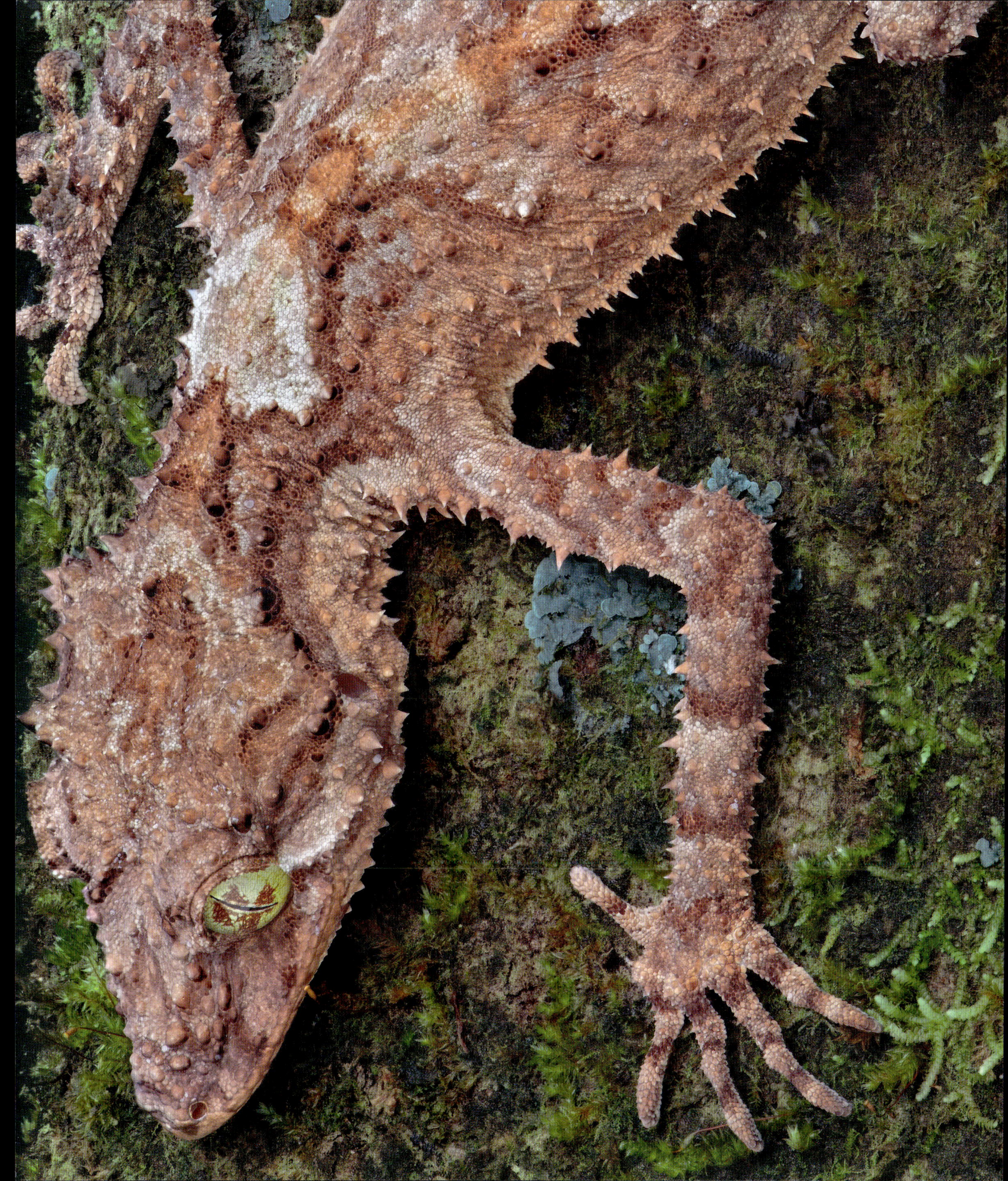

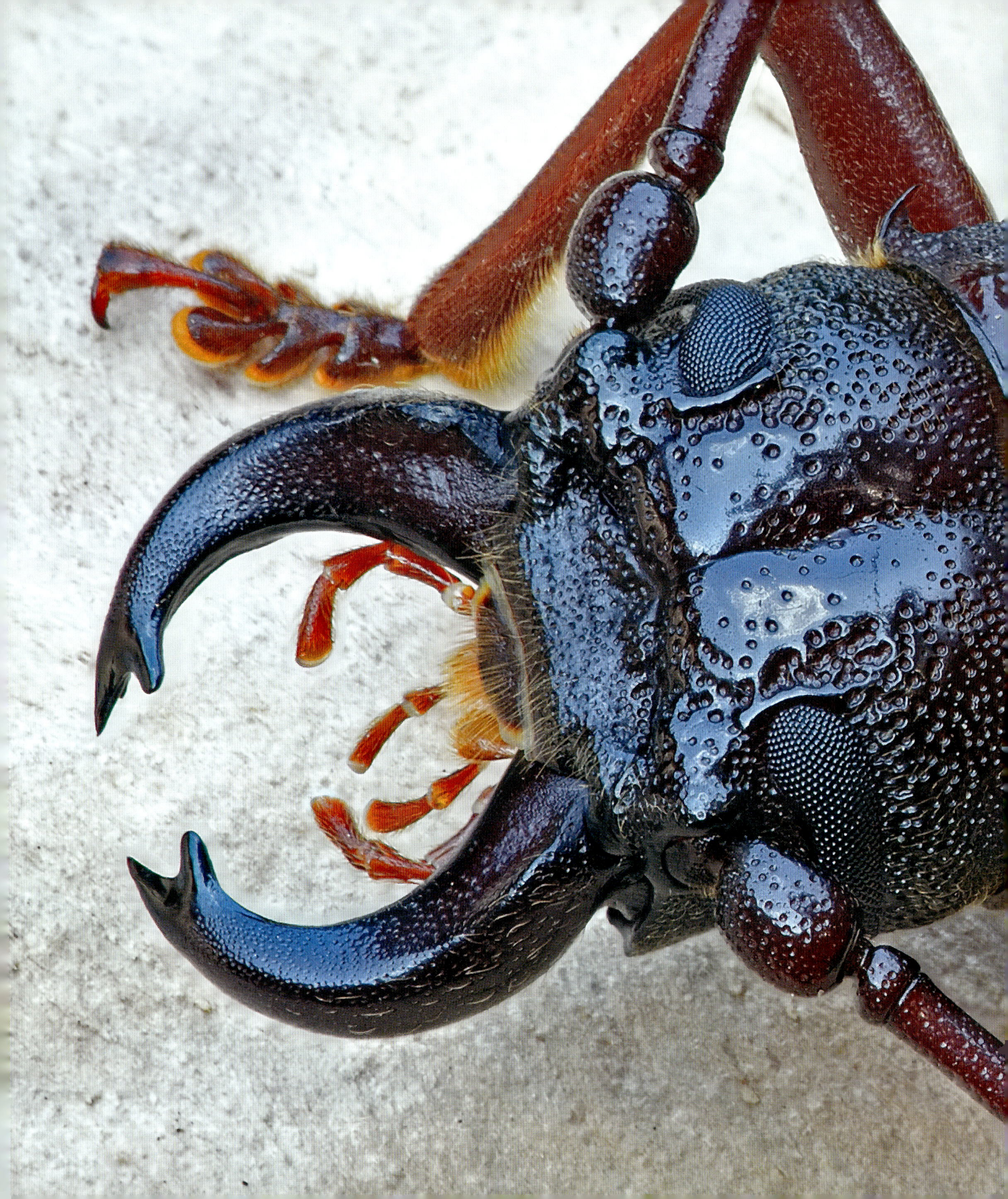

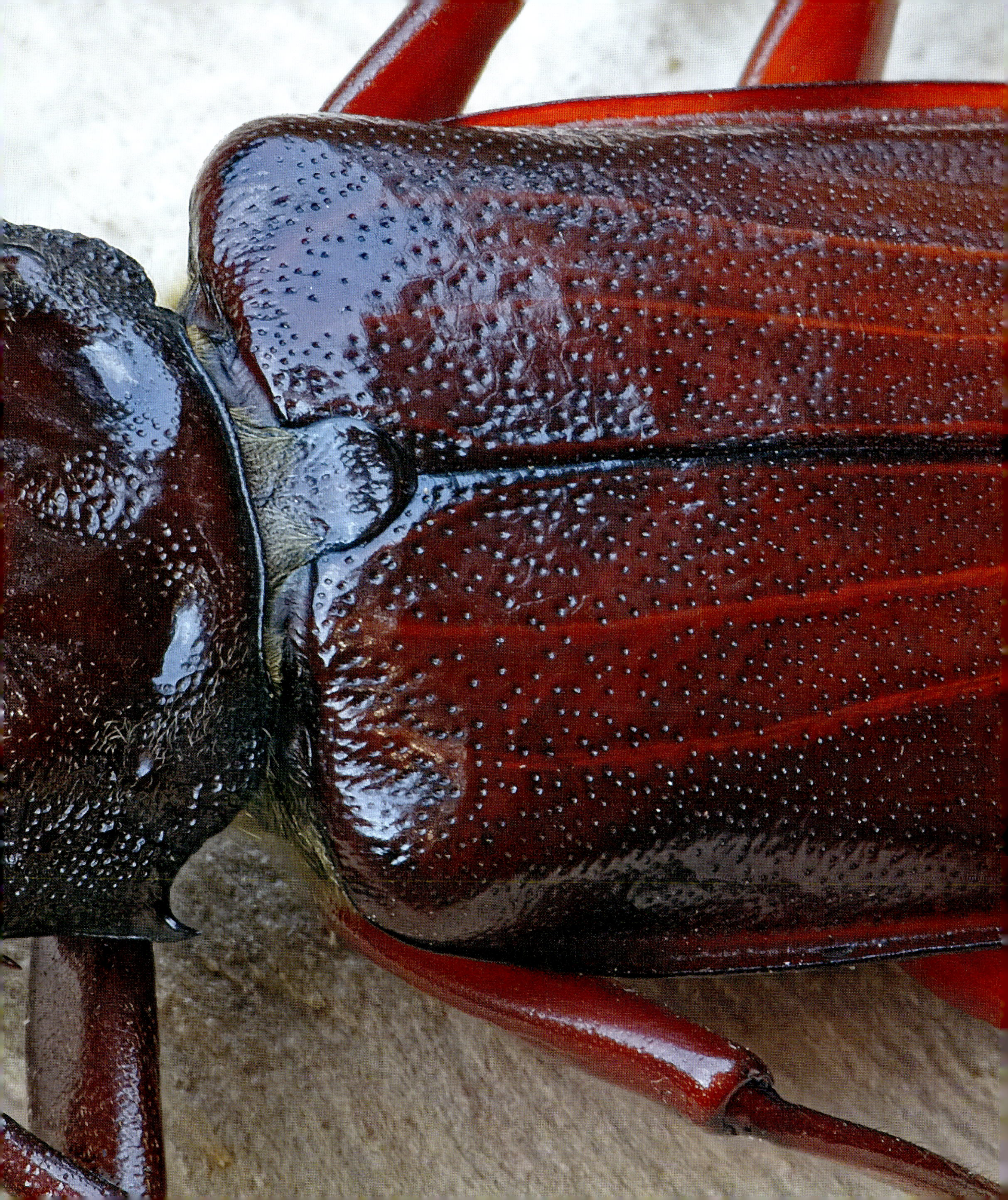

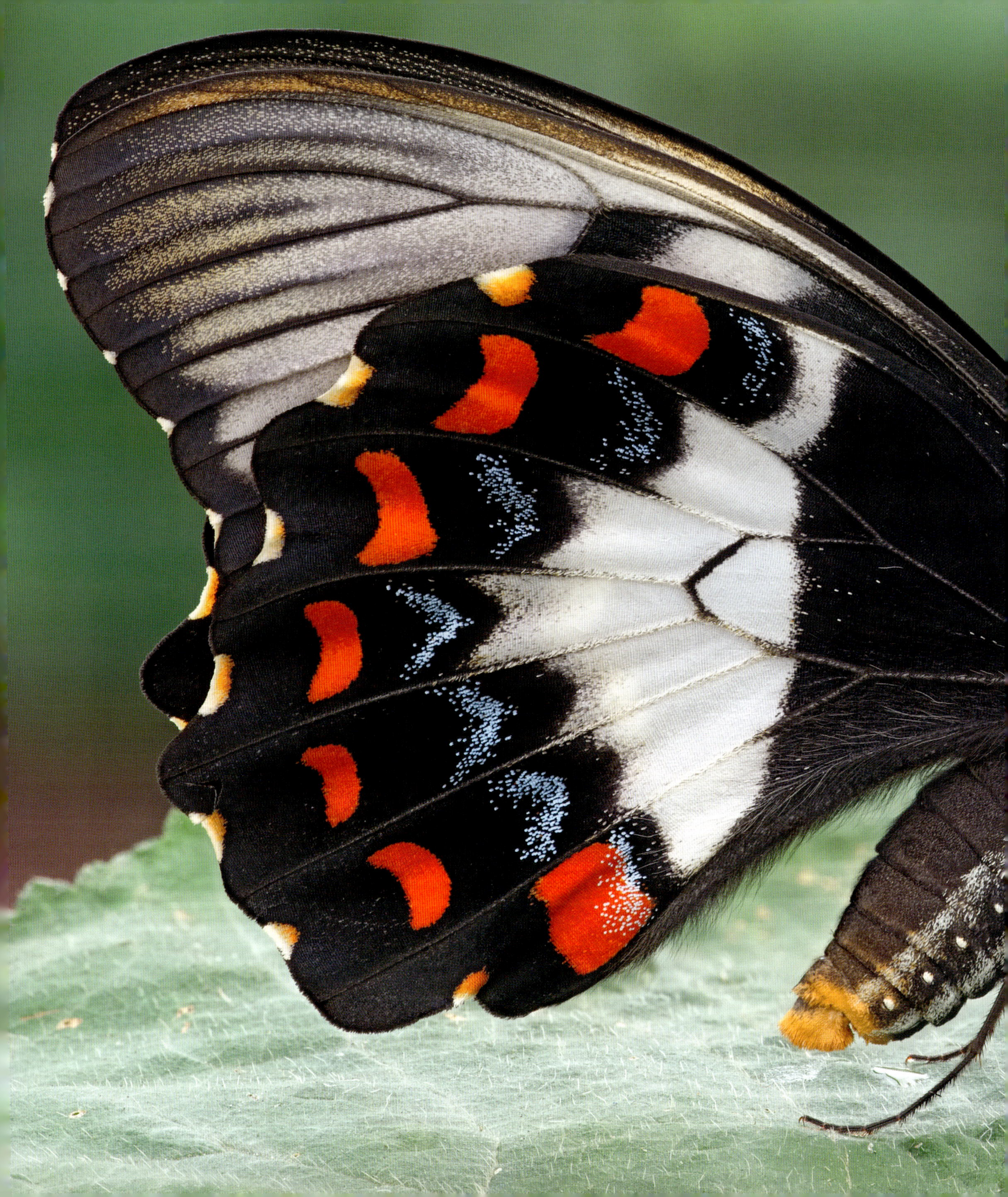

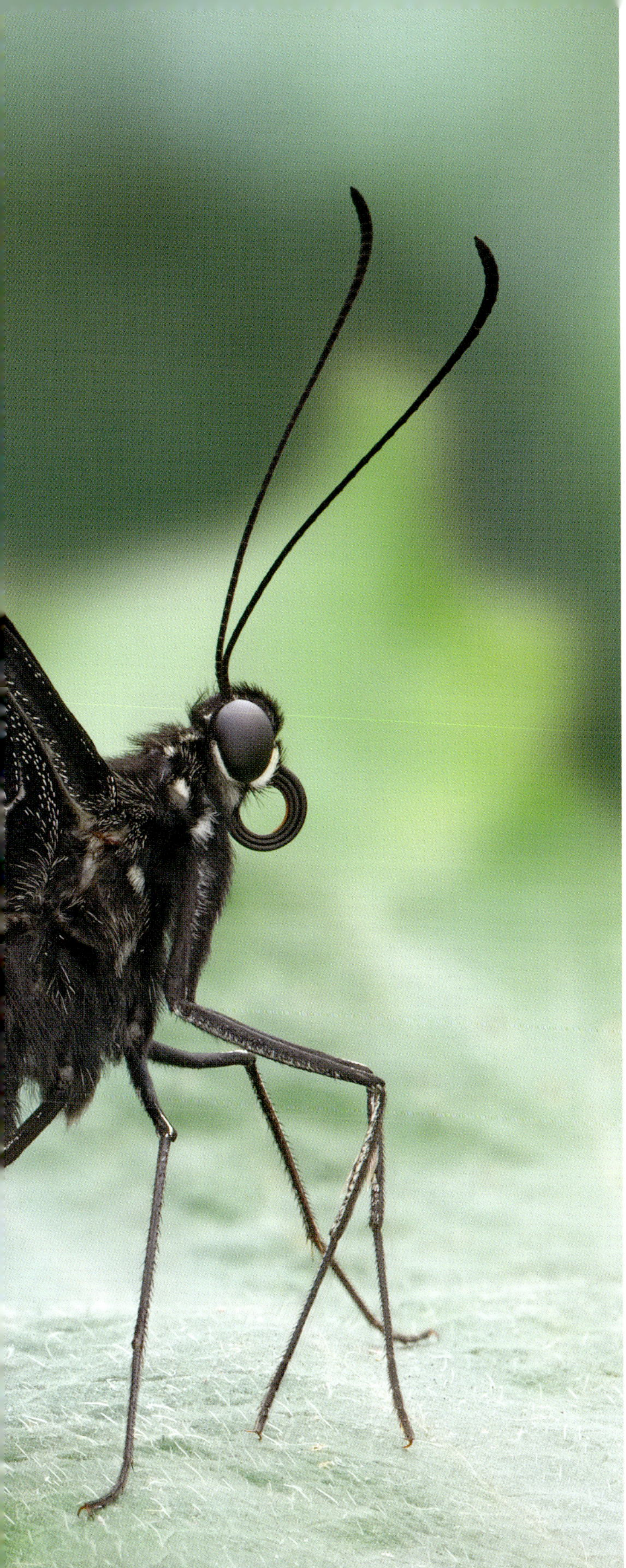

Preceding pages

Despite its formidable appearance this longicorn beetle, *Cacodacnus planicollis*, is not a predator. Its armour and crushing jaws are for defence. Like most of its kind it feeds on leaves, flowers, bark and tree sap. It is a rare beetle with an unusual distribution. Most have been found in the rainforests of northeast Queensland. There are a few records from around Adelaide and a single one from the forests of the southwest.

Left

Female Orchard Butterfly, *Papilio aegeus*. The male is mostly black. The caterpillars feed on a wide variety of plants. Their favourites, however, are citrus trees, especially those in backyards and orchards. That may be why it is one of the most widely distributed of our butterflies.

Page 46

Caterpillars of the emperor moth *Opodiphthera fervida*. They grow into large moths (see page 50).

Page 47

In this defence posture the caterpillar of the Fruit-piercing Moth, *Eudocima fullonia*, has stretched segments of its body so enlarging the 'eyes' on its skin – a ploy to discourage predators. The moth (following pages) is as striking as the caterpillar.

Pages 48–49

Close-up of the wings of the Fruit-piercing Moth, *Eudocima fullonia*. The moth's proboscis is tipped with a sharp spike with which it pierces the skin of fruit to get at the juices. It easily drills through the rinds of oranges and other citrus.

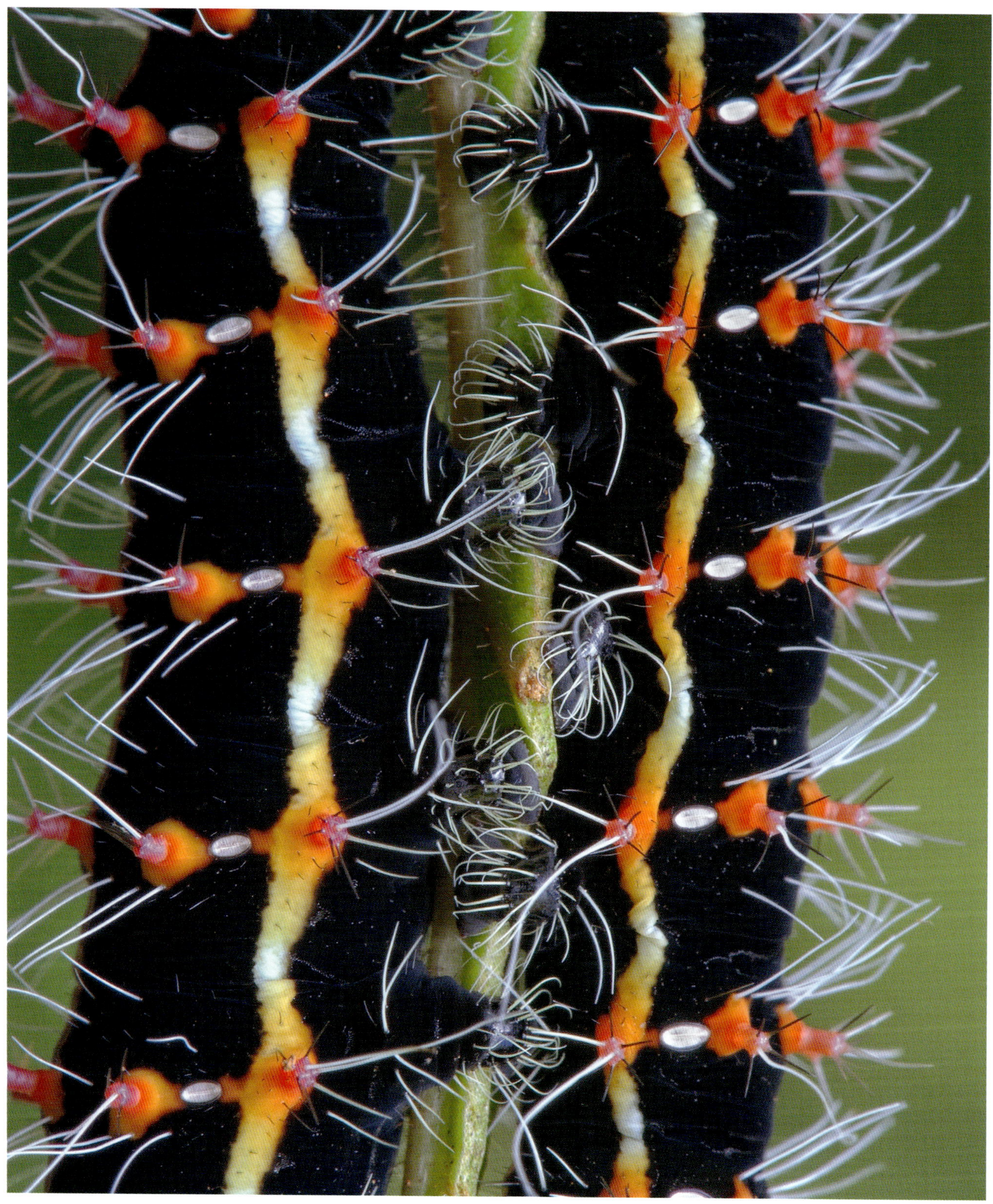

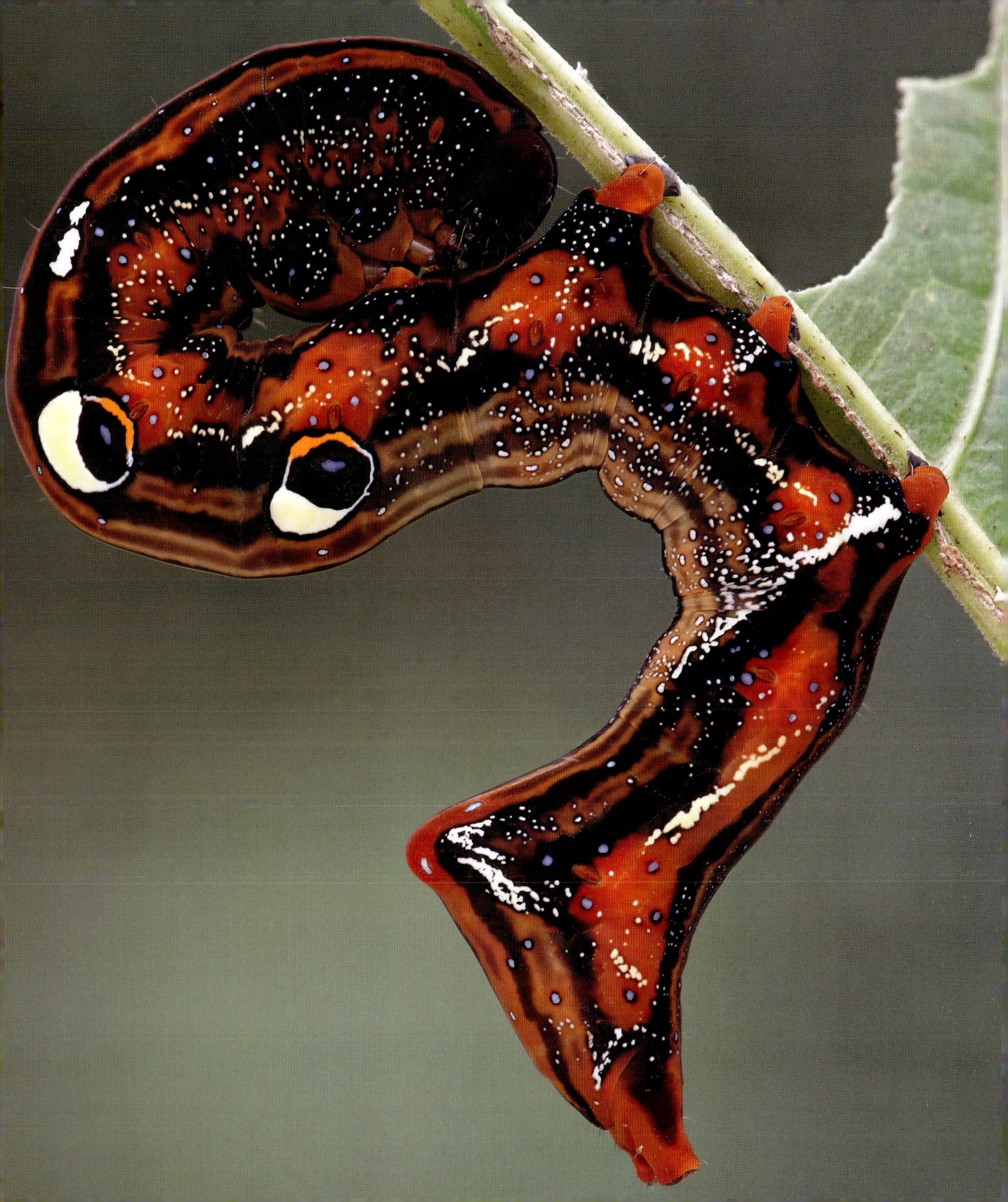

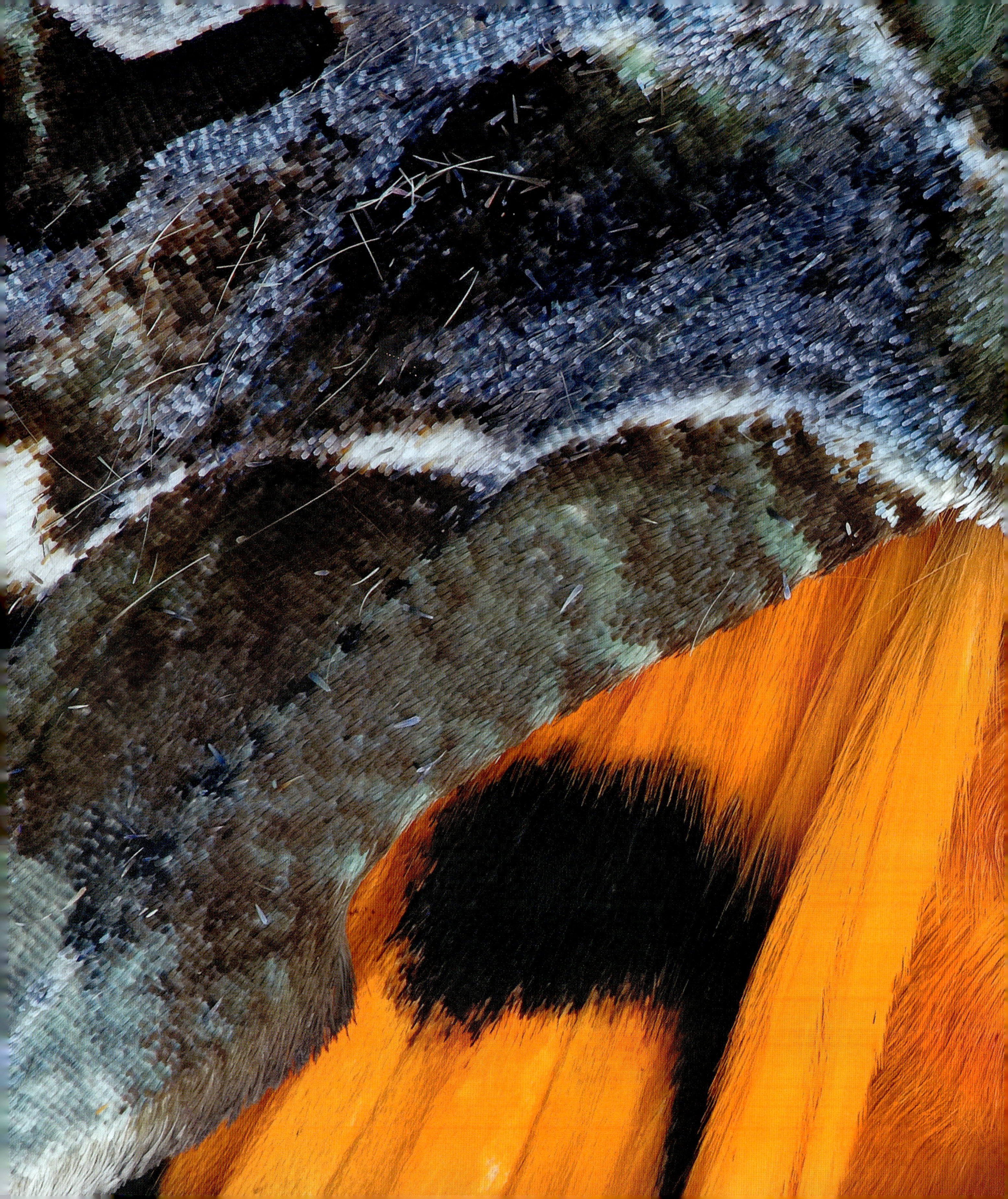

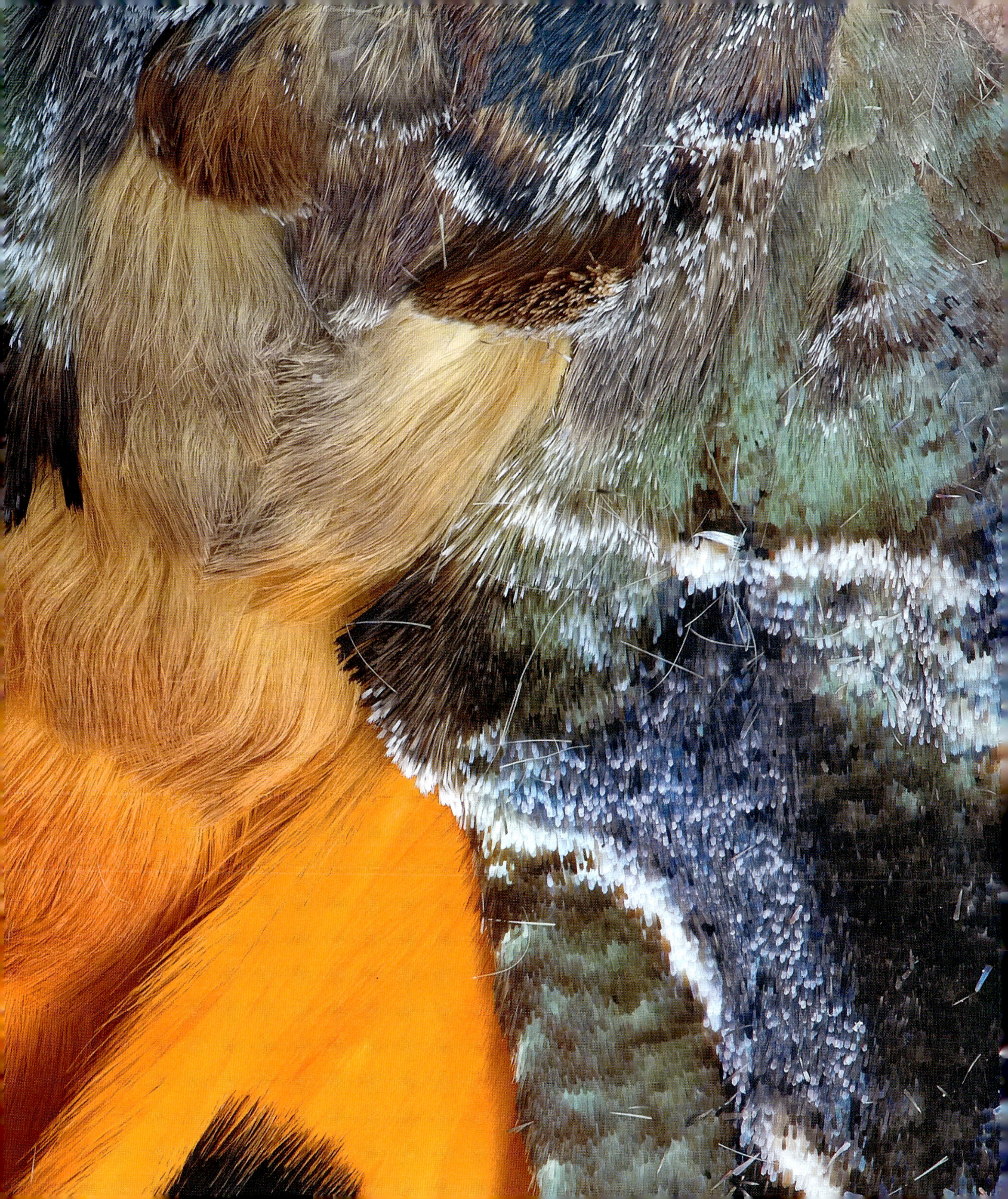

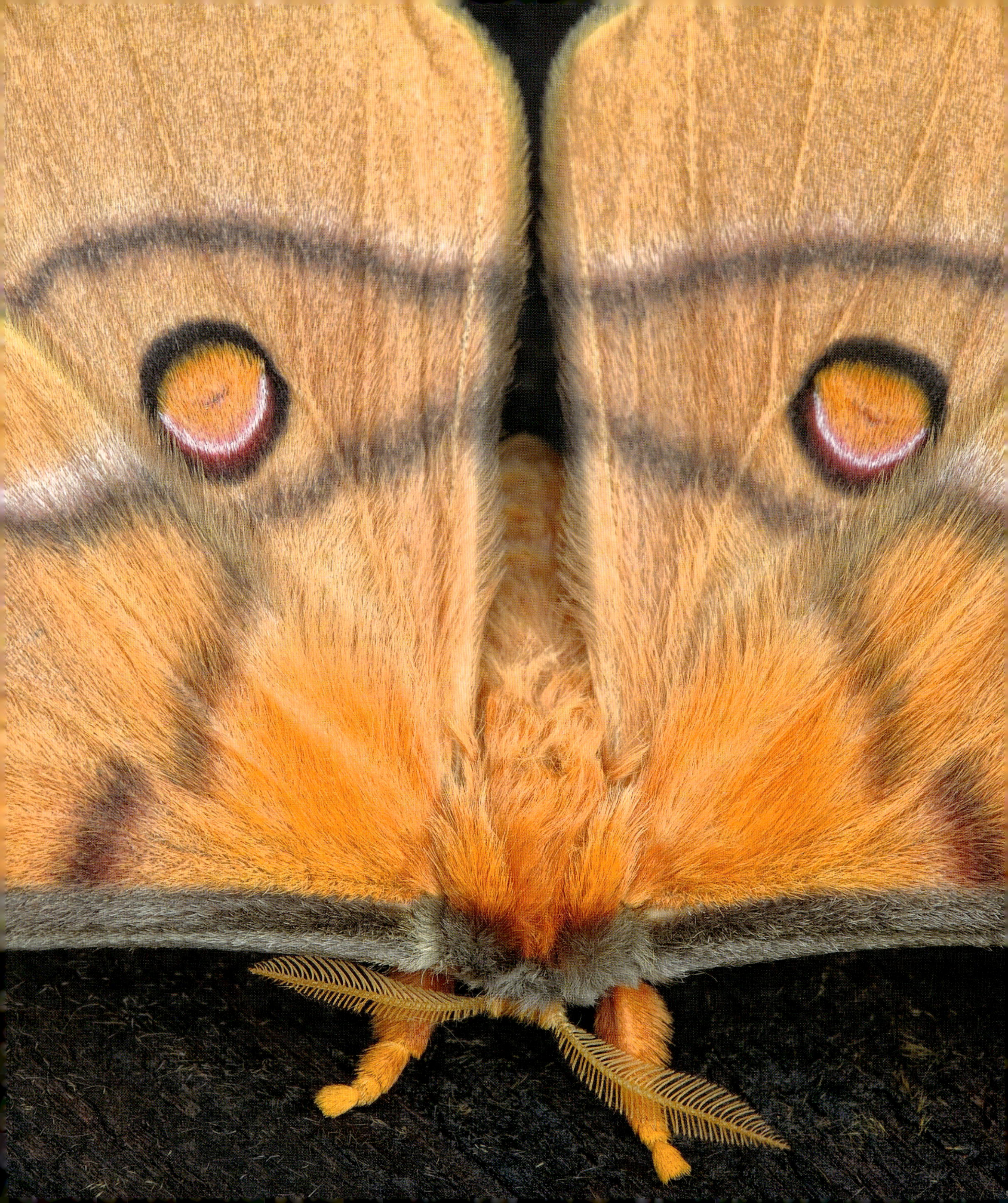

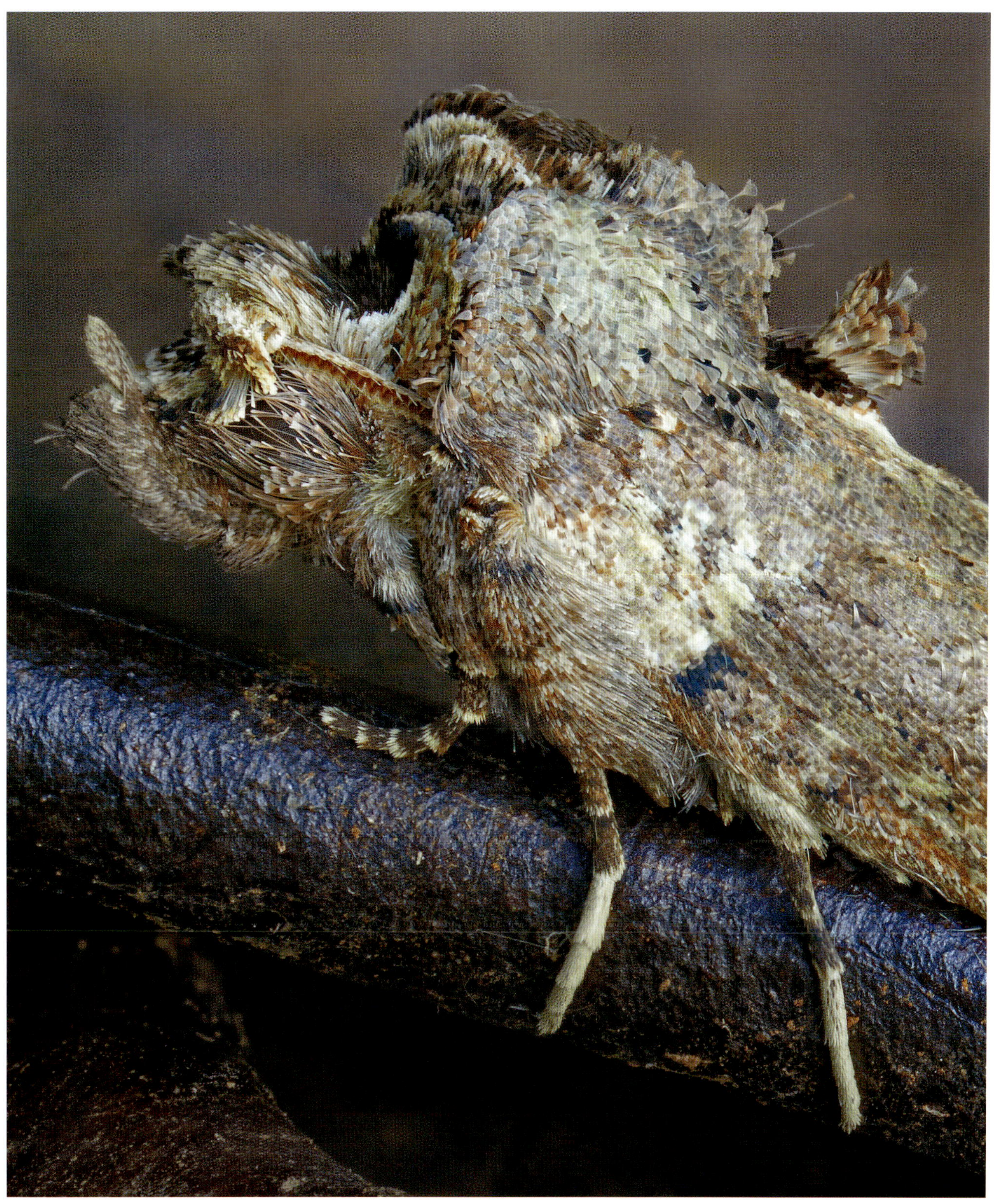

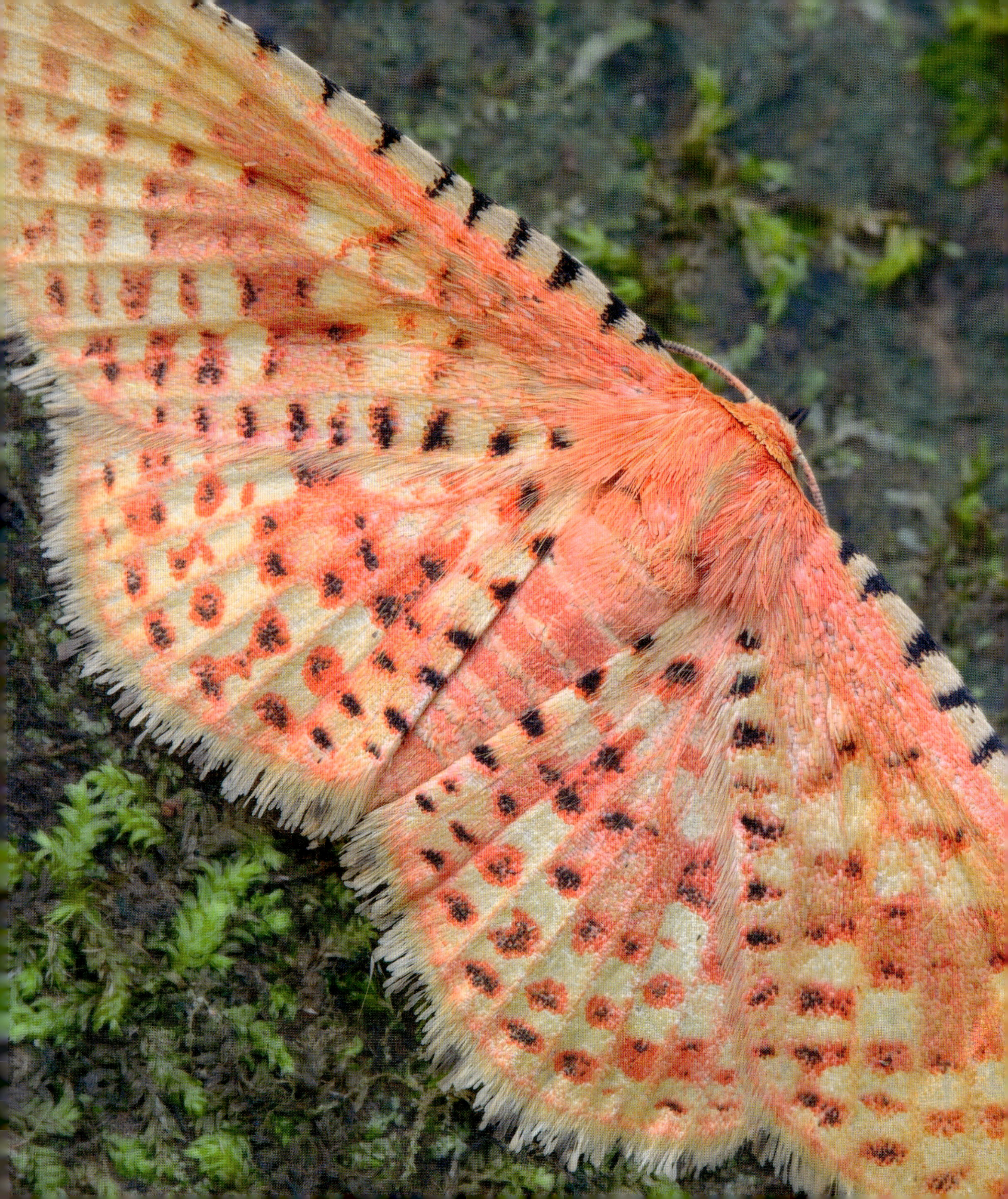

Page 50

When threatened, the emperor moth *Opodiphthera fervida* tucks its head in and suddenly spreads its large wings to flourish an intimidating stare from a pair of 'eyes'.

Page 51

This tiny unidentified moth, just 23 mm long, resembles a broken dead stick. But when enlarged, the 'broken' end discloses the true nature of the disguise. It is an intricate pattern of earth colour and fans of scales. The moth's eyes are just visible behind one of these fans. ☙

Of all the miniatures that inhabit the bush, none entrances us more than the moths. Over 10,000 species can be found on the continent. There is an infinite variety in the combinations of colour, pattern and shape – from cryptic species resembling leaves, bark, sticks or lichen to those daringly coloured. From just a few millimetres long to a wingspan of 270 mm, they offer an unending kaleidoscope.

Opposite

Aglaopus gemmulosa from the tropical rainforest has a wingspan of 45 mm.

Below

We've called *Problepsis apollinaria* the Mercury Moth after its pattern resembling dribbled quicksilver. ☙

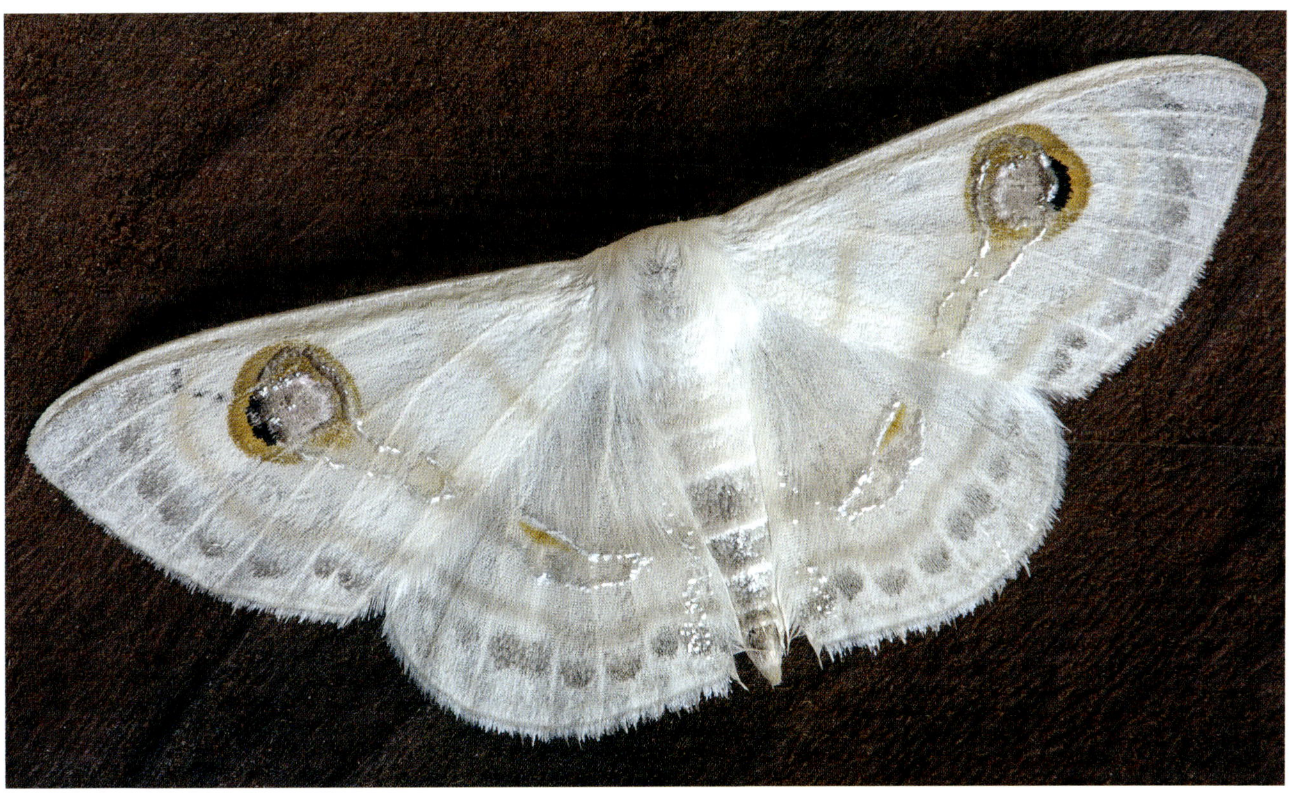

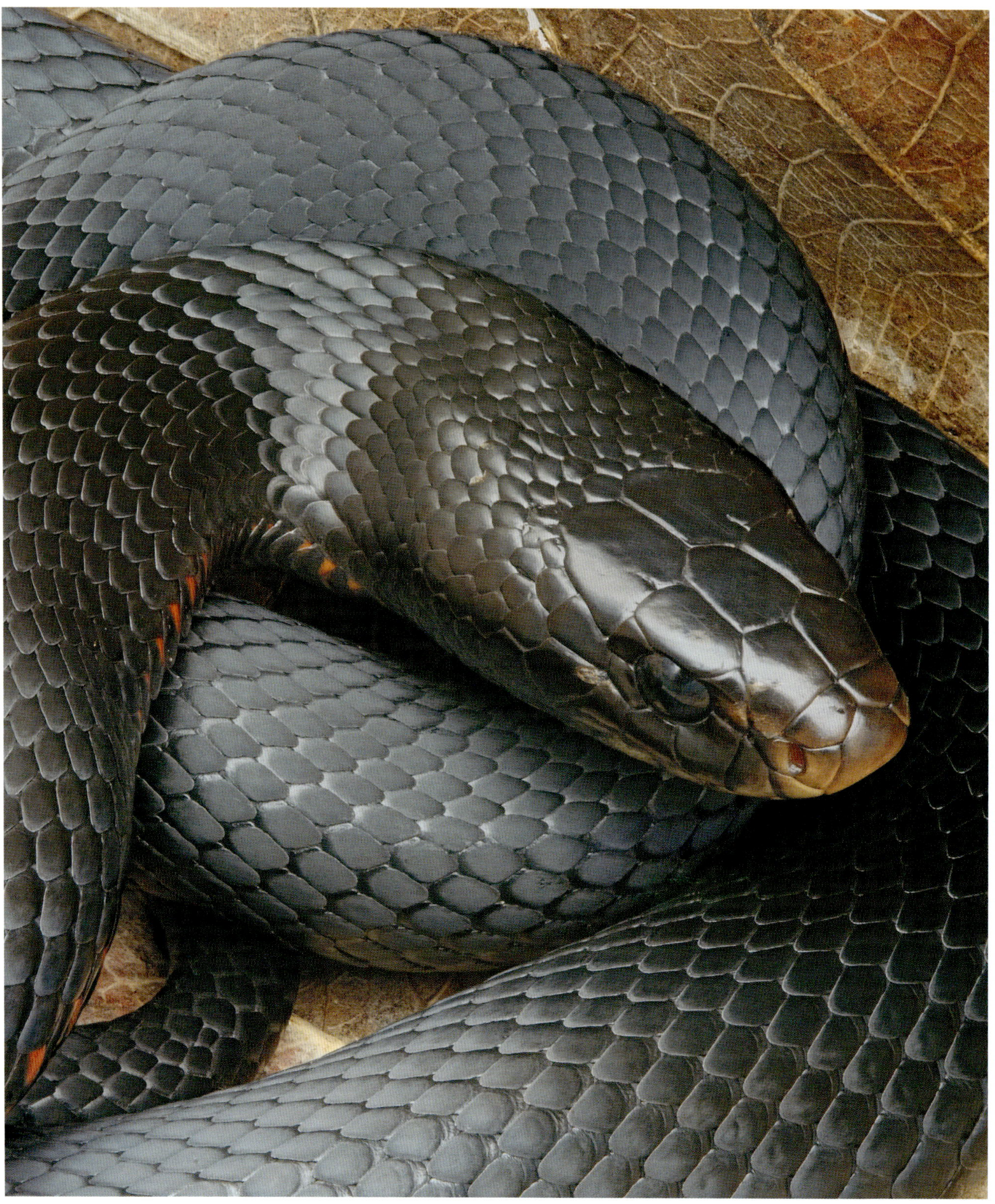

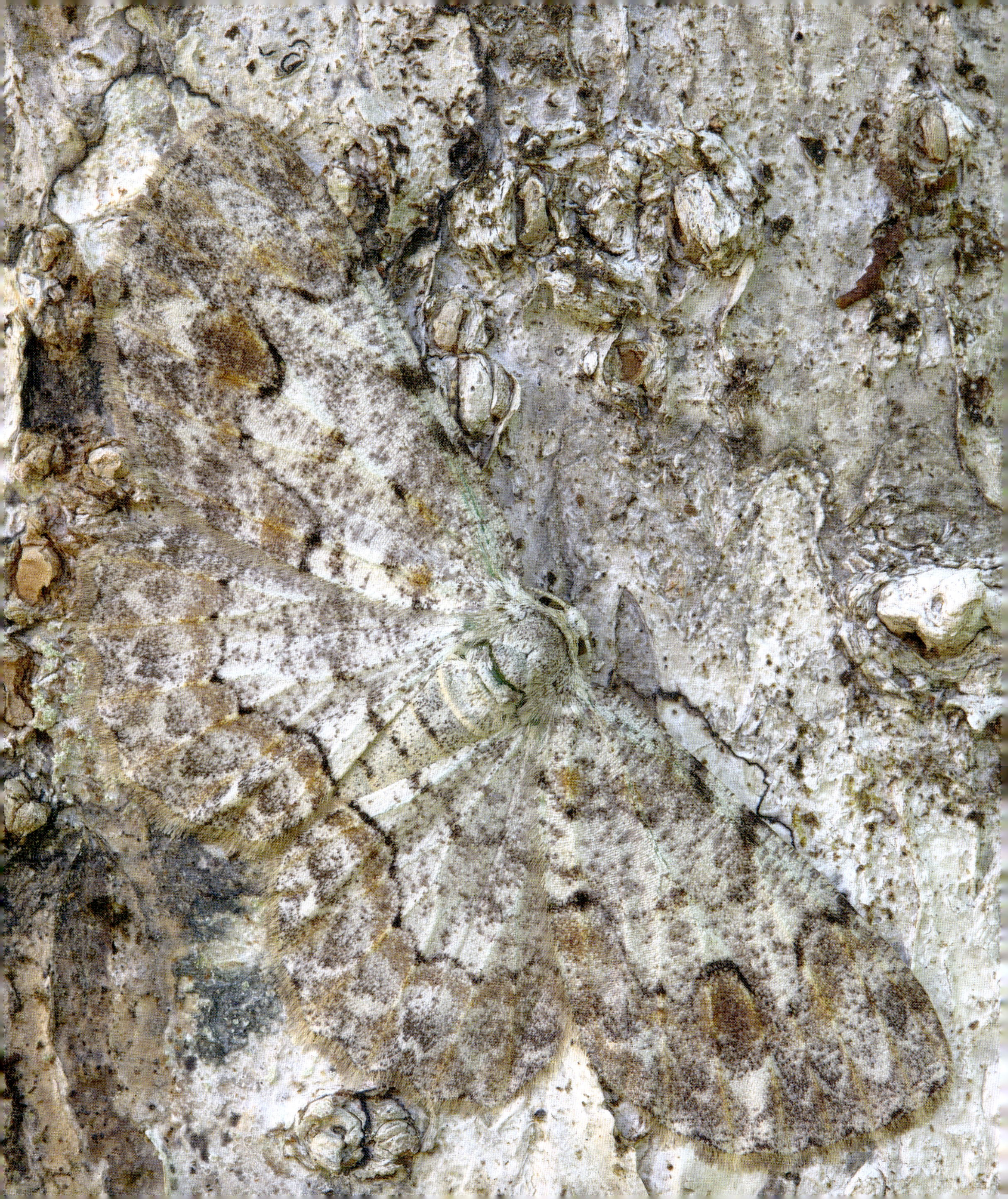

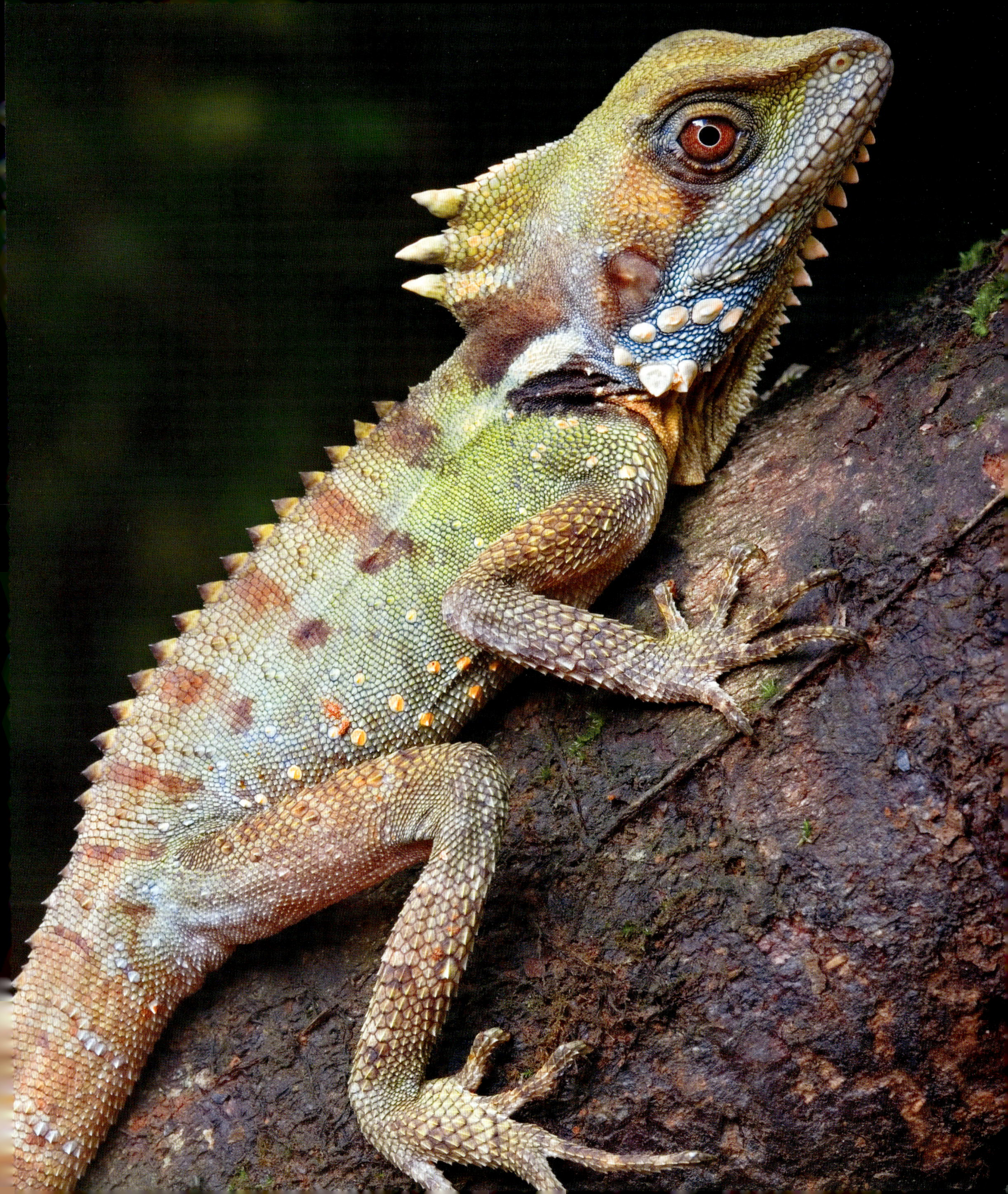

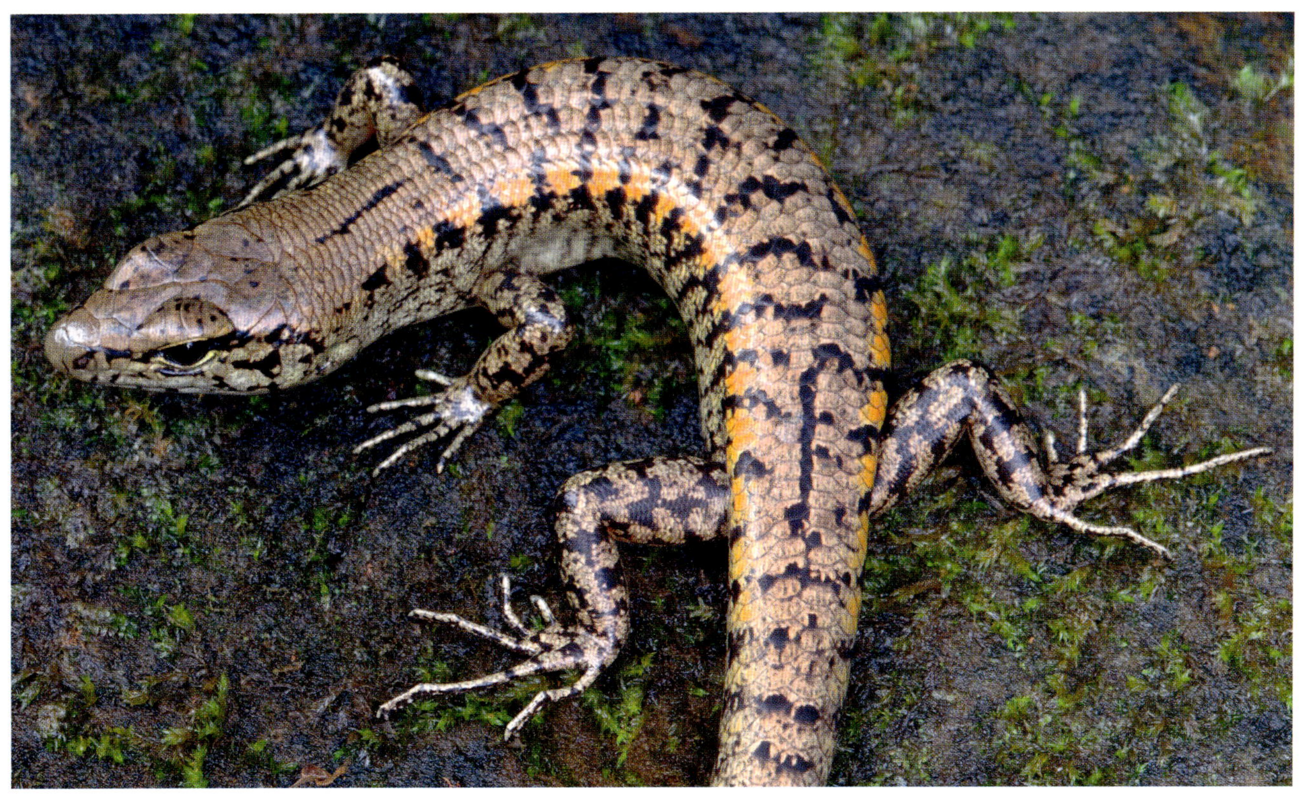

Page 54

Red-bellied Black Snake, *Pseudechis porphyriacus*. The red in some individuals is minimal.

Page 55

This moth of the genus *Cleora* is a perfect match for lichen growing on the bark of a celerywood.

Opposite

Despite its colourful pattern, Boyd's Rainforest Dragon, *Hypsilurus boydii*, is well camouflaged in sun-dappled forests.

Above

The Tiger Skink, *Concinnia tigrina*, lives in the coolness of dense rainforest. It is often seen basking in patches of sunlight.

Following pages

The Shingleback or Pine-cone Lizard, *Trachydosaurus rugosus*, was named after the large, wrinkled scales on its back. Its scientific name translates as 'wrinkled rough lizard'. It is common across southern Australia.

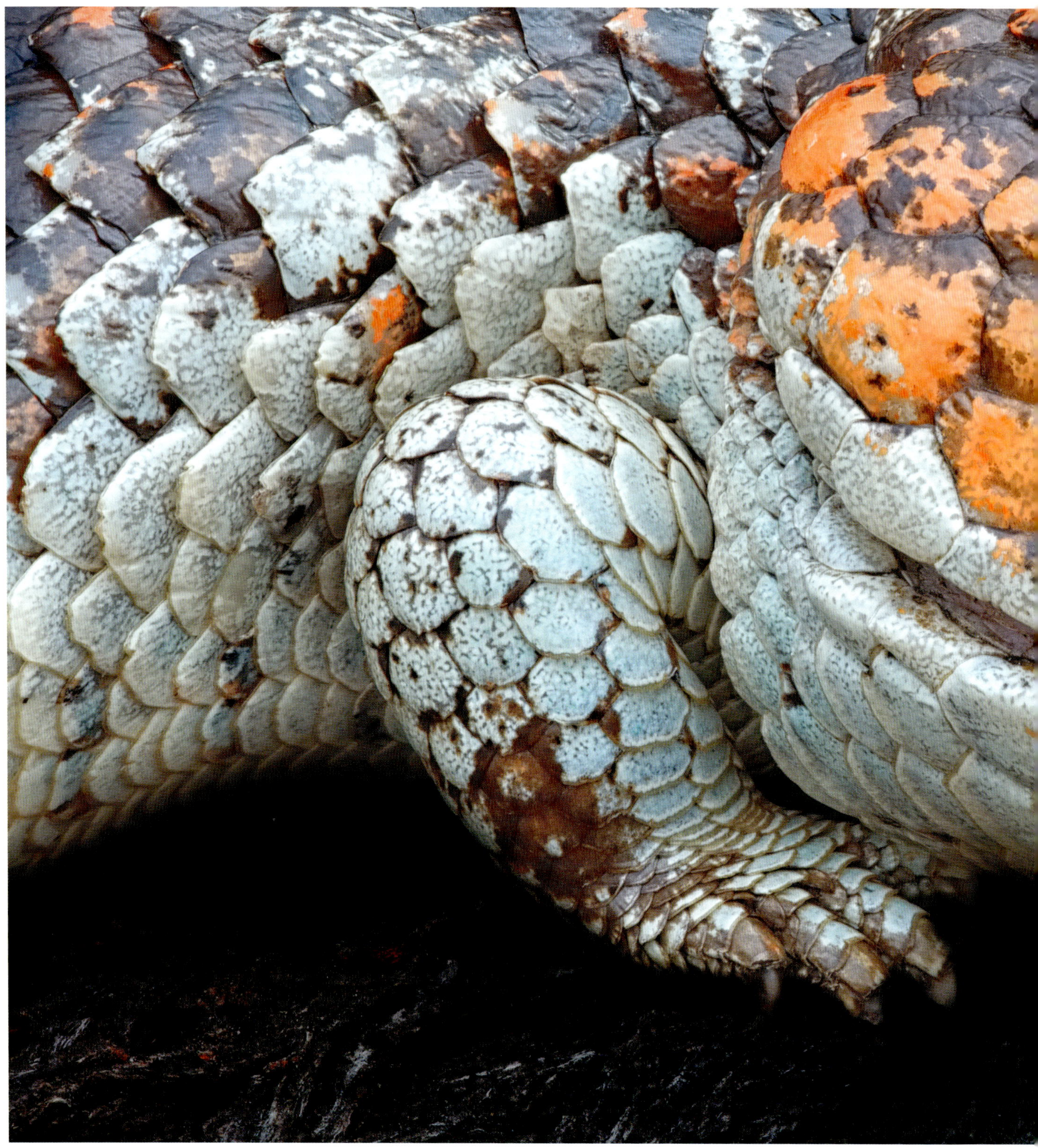

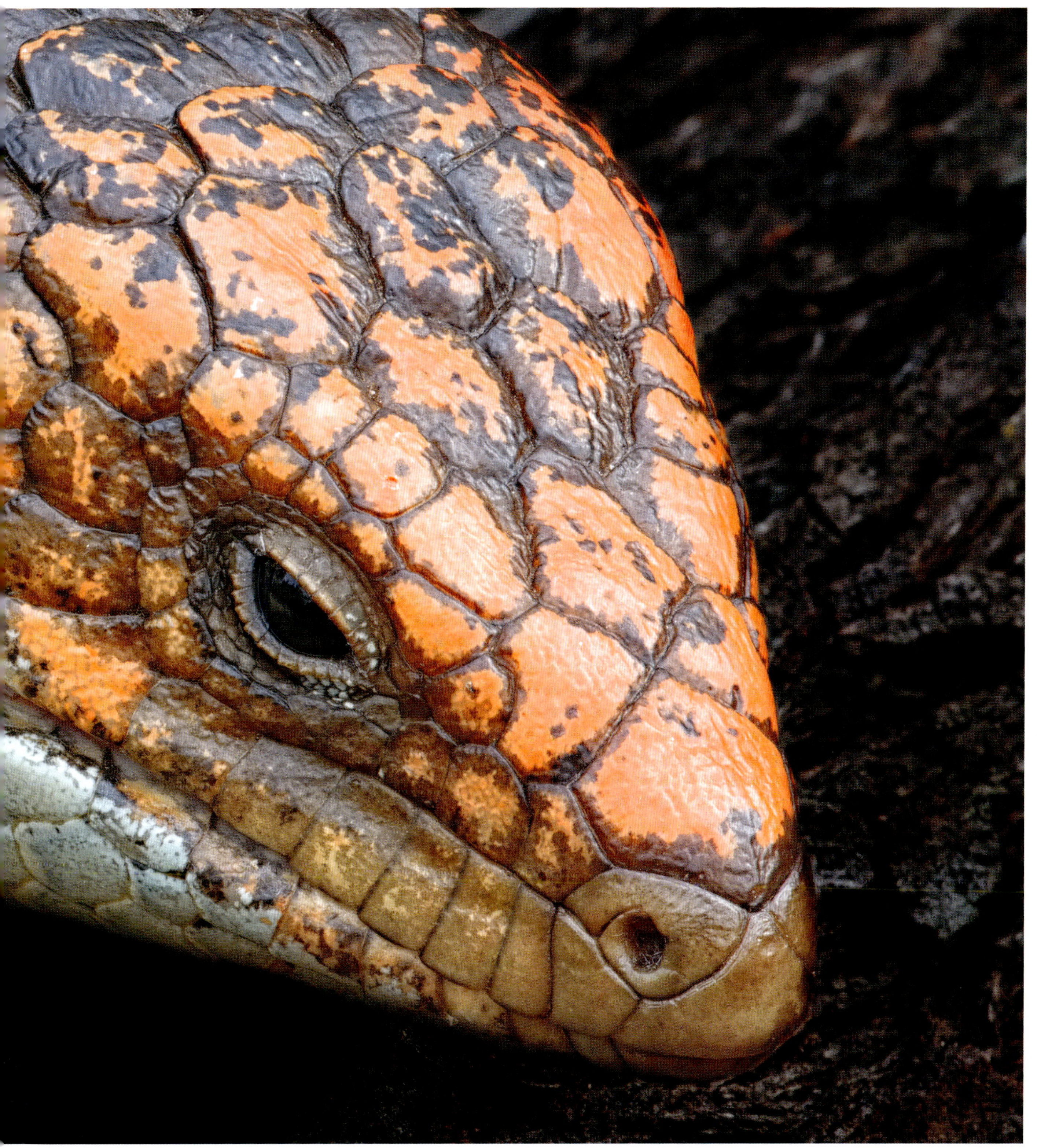

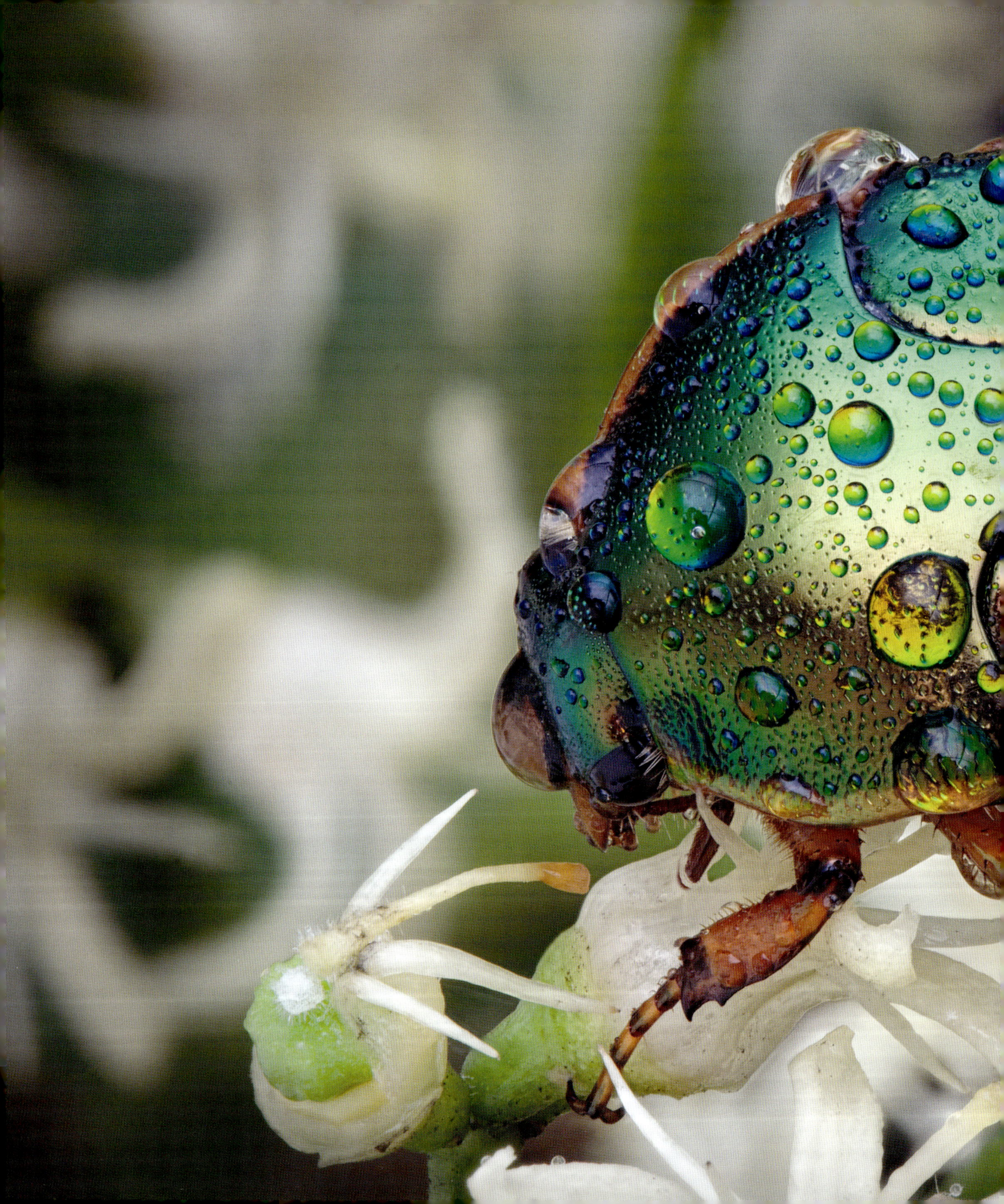

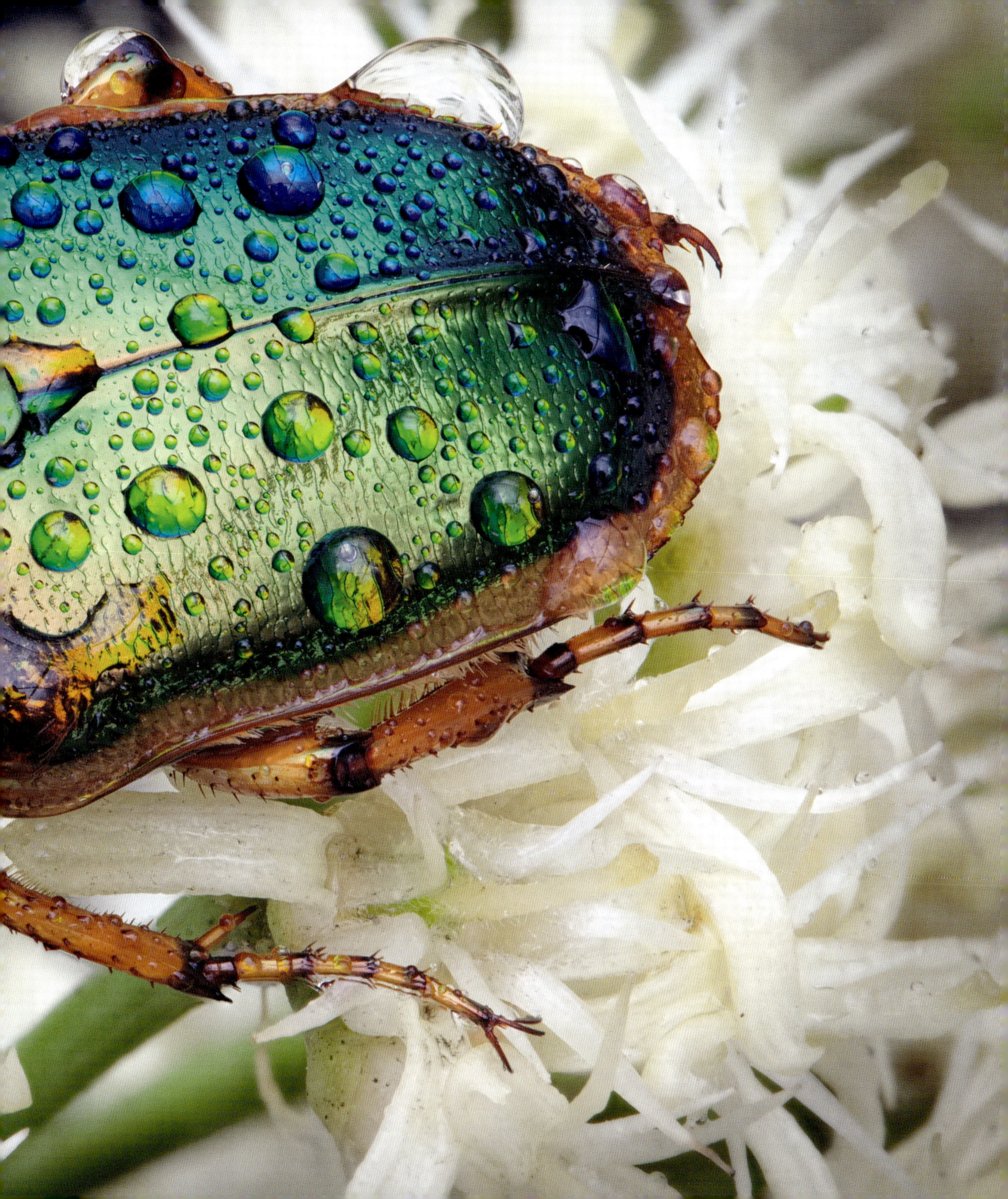

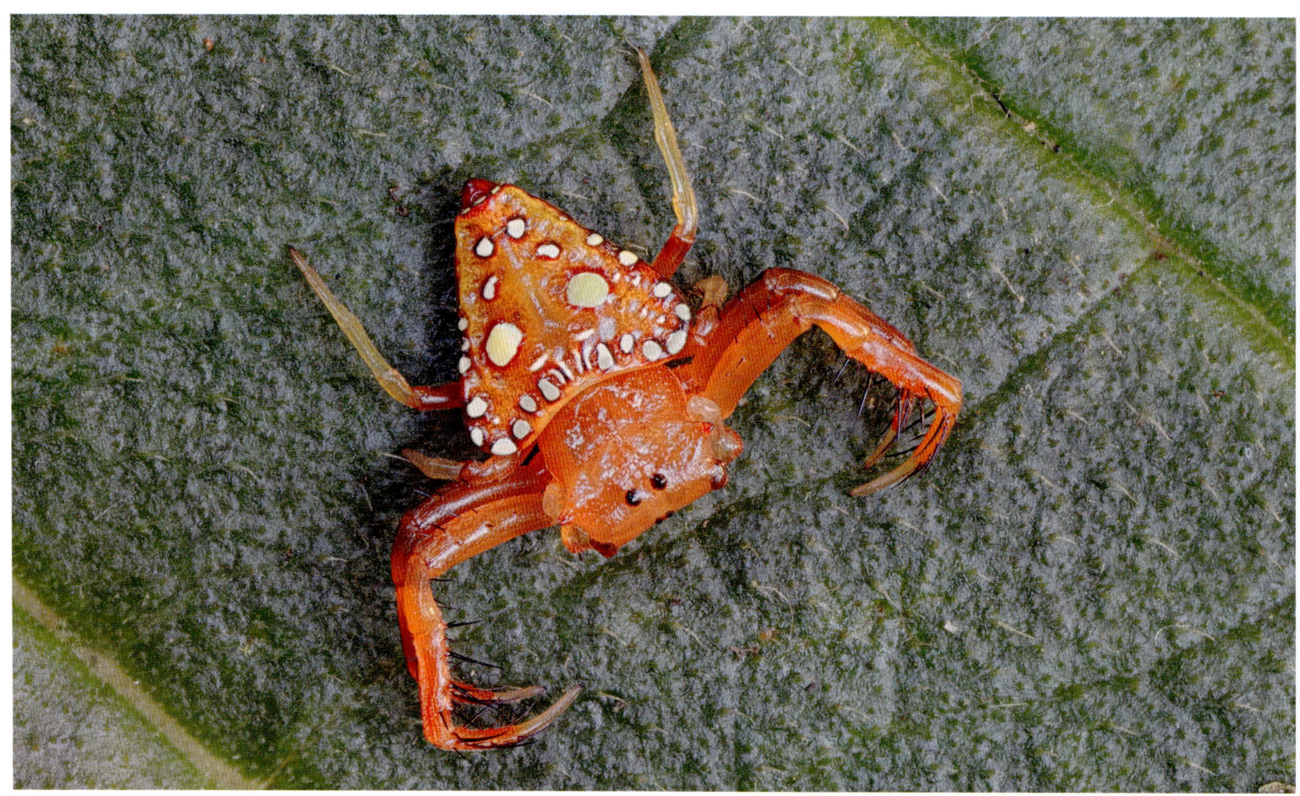

Preceding pages

Mycterophallus duboulayi is a chafer beetle and like all of its kind it loves flowers and hot sunny weather. A flowering shrub or tree can be abuzz with scores and sometimes hundreds of chafers of many species. When it rains and is cooler they will rest on a flower or leaf. ☙

Above

Though only 7 mm long the Triangle Spider, *Arcys* sp., is a fearsome predator. It lies in wait for possible prey on leaves and flowers. Any fly or other small insect that wanders within range of its jackknife front legs is seized and devoured.

Opposite

Australian cicadas are held in great affection. This is reflected in the common names they have been given – Greengrocer, Double Drummer, Black Prince, Floury Baker, Cherrynose and many others. Members of the genus *Tamasa* have become known as Bunyips! This is an undescribed species of Bunyip (*Tamasa* sp.). Its pristine silver and golden hairs tell us it has only just emerged from its nymphal case. ☙

Following pages

Underside of a wing of a Rainbow Lorikeet, *Trichoglossus haematodus*.

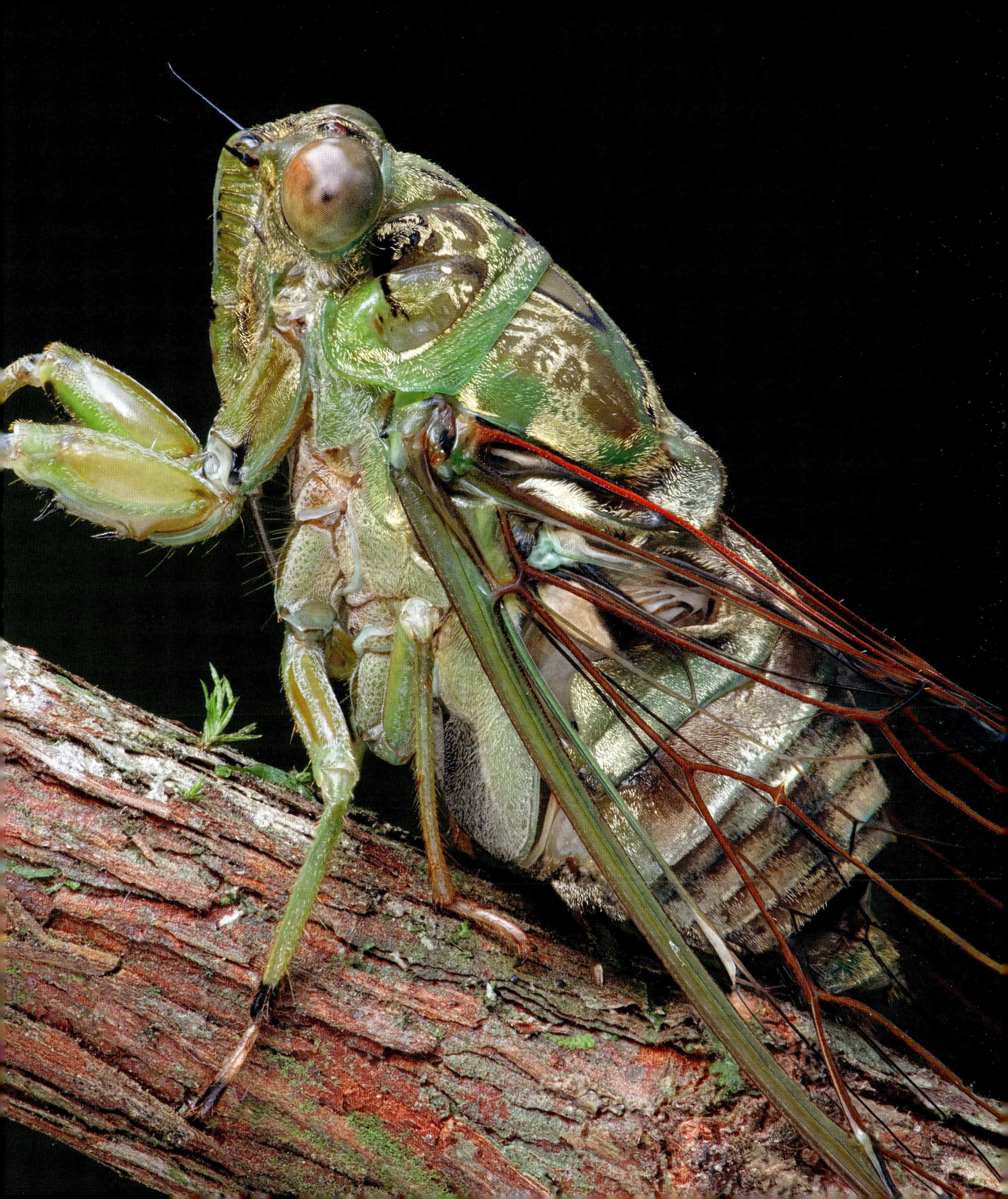

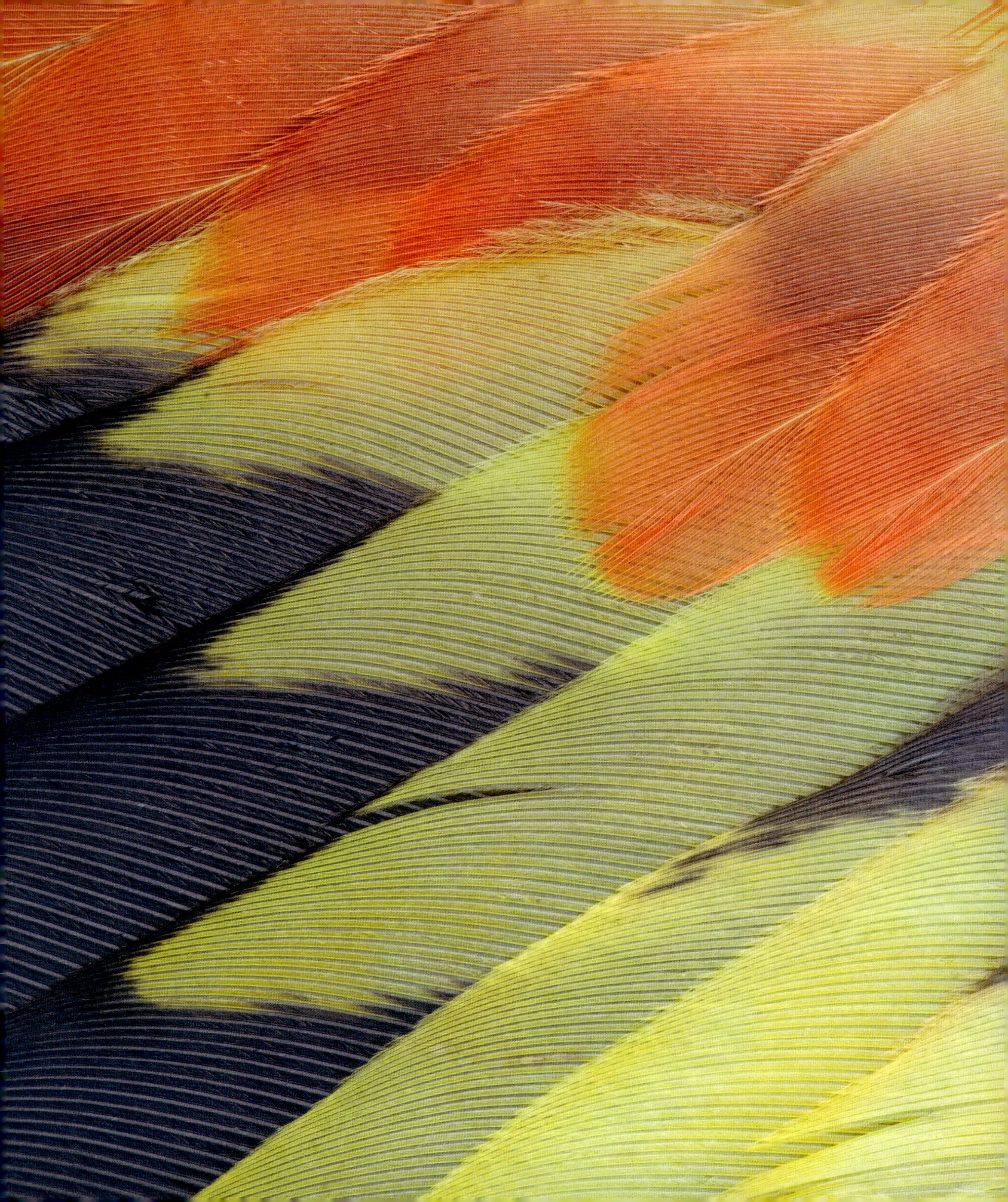

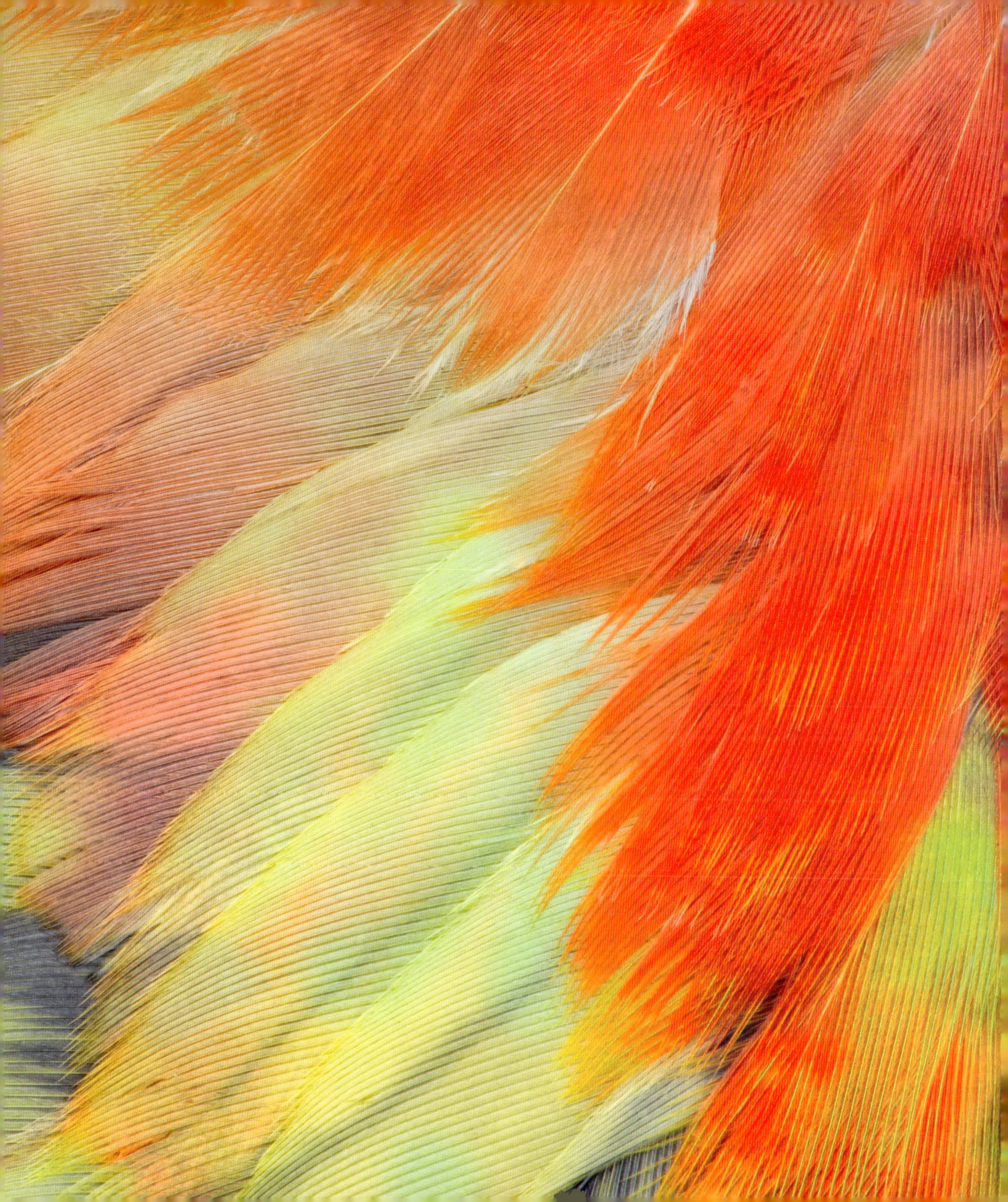

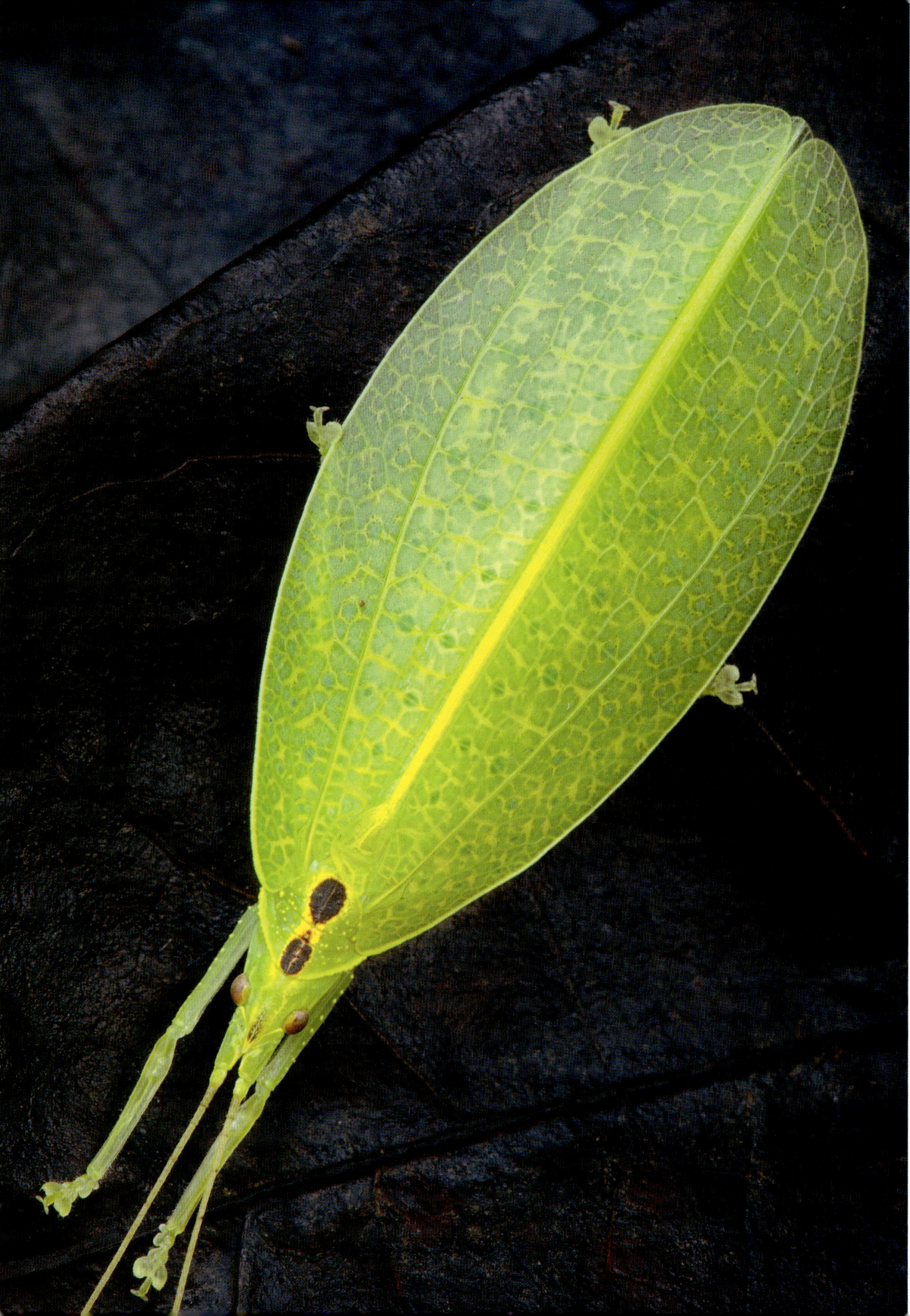

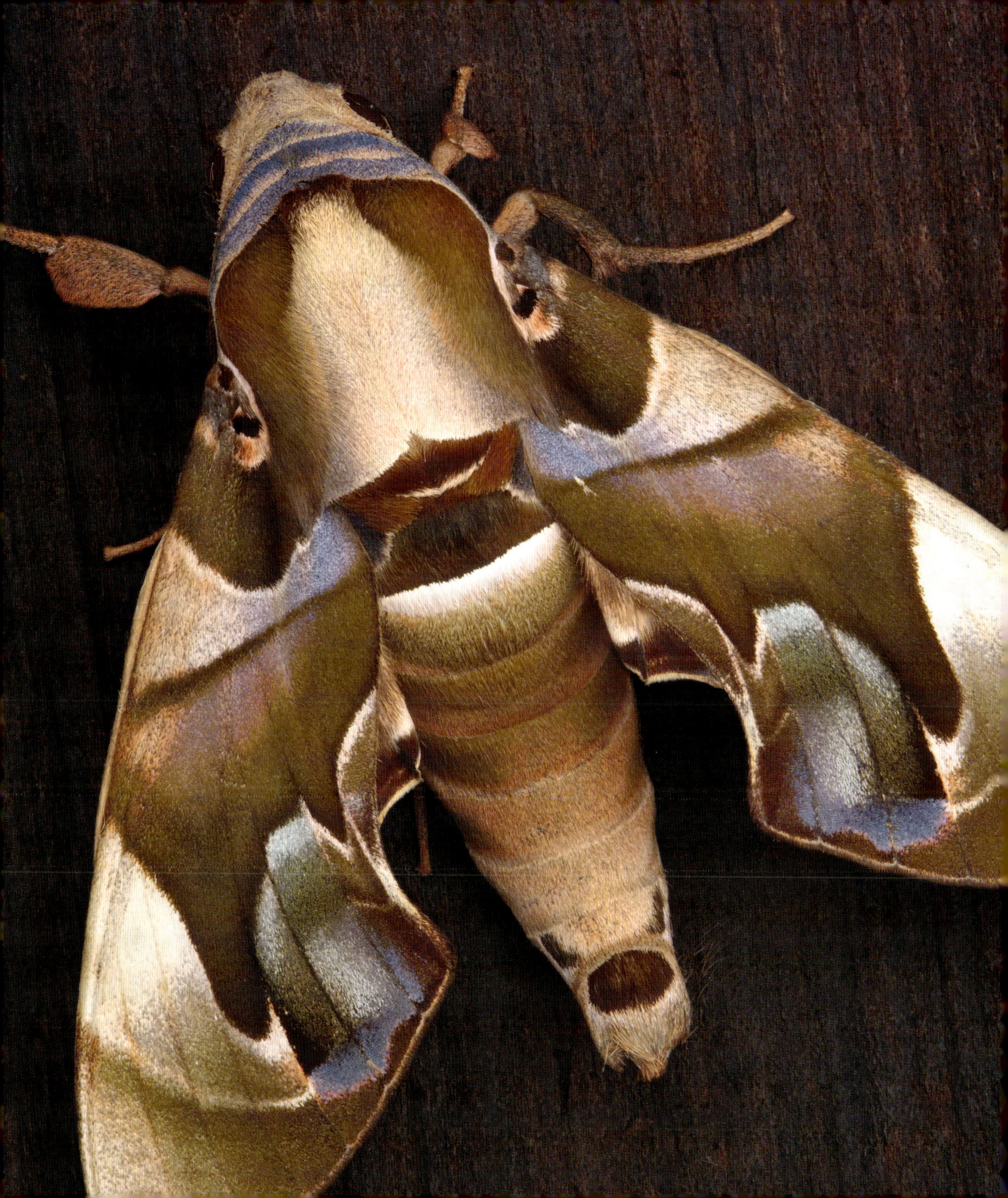

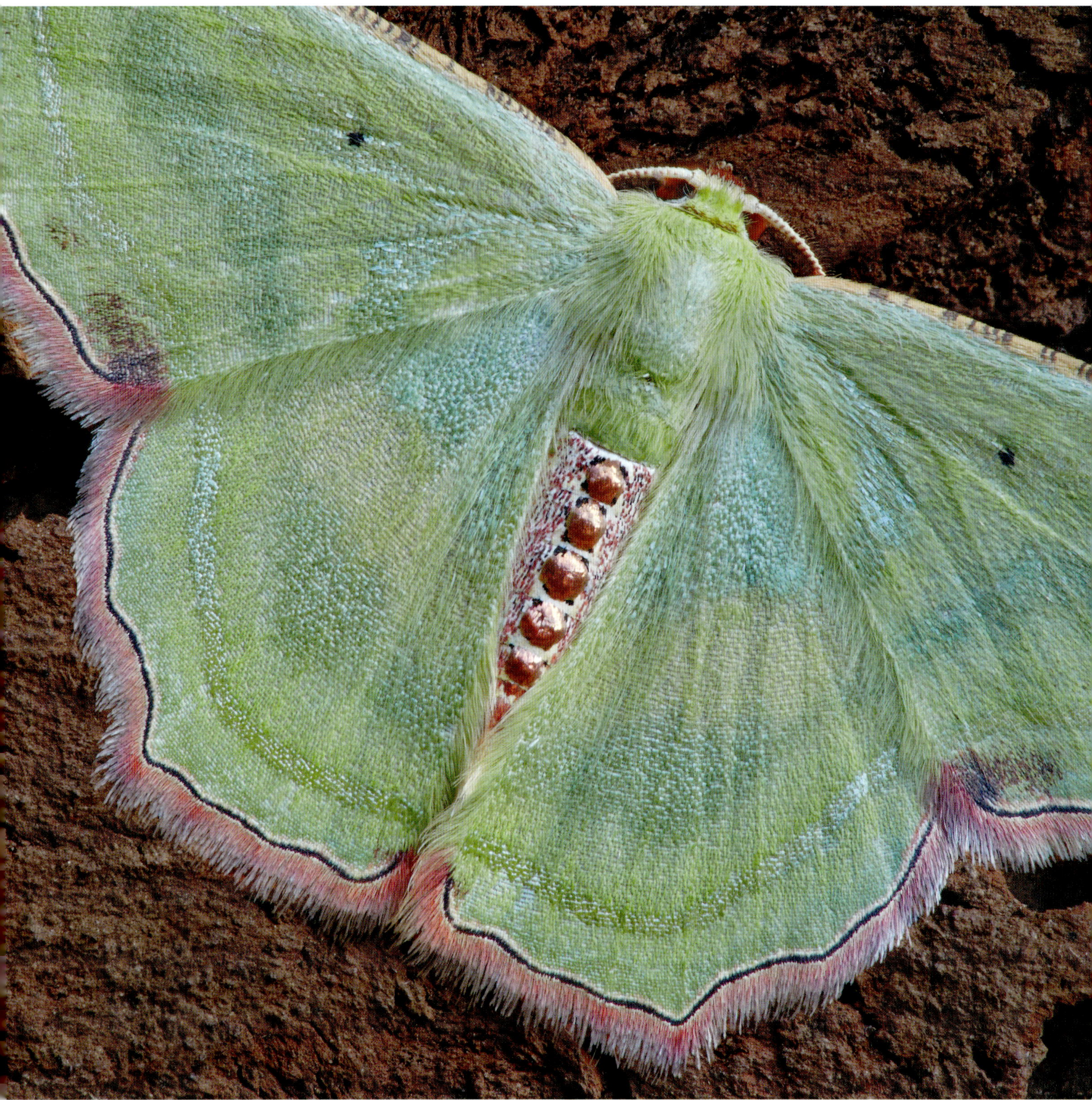

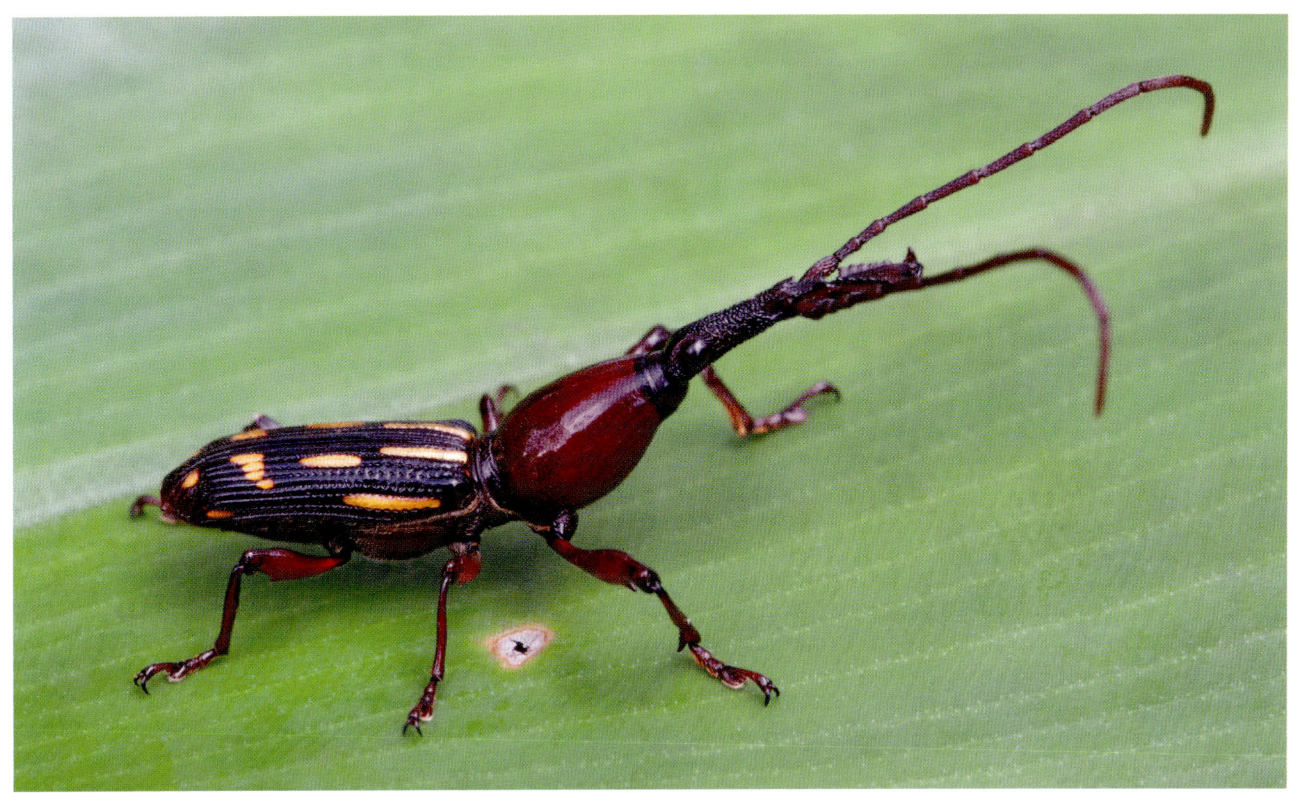

Page 66

Only when the Leaf-mimicking Katydid, *Acauloplacella hasenpuschae*, settles on a contrasting background can its true shape and colours be appreciated.

Page 67

Daphnis protrudens, a species of hawkmoth, is powerfully built for fast, buzzing flight. At night it seeks out flowering rainforest trees. Hovering in front of the flowers, it extracts their nectar with its long proboscis. Hawkmoths are important pollinators.

Opposite

The Brass-button Moth, *Metallochlora lineata*, is one of about two score small, green-patterned species in the Geometrid family. They all have looper caterpillars. ☙

Above

There are more than 300,000 species of beetles in the world. About 30,000 of them live in Australia. Of all the families of beetles, the weevils have the most species – about 8,000 in Australia alone. No other animal family has so many species. All weevils have a long 'snout' or rostrum. The 25 mm long *Ectochemus decimmaculatus* has taken this rostrum to extreme lengths. ☙

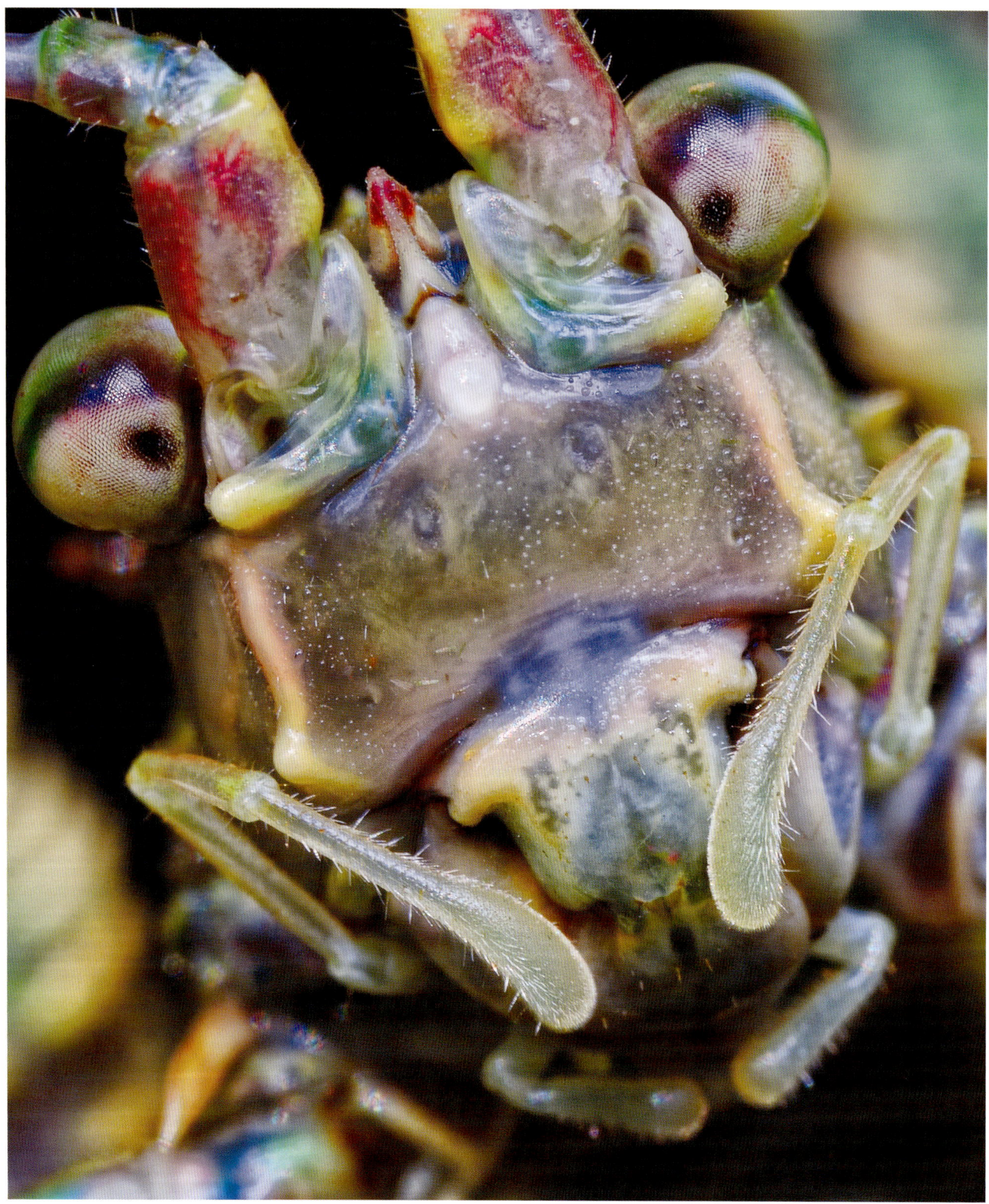

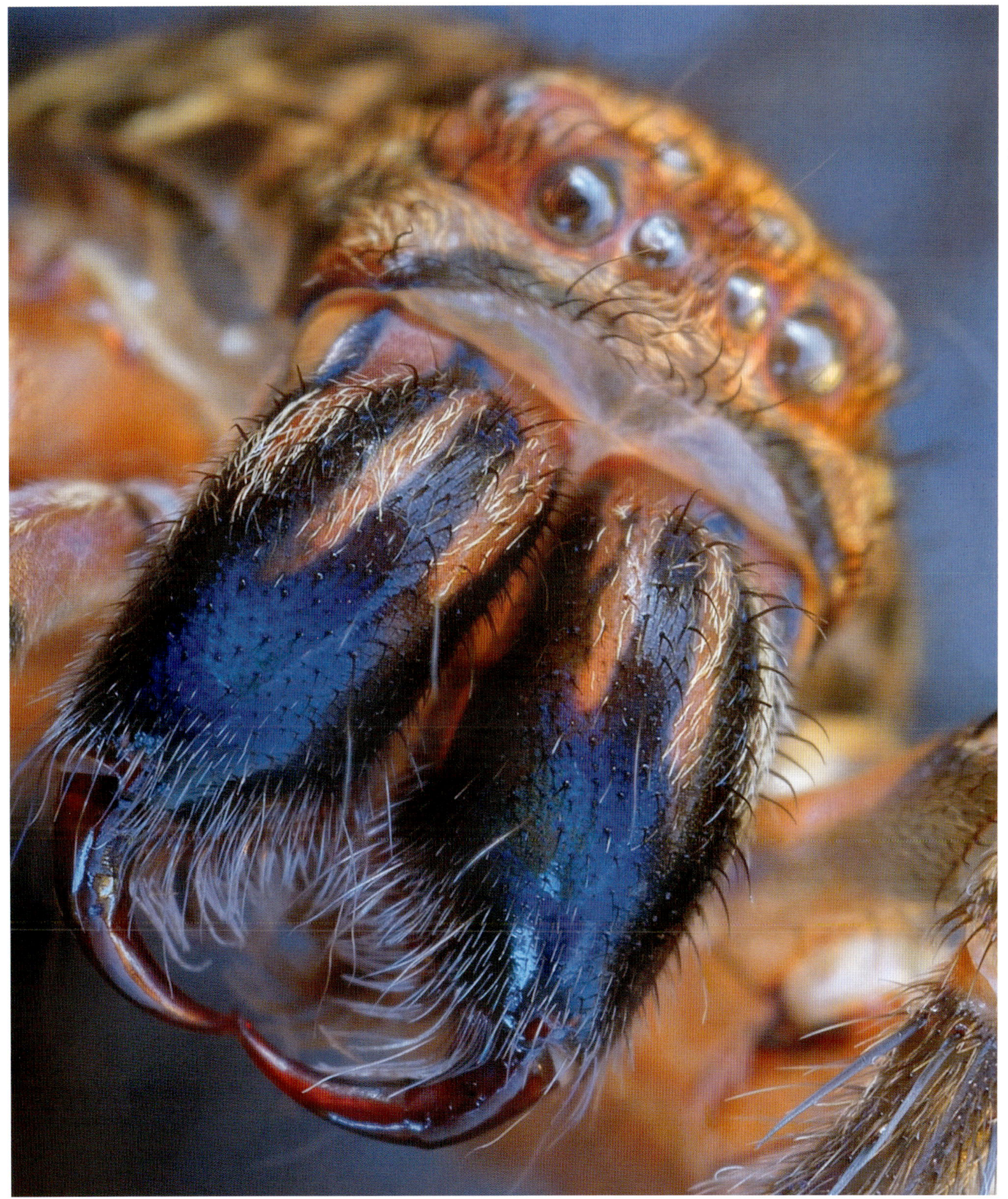

Page 70

Portrait of the Spiny Katydid, *Phricta spinosa*.

Page 71

Not a face but a mask – the empty exoskeleton of a huntsman spider. The 'skin' in insects and spiders cannot grow, only expand to a limited degree. When this limit is reached the exoskeleton splits and the spider emerges in a new, roomier 'skin'. The old one, a perfect but hollow replica, is discarded.

Right

Stag beetles like this splendid Mueller's Stag Beetle, *Phalacrognathus muelleri*, are not endowed with antlers but with enlarged and reinforced mandibles. The 'antlers' are really its jaws (see also page 32).

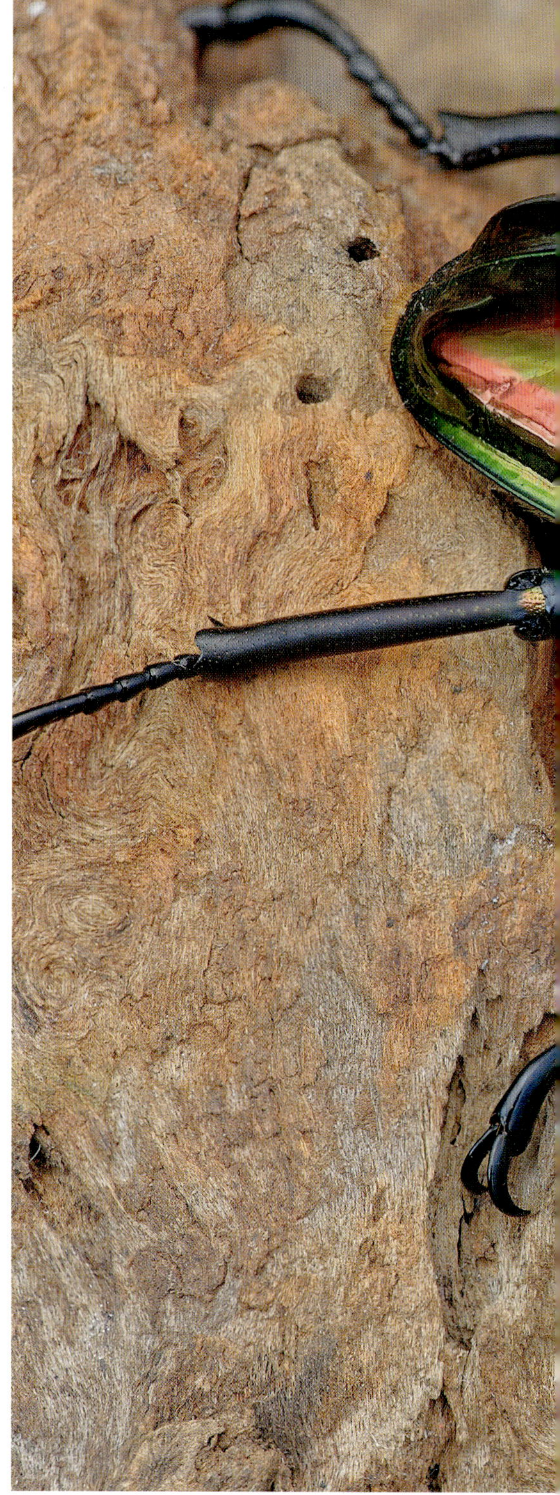

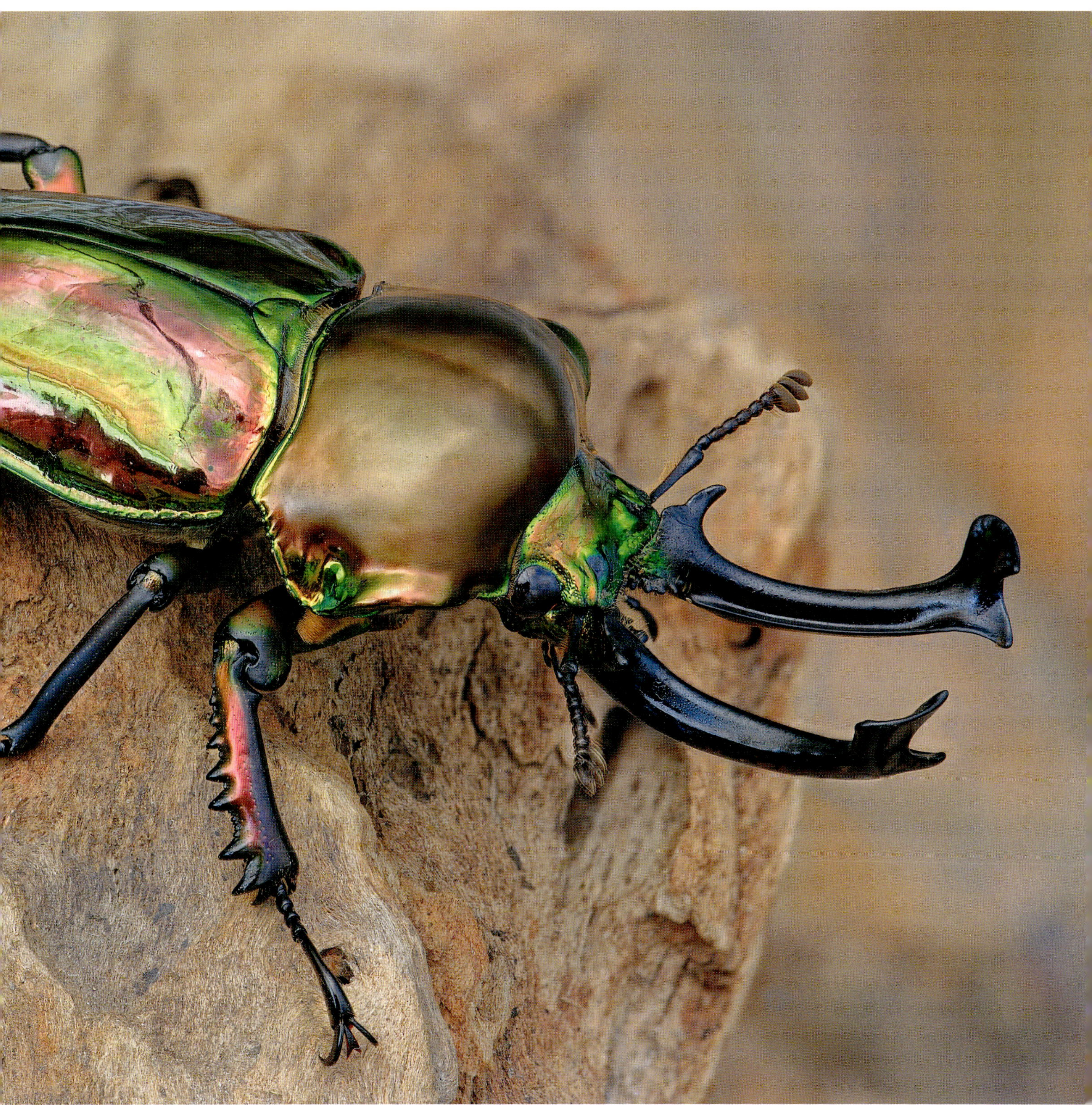

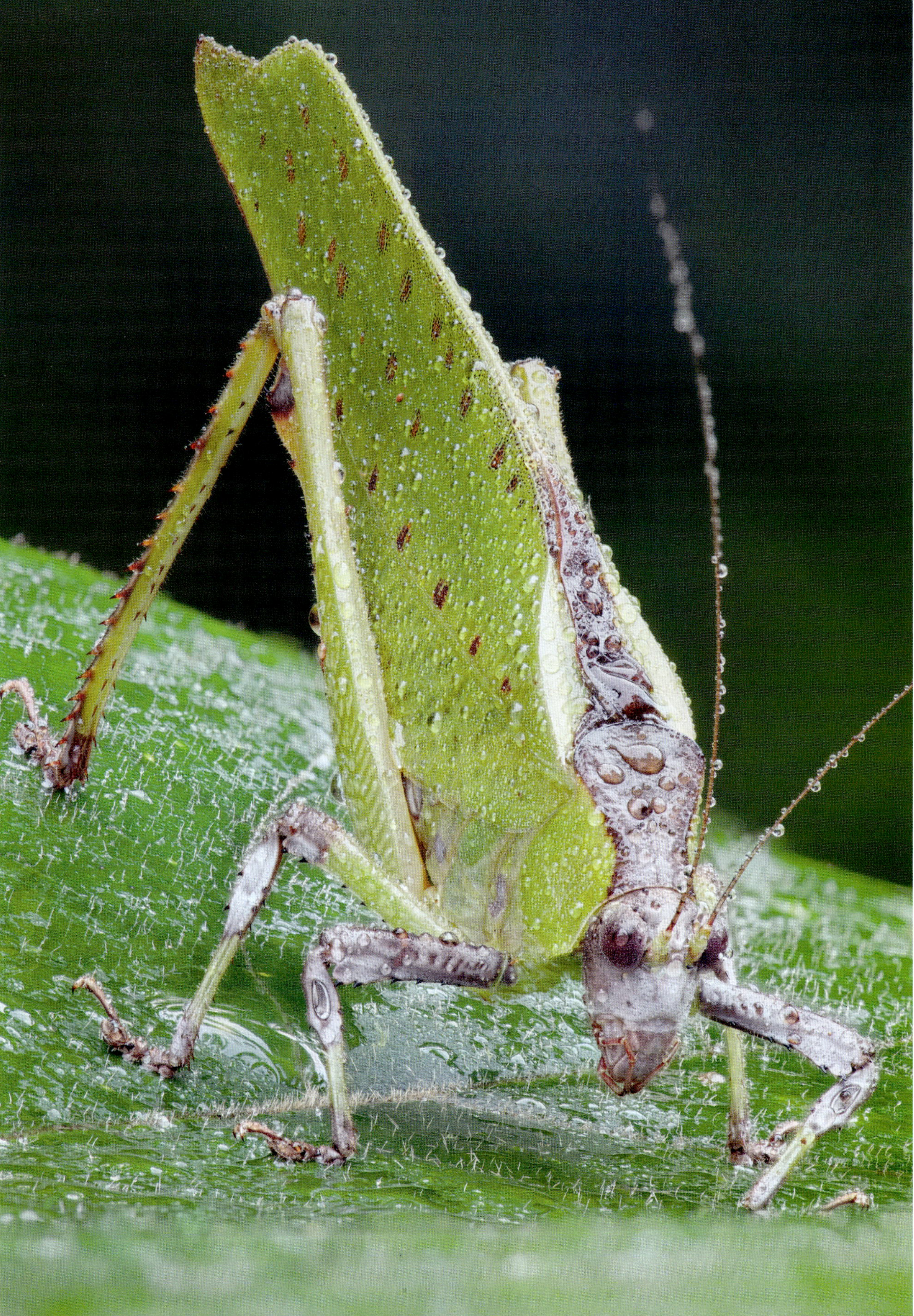

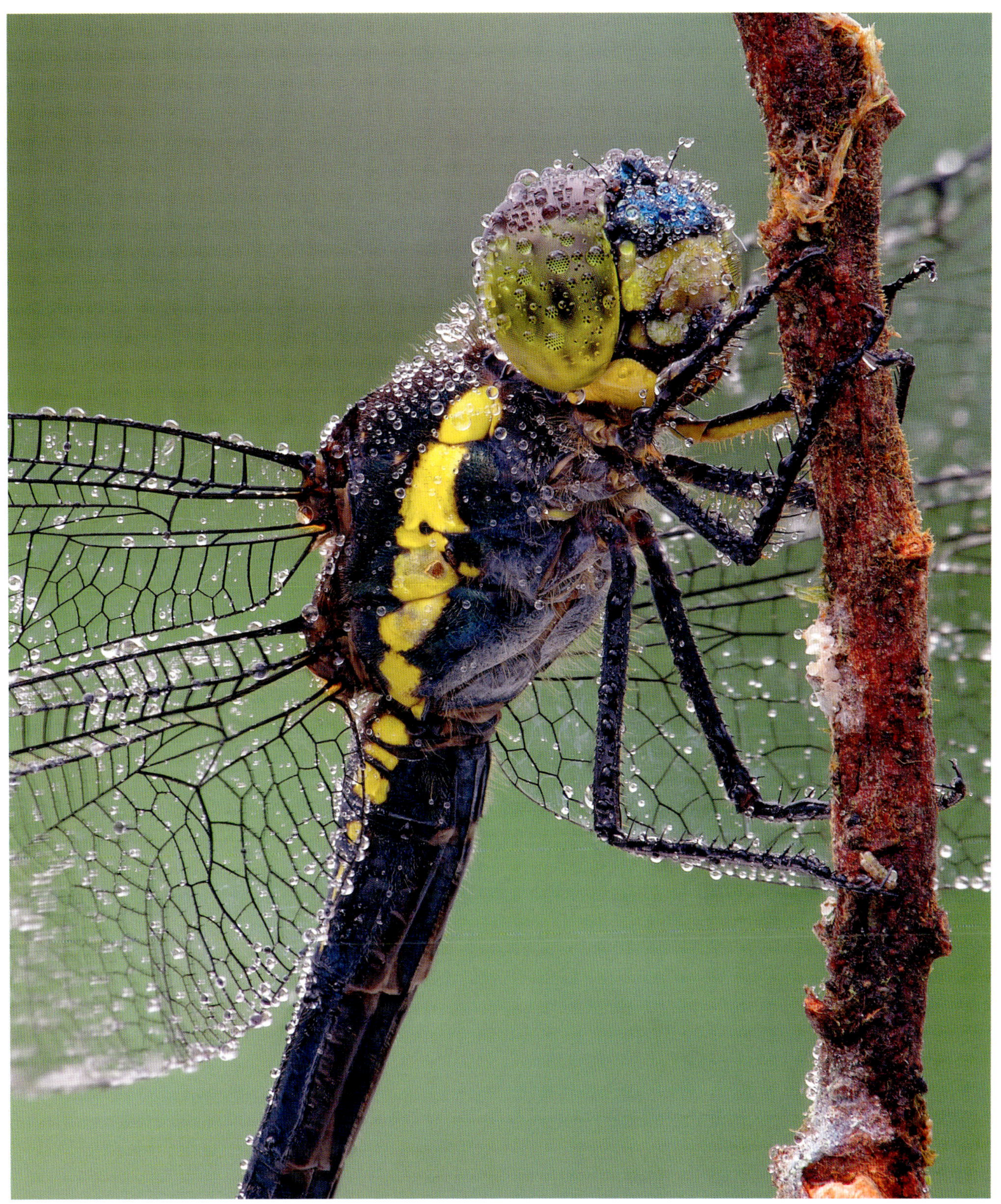

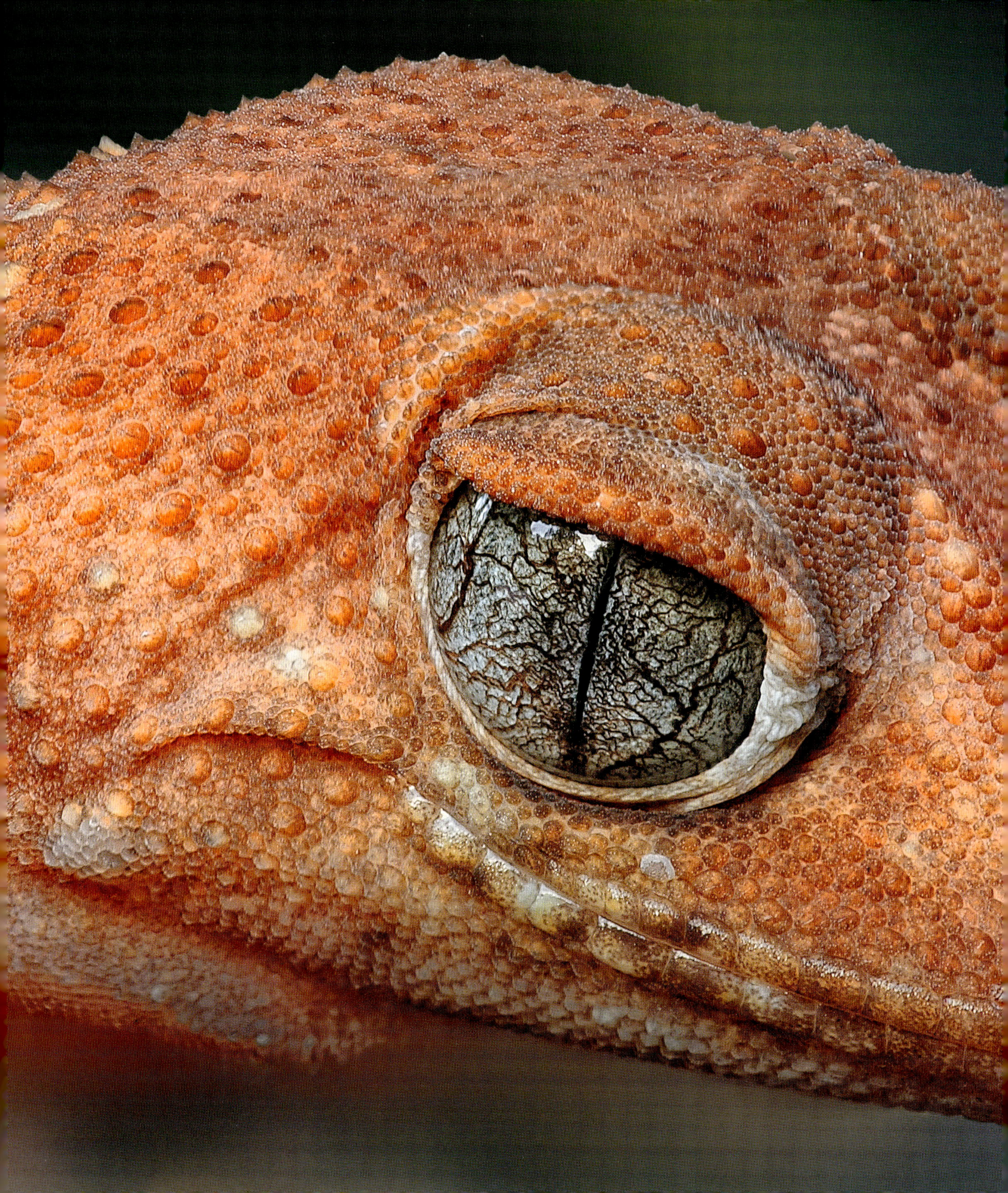

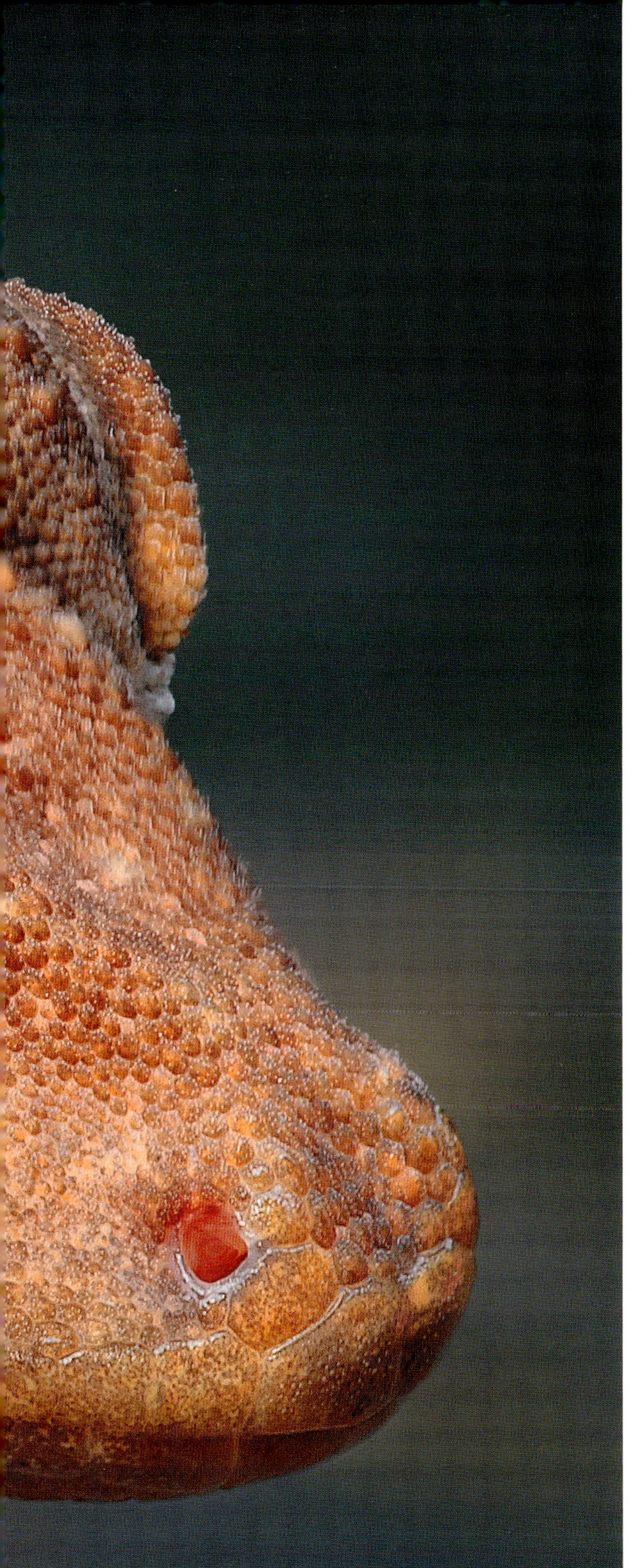

Pages 74 and 75

Most insects will hide under leaves or in tree hollows during downpours. But some – like the Brown-faced Katydid, *Ephippitytha kuranda* (page 74) and Striped Swamp Dragonfly, *Agrionoptera longitudinalis* (page 75) – seem to welcome the rain.

Left

The Pilbara Barking Gecko, *Underwoodisaurus seorsus*, has so far only been found in the Pilbara region of Western Australia. It is a terrestrial lizard that emerges from its hiding place at night to hunt for insects and other small animal life.

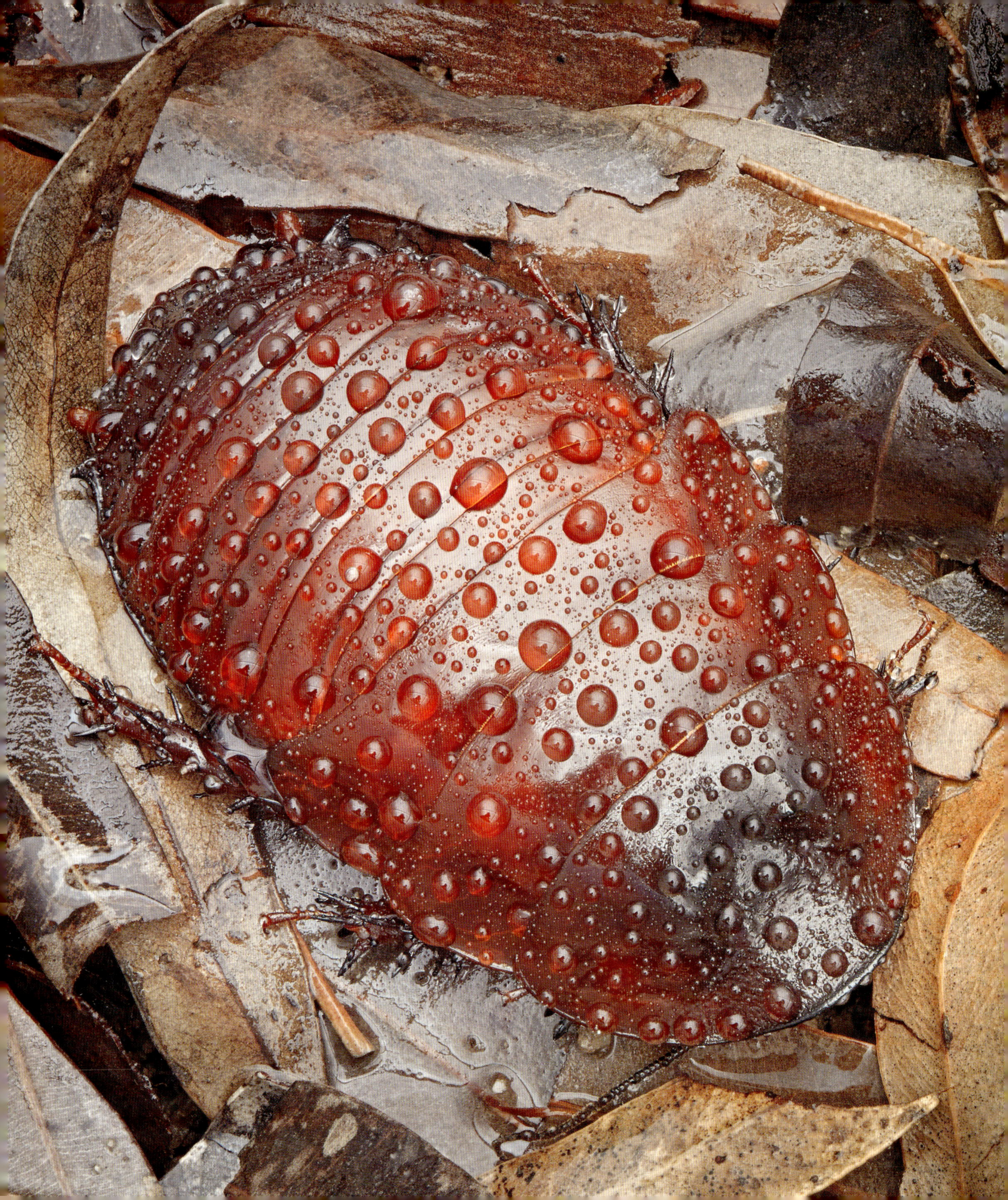

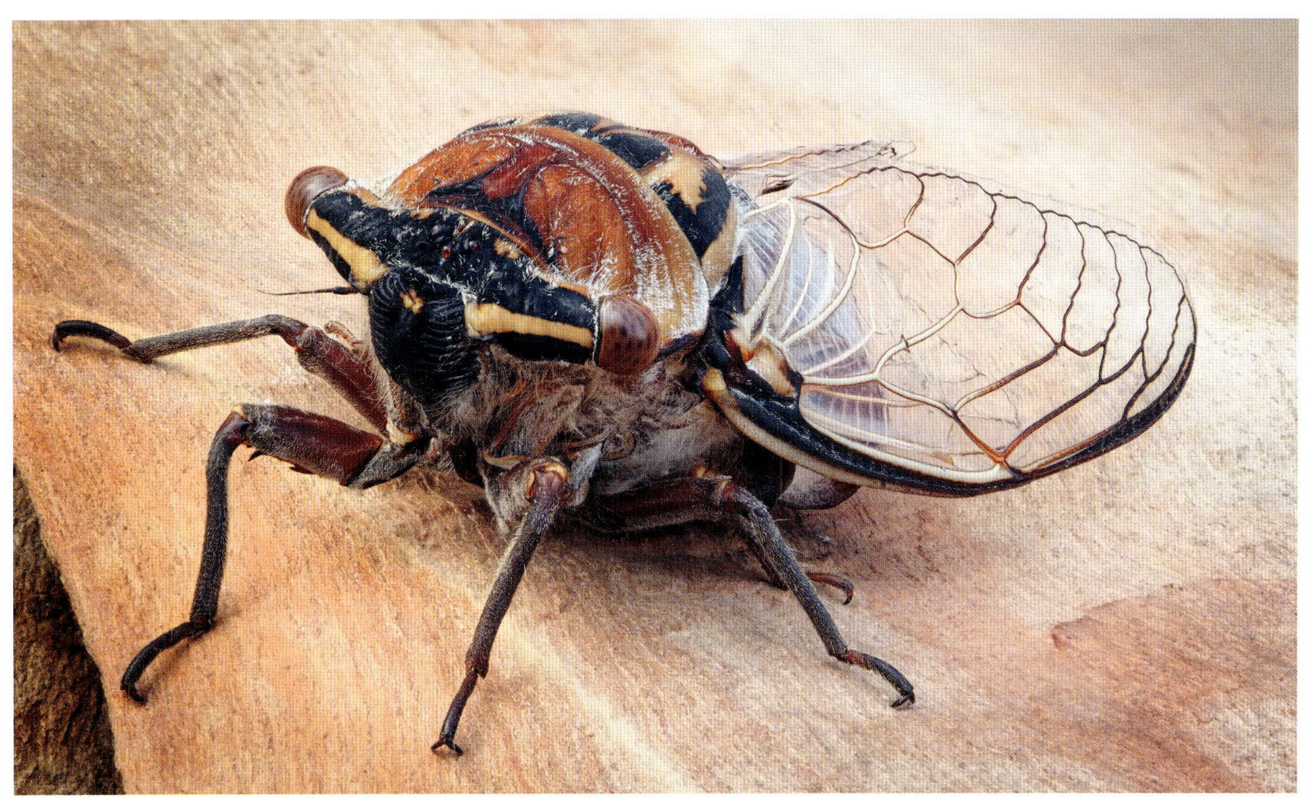

Opposite

The Giant Burrowing Cockroaches, *Macropanesthia rhinoceros*, rarely see daylight; they spend most of their seven-year lifespan in burrows they excavate in sandy soils. A male and female may live together in a chamber at the end of the burrow. At night they emerge to gather dry eucalypt leaves on which they feed. The female gives birth to as many as 30 young in a season. These stay with their parents for some time. During wet-season rains males emerge from their burrows, swarming over the countryside to look for mates. At 65 mm long, they are so large that they have been mistaken for baby turtles. At 30 grams, they are also among the heaviest of all insects. They are much too heavy to fly and have no wings.

Above

The Double Drummer, *Thopha saccata*, is Australia's largest cicada. It is so named after its particularly well developed and prominent musical instruments. There is one on each side of the male's body. But the instruments are not drums, they are known as tymbals – membranes that buckle in and out at a rate of 100–400 times a second to produce remarkably penetrating sounds. See also pages 63, 92–93.

Following pages

A Grey and Orange Hypsidia, *Hypsidia robinsoni*, at rest (left). When you get too close, the moth transforms itself, flashing its red and white pattern (right). This may well startle and distract a predator. The bright colours could also be a warning that the moth is poisonous and distasteful.

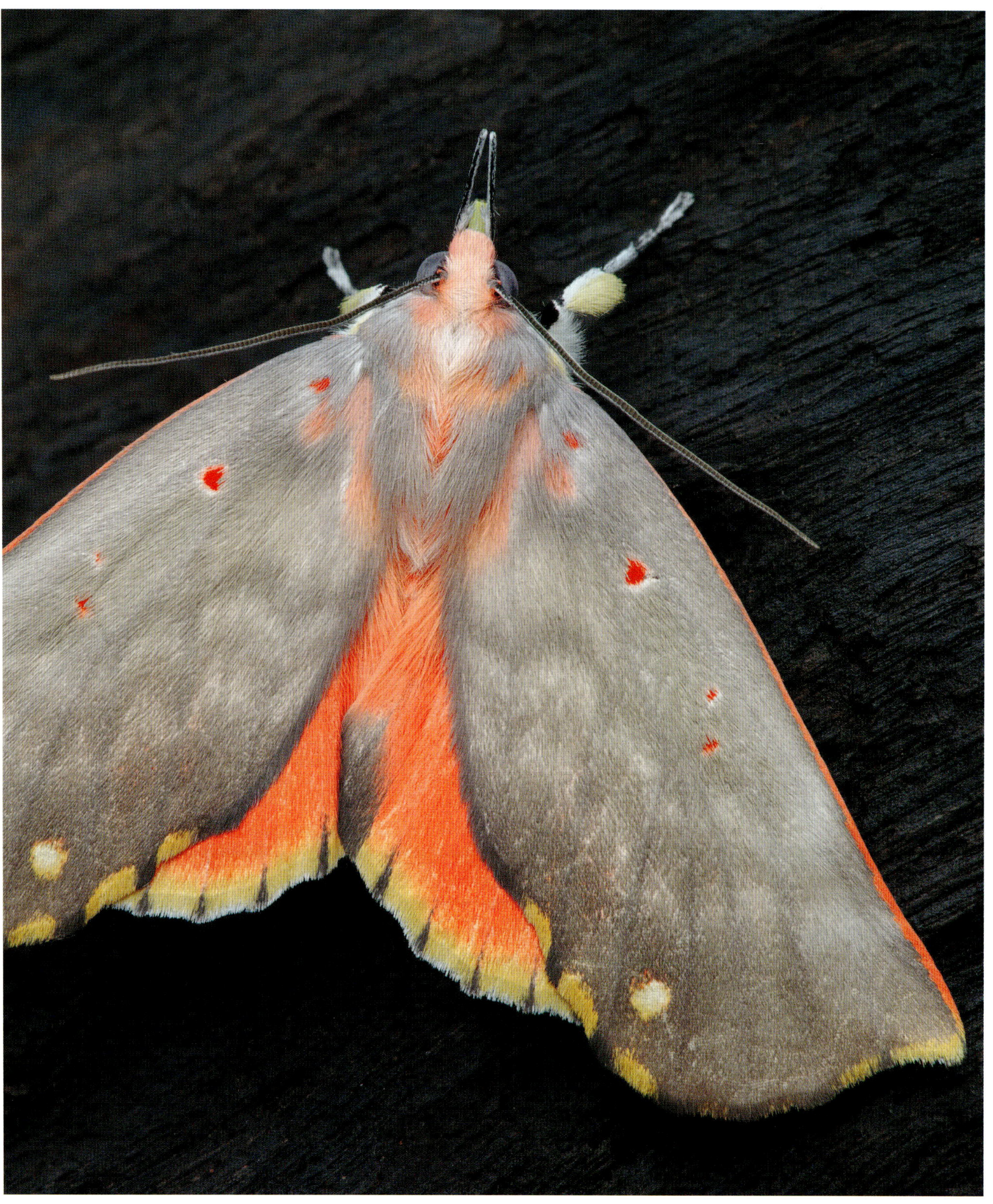

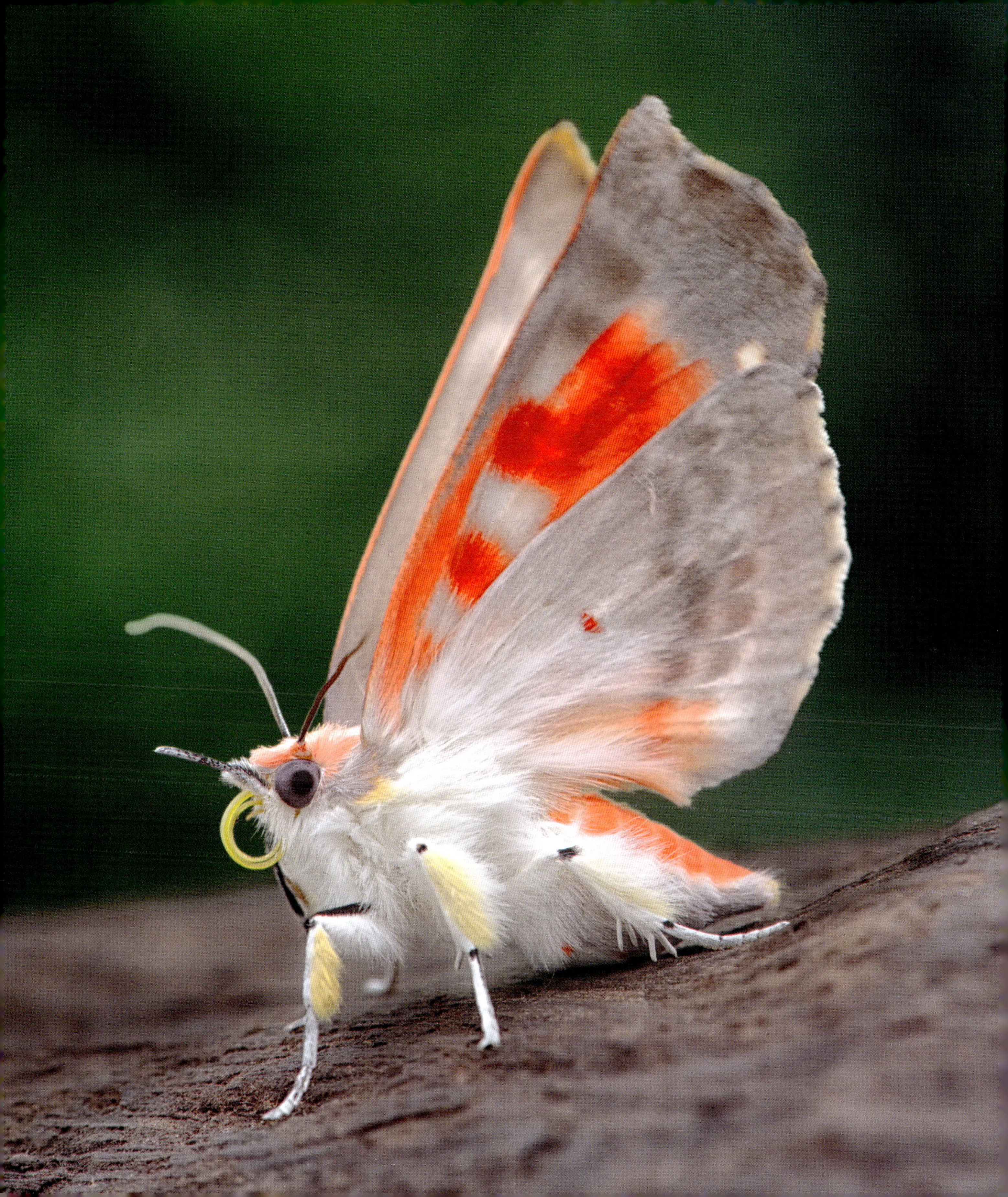

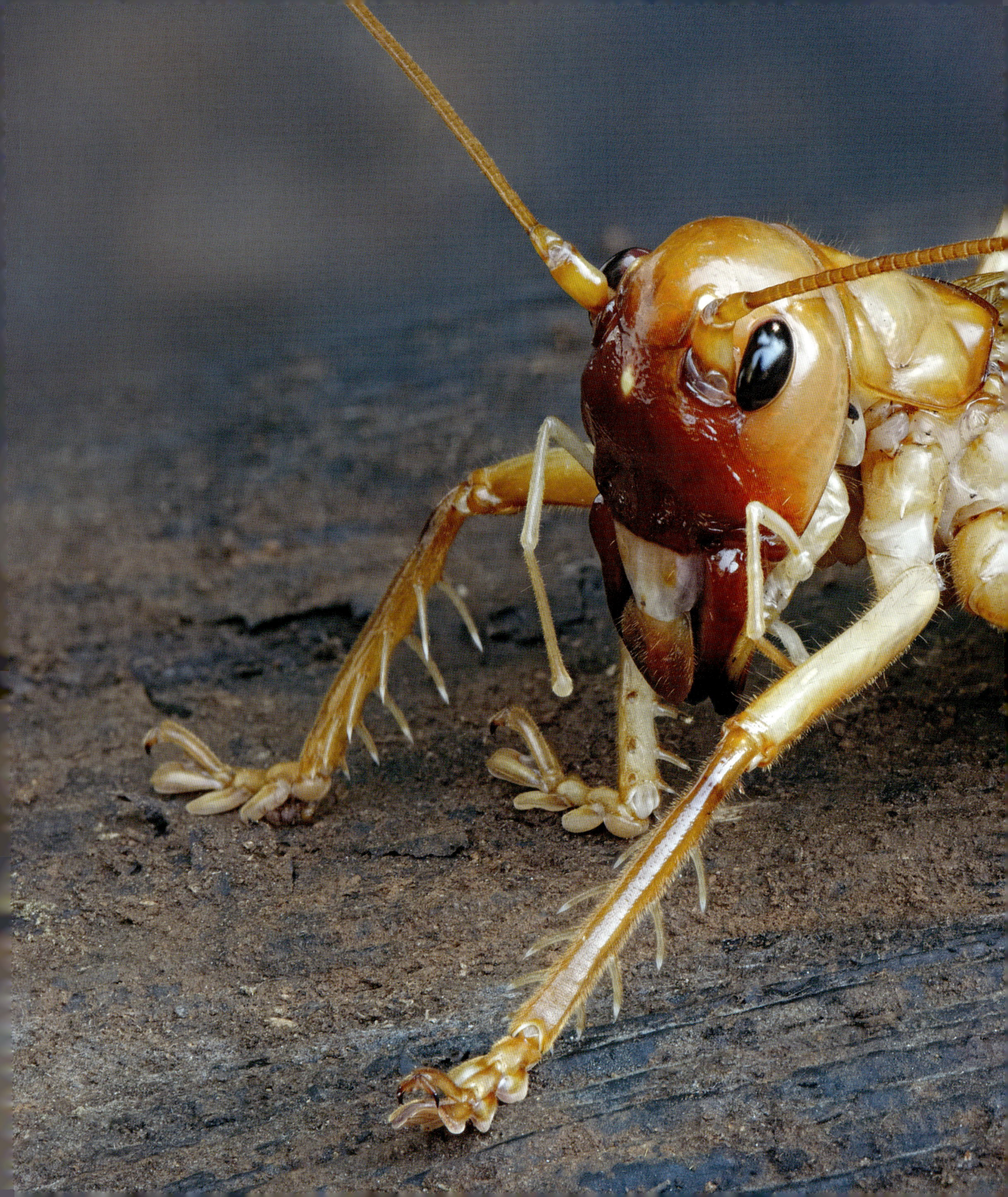

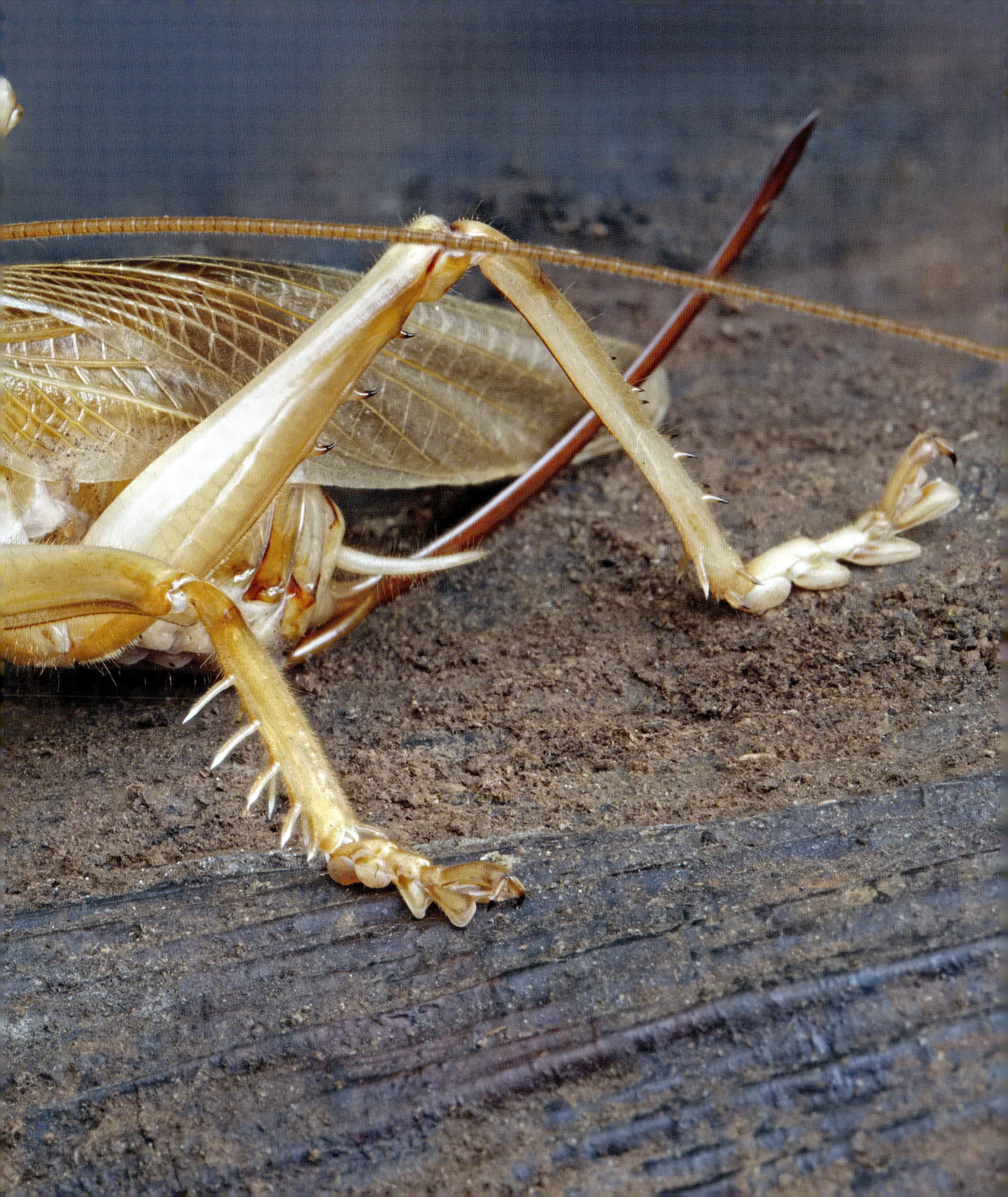

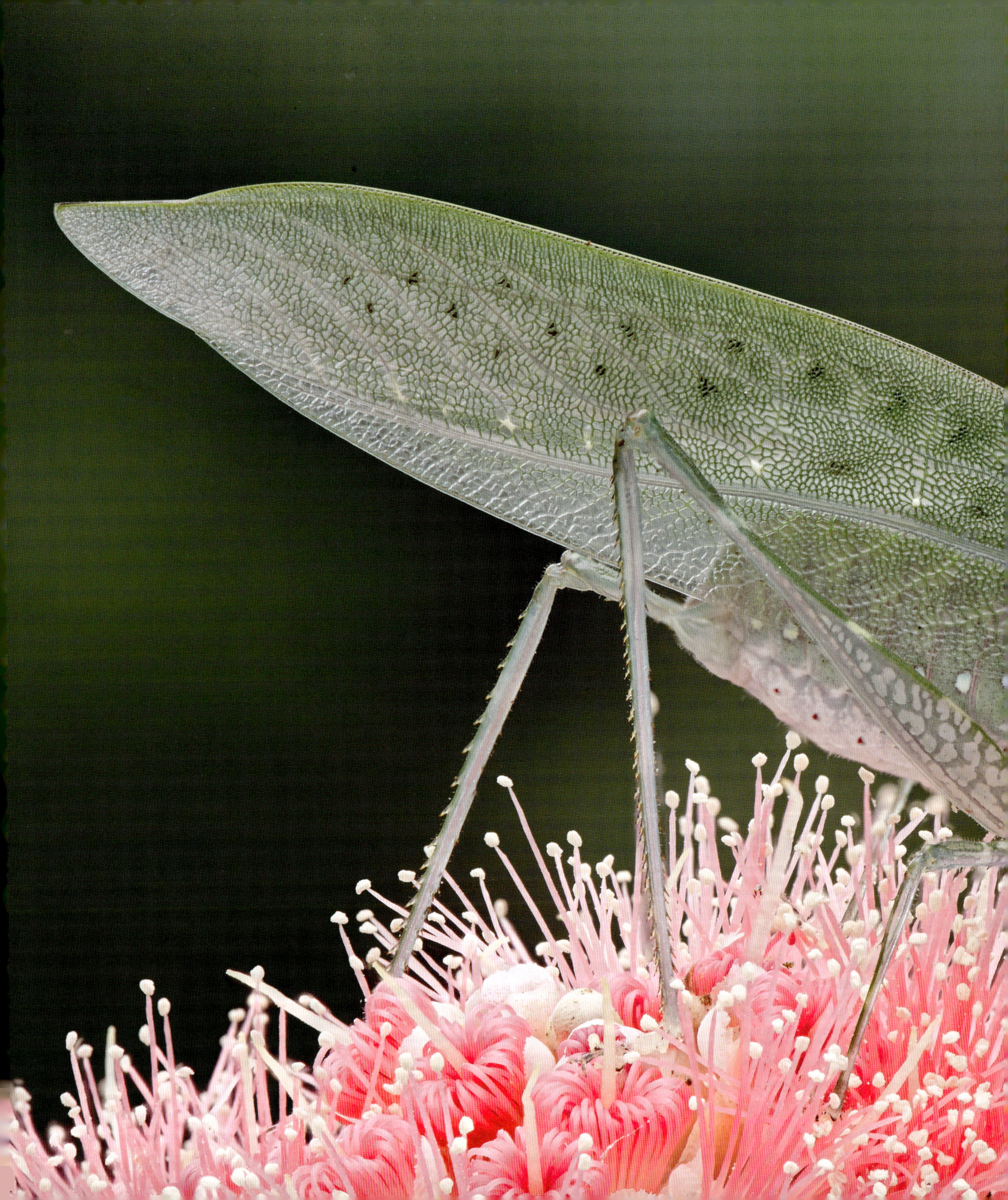

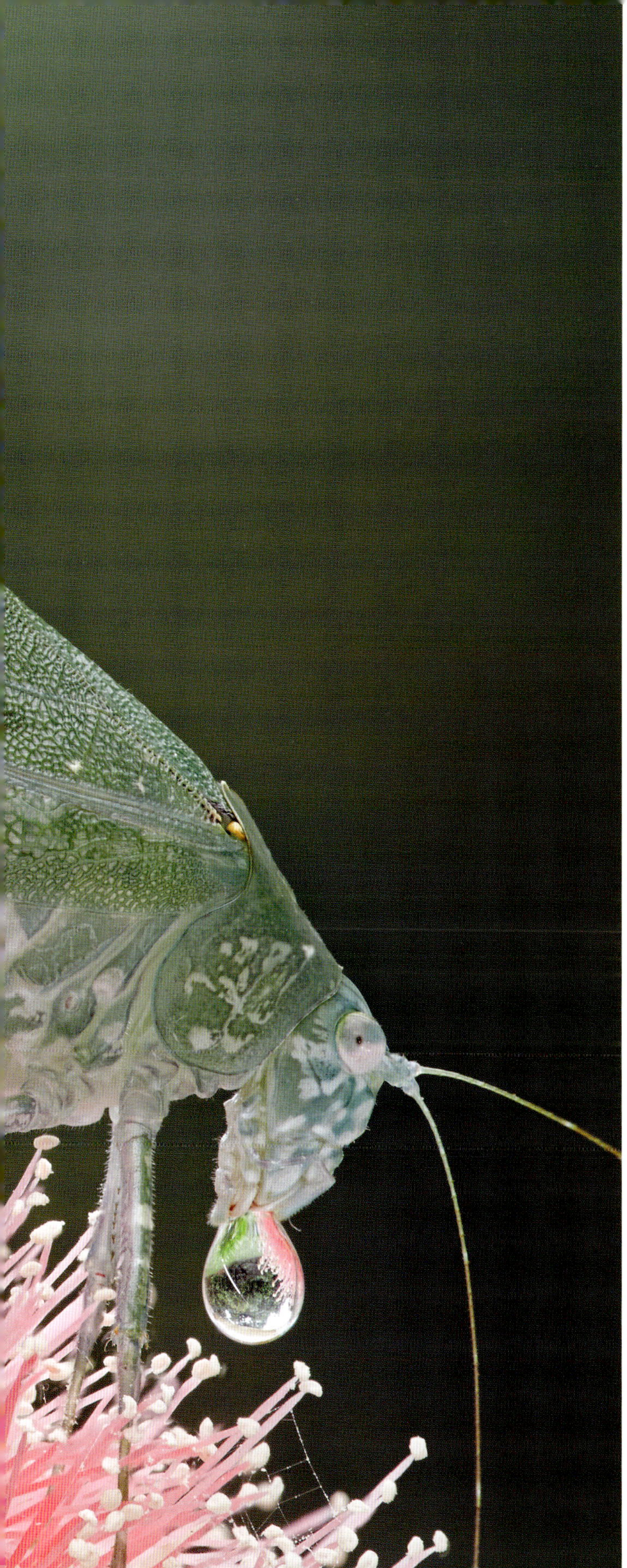

Preceding pages

There are many large and athletic crickets about in the rainforest at night. Some are flightless (see page 40), but this Raspy Cricket, *Mooracra* sp., is capable of strong, fast flight. The 'sword' that this female carries is her ovipositor, a kind of skewer she pushes into the soil to lay her eggs.

Left

The Bush Katydid, *Caedicia webberi*, feeding on the rain-sodden flowers of a Powderpuff Satinash, *Syzygium wilsonii*. After extracting the proteins from the pollen and nectar the katydid expels the excess water in a clear drop.

Following pages

Carpet Python, *Morelia spilota*. The greater clarity of digital photography emphasises both the power and sinuousness of the snake's coils.

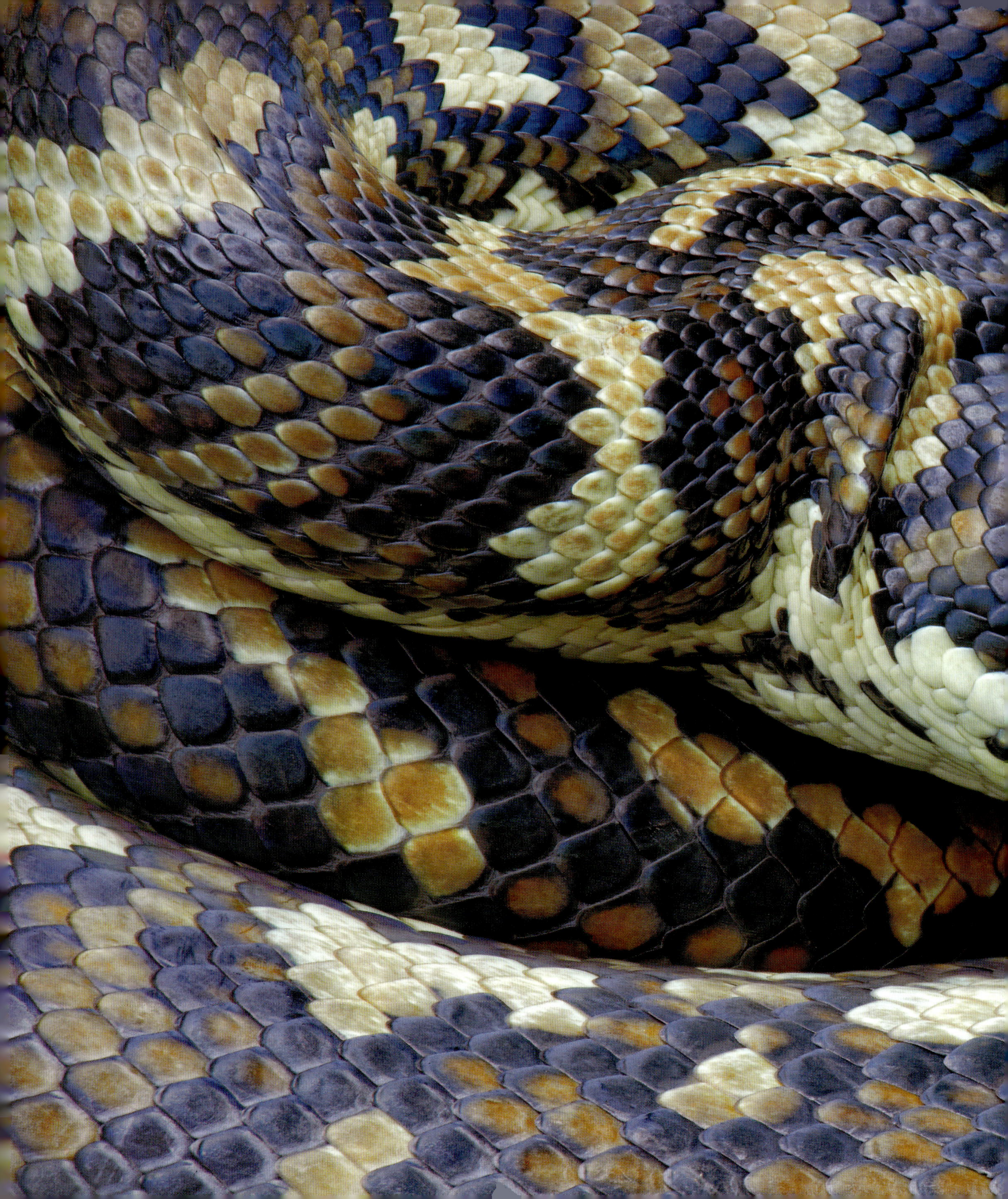

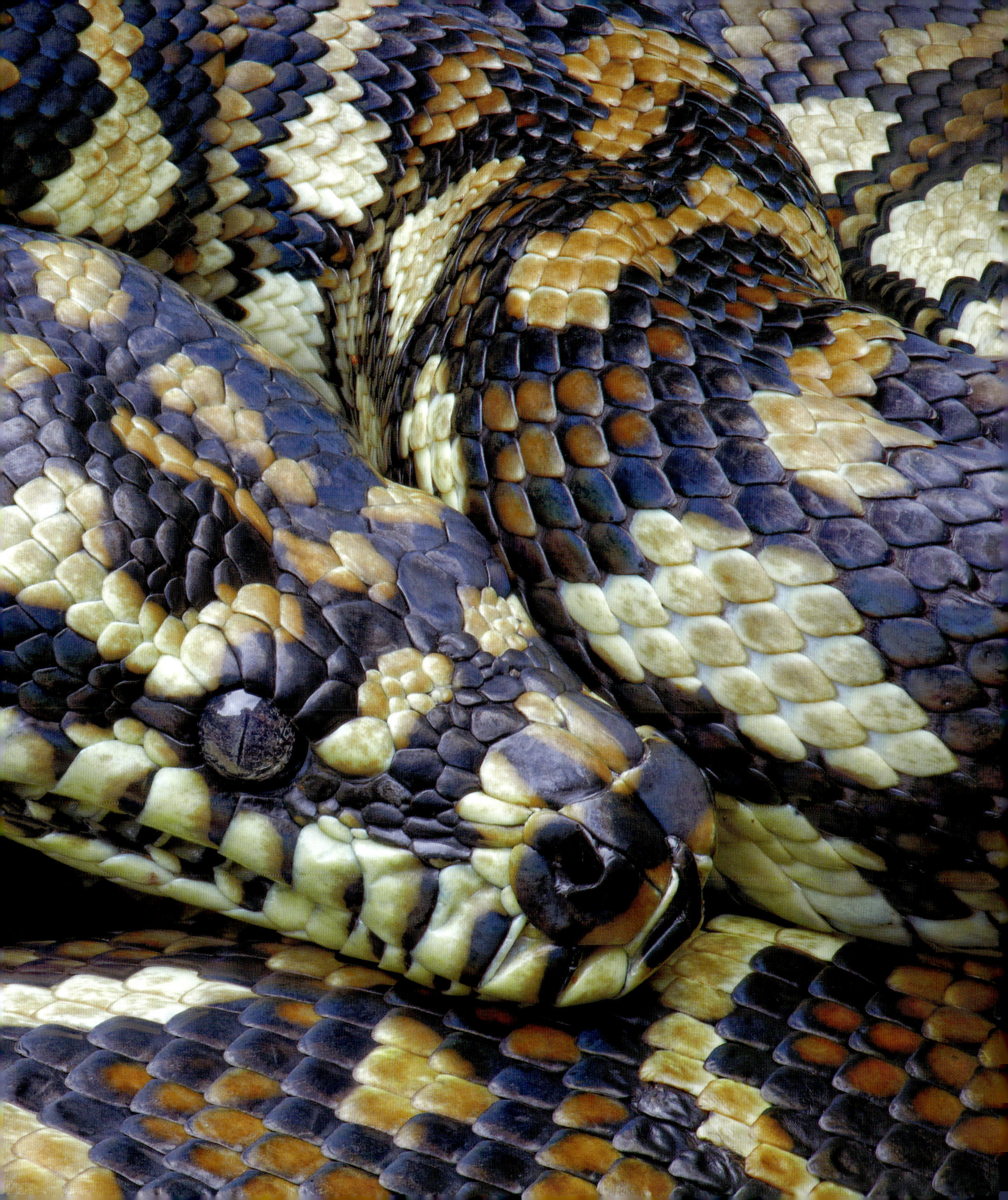

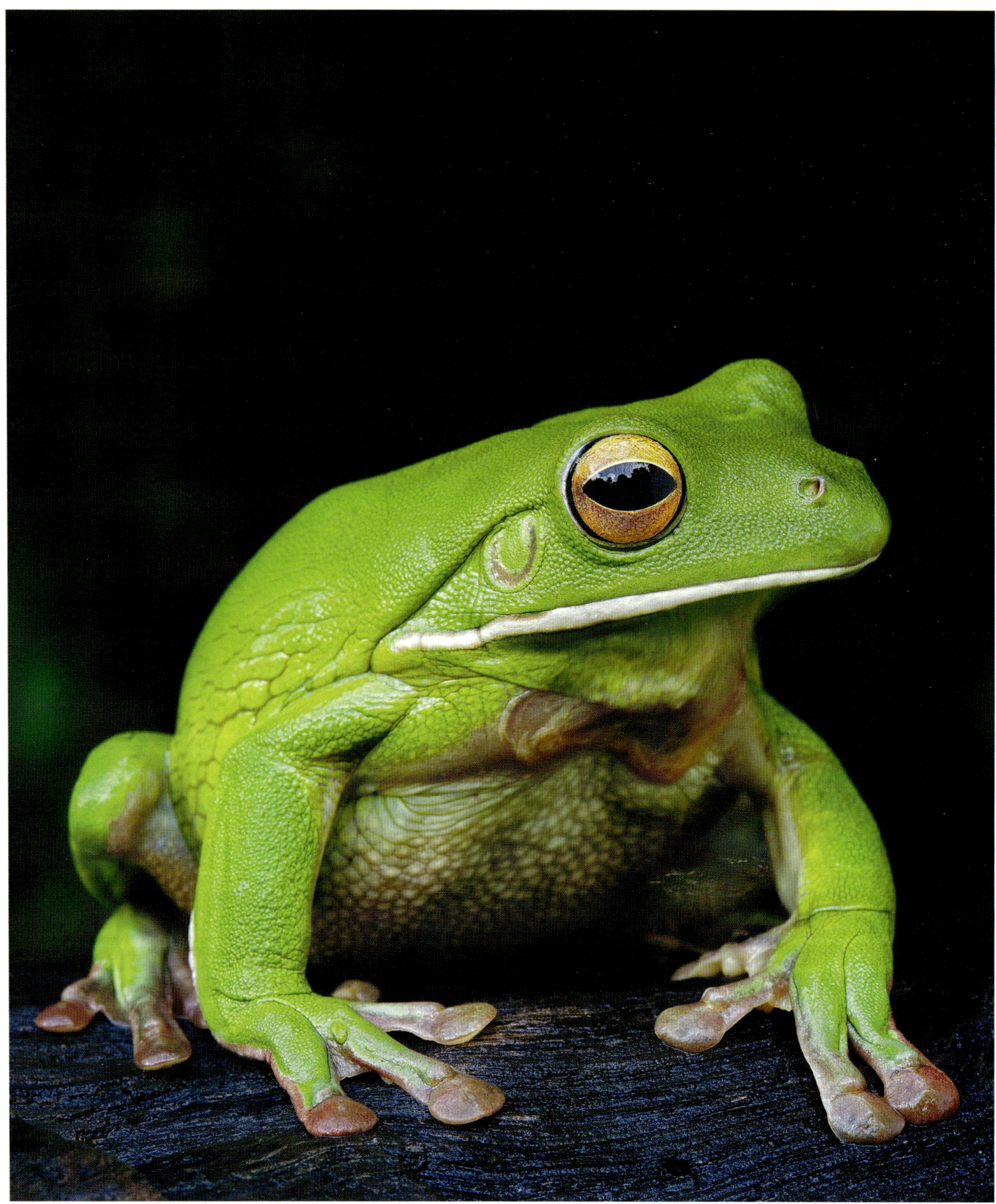

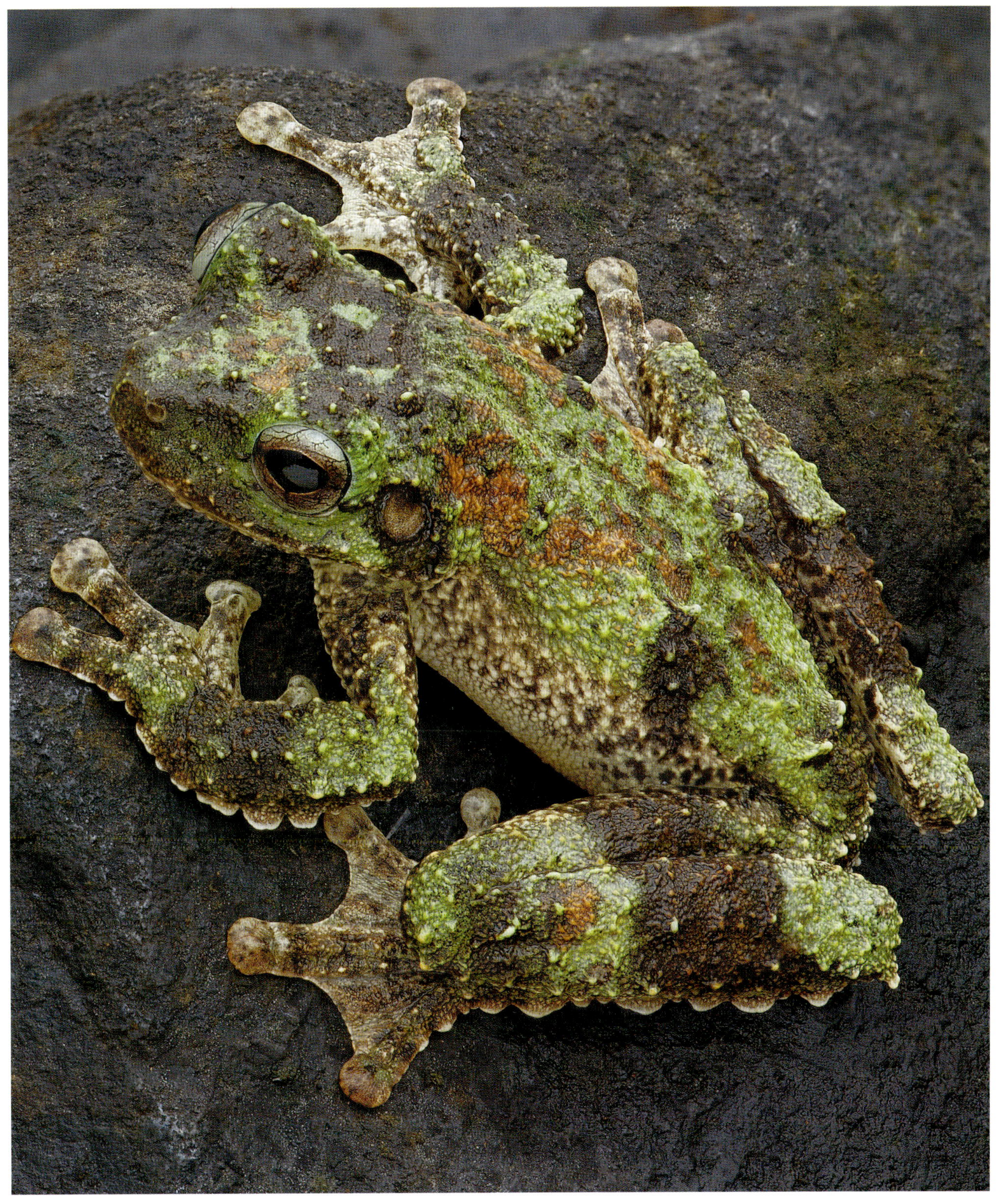

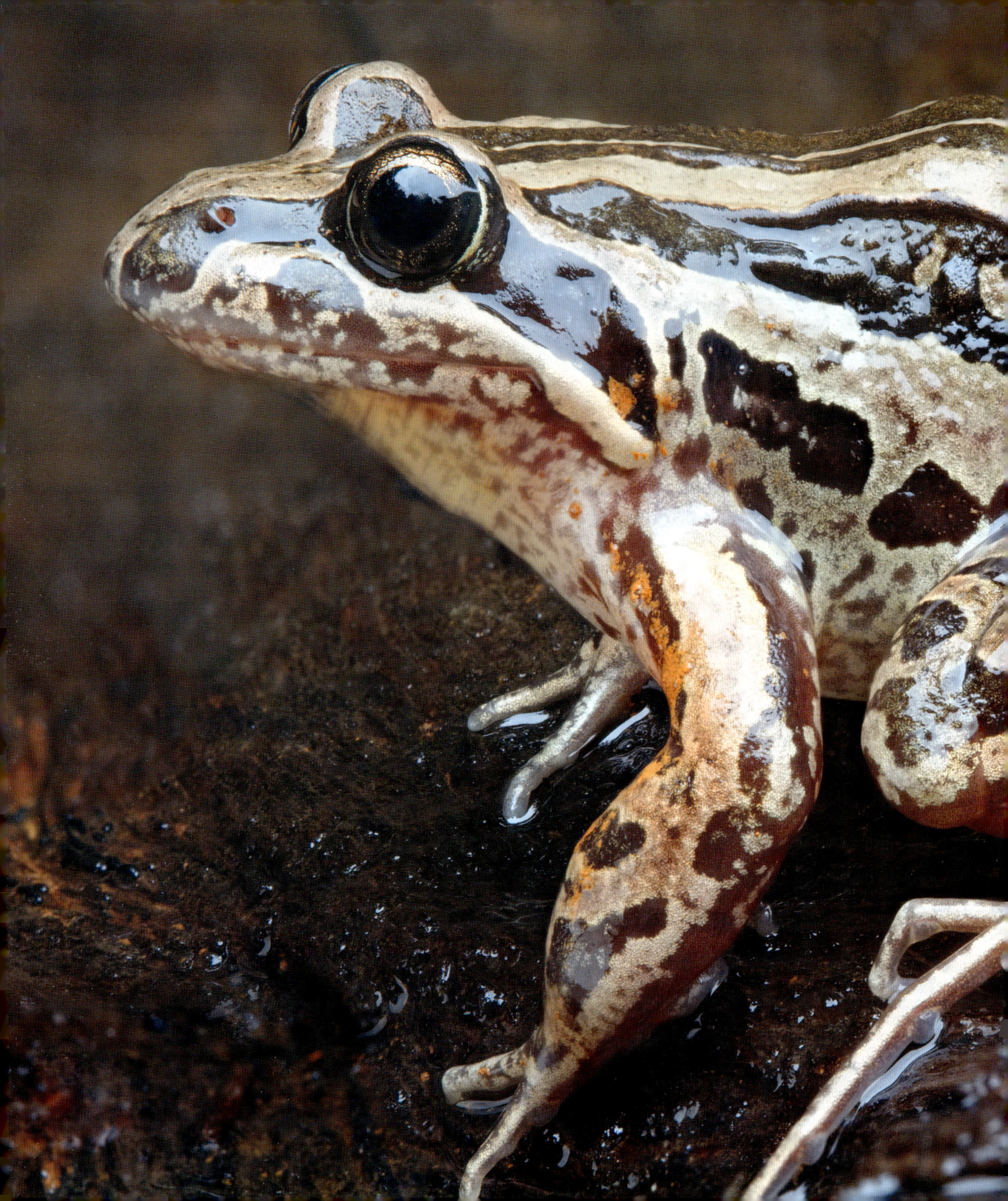

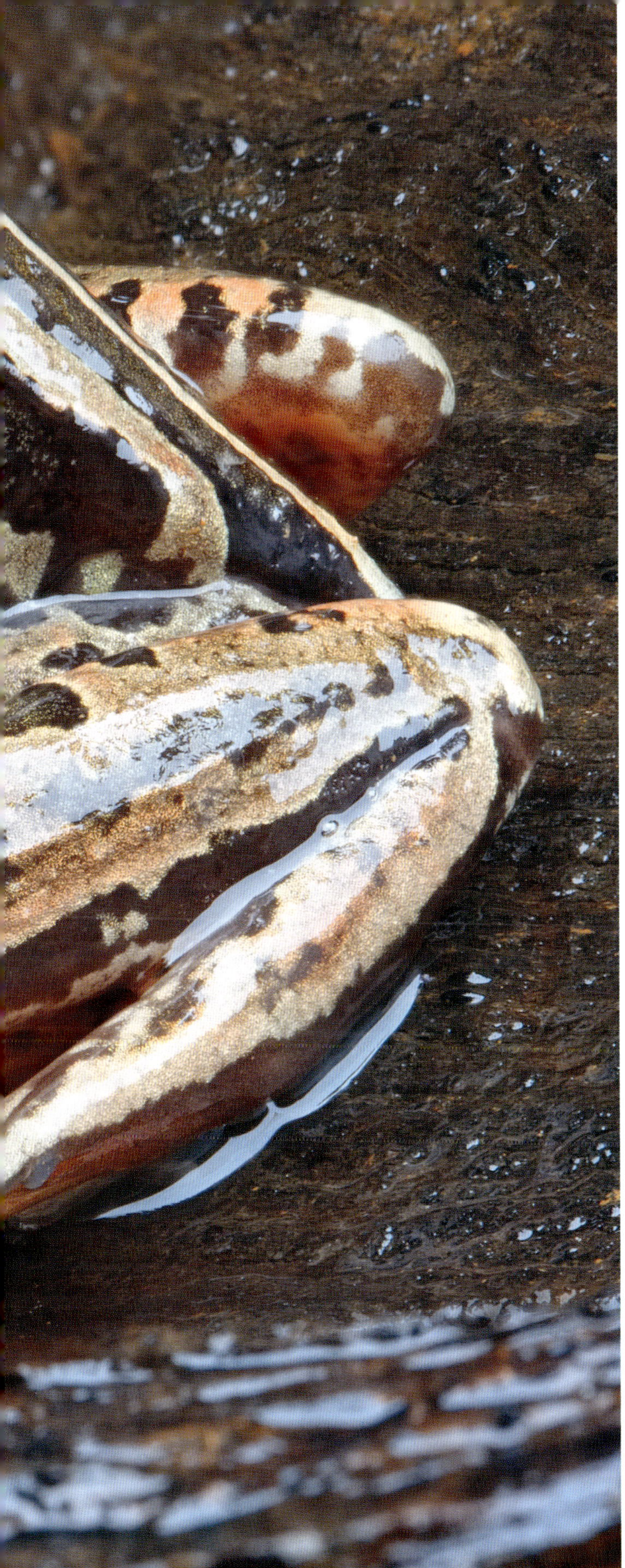

Page 88

In the wet season White-lipped Tree Frogs, *Litoria infrafrenata*, congregate around swampy areas in the tropical lowlands. The males' calls of 'che-check' to attract females resemble the sound of matches being shaken in their box.

Page 89

Green-eyed Tree Frogs, *Litoria serrata*, look like the mossy rocks of their habitat along fast-flowing streams. Their calls are a series of soft 'toc's, barely audible above the sound of the rushing water.

Left

Unlike the previous two species the Striped Marsh Frog, *Limnodynastes peronii*, can be found in any swampy area along Australia's east coast. The blur of the pulsing throat reveals the duration of time it took to create this focus stack of 25 exposures. This effect can also be seen on pages 76–77 and 88. ☙

Following pages

Northern Greengrocer, *Cyclochila virens*. These cicadas set the forest ringing with their songs at dusk during the warmer months. They are so loud you cannot hear yourself speak. See also pages 63 and 79.

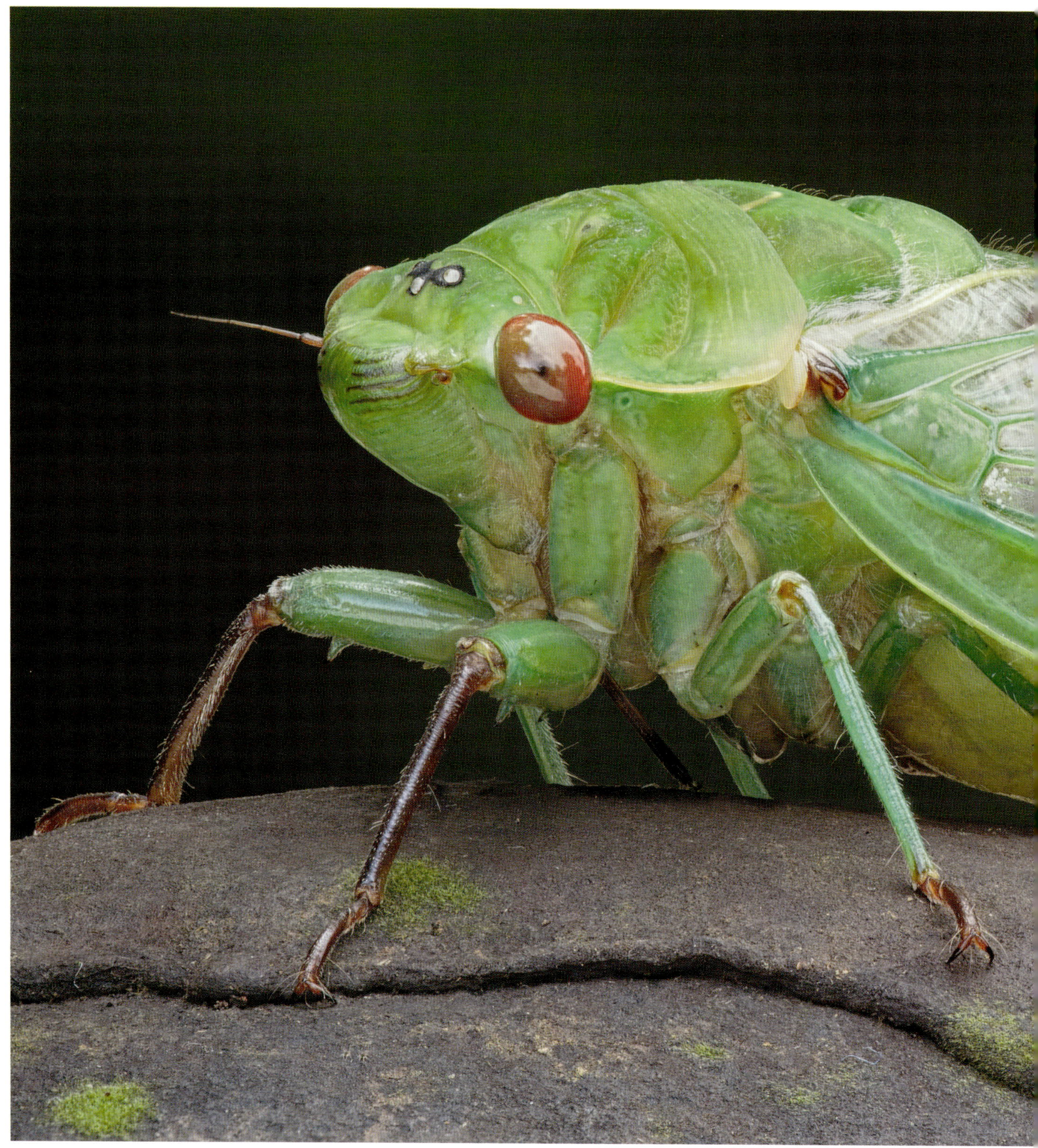

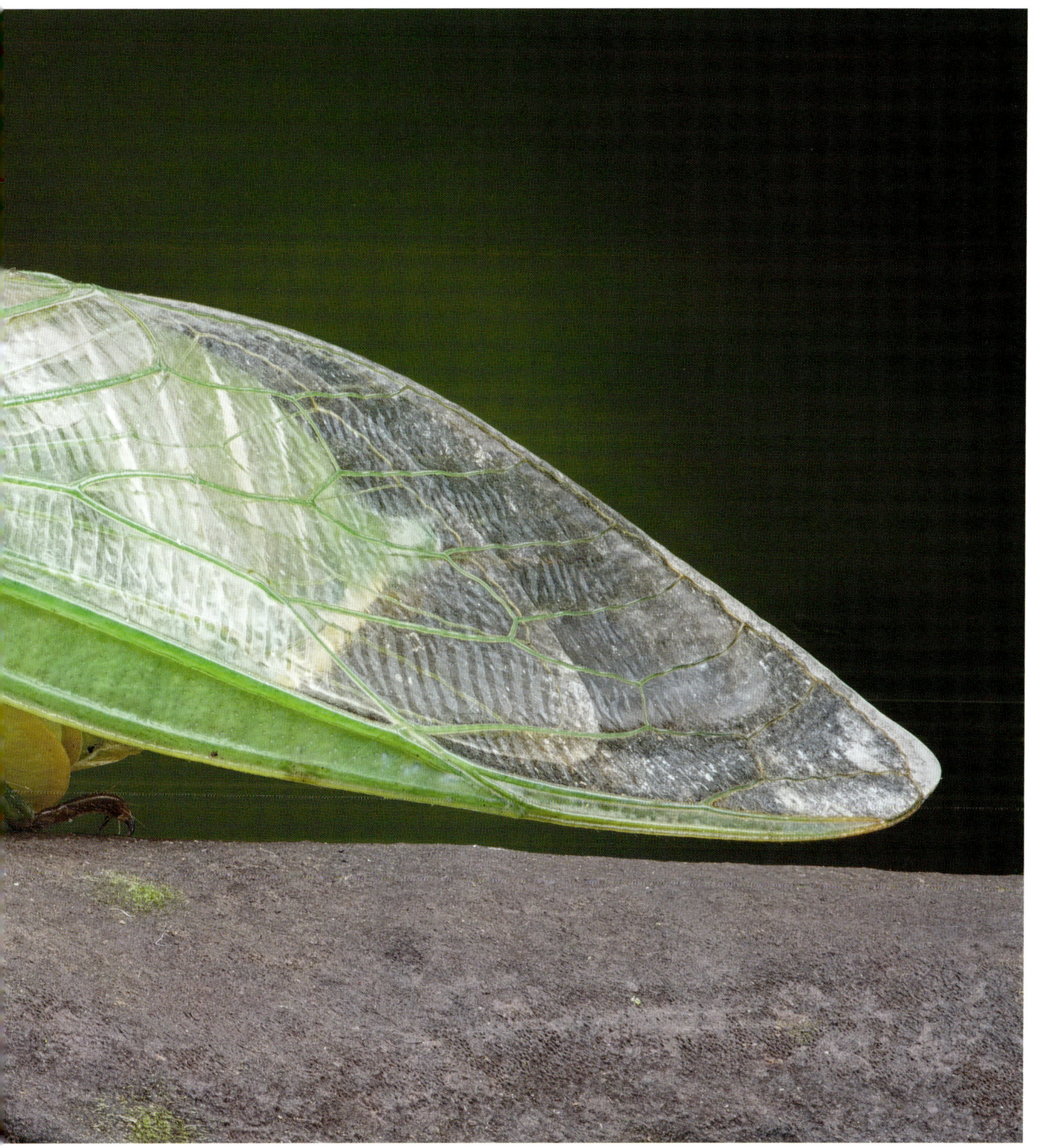

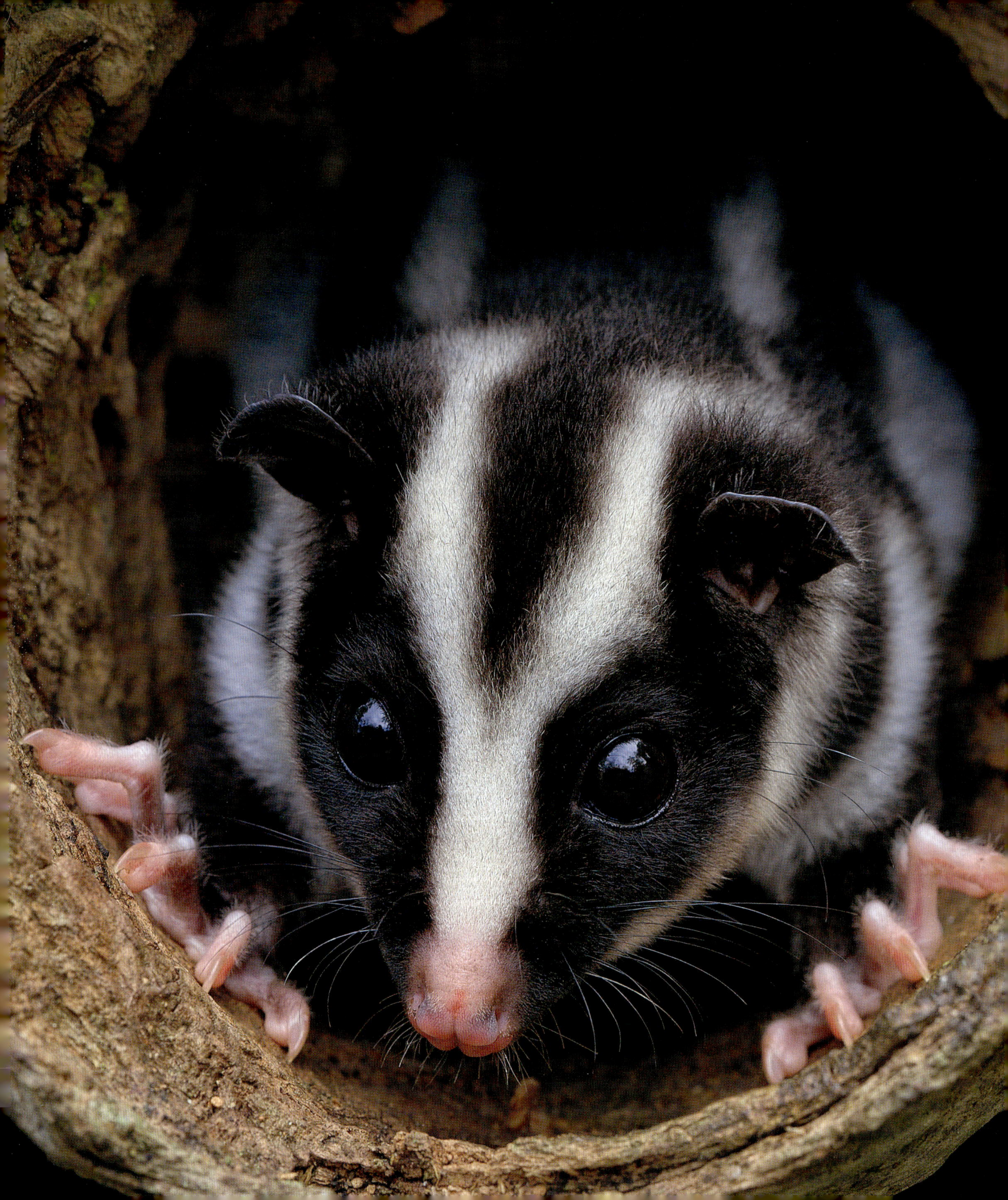

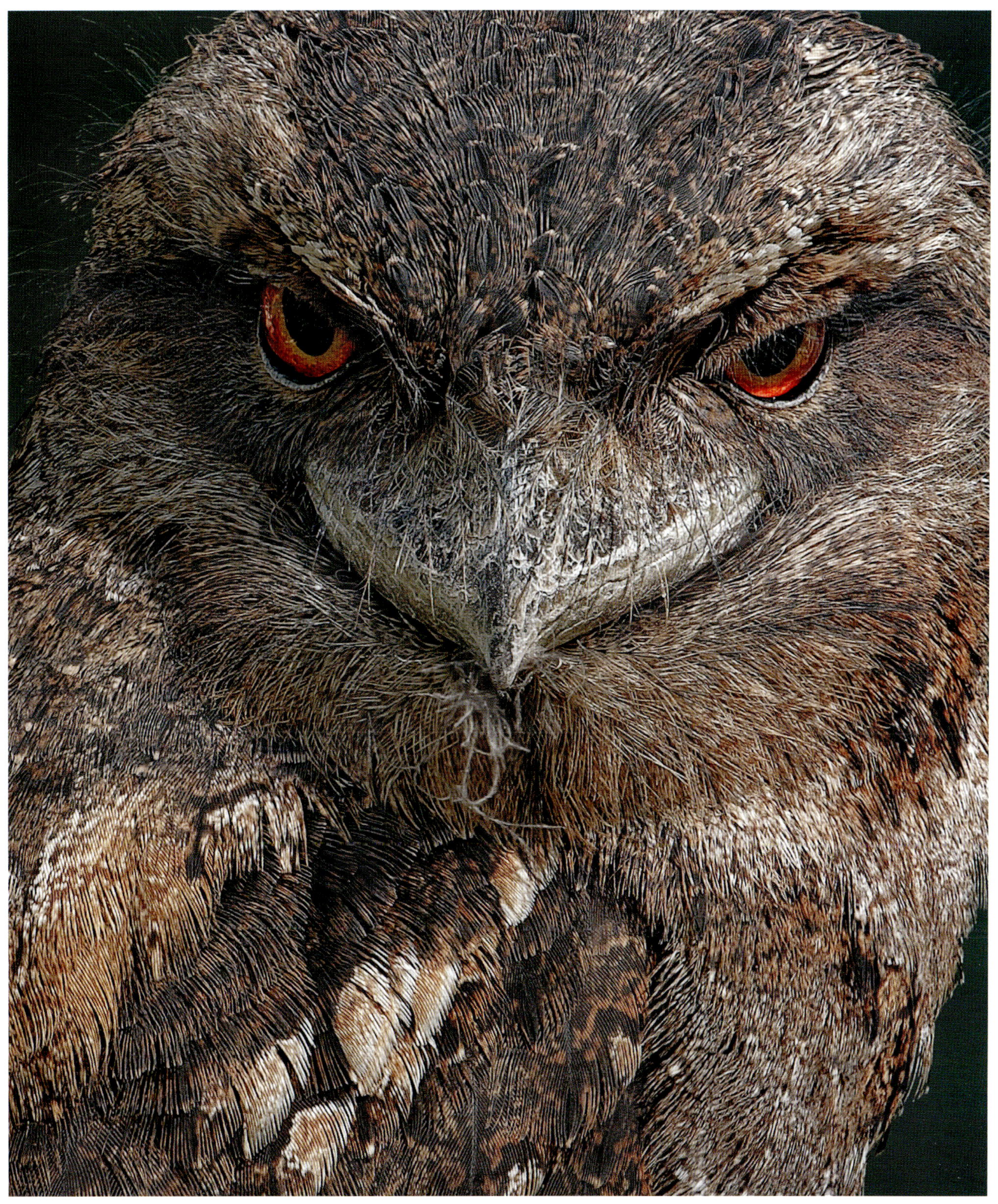

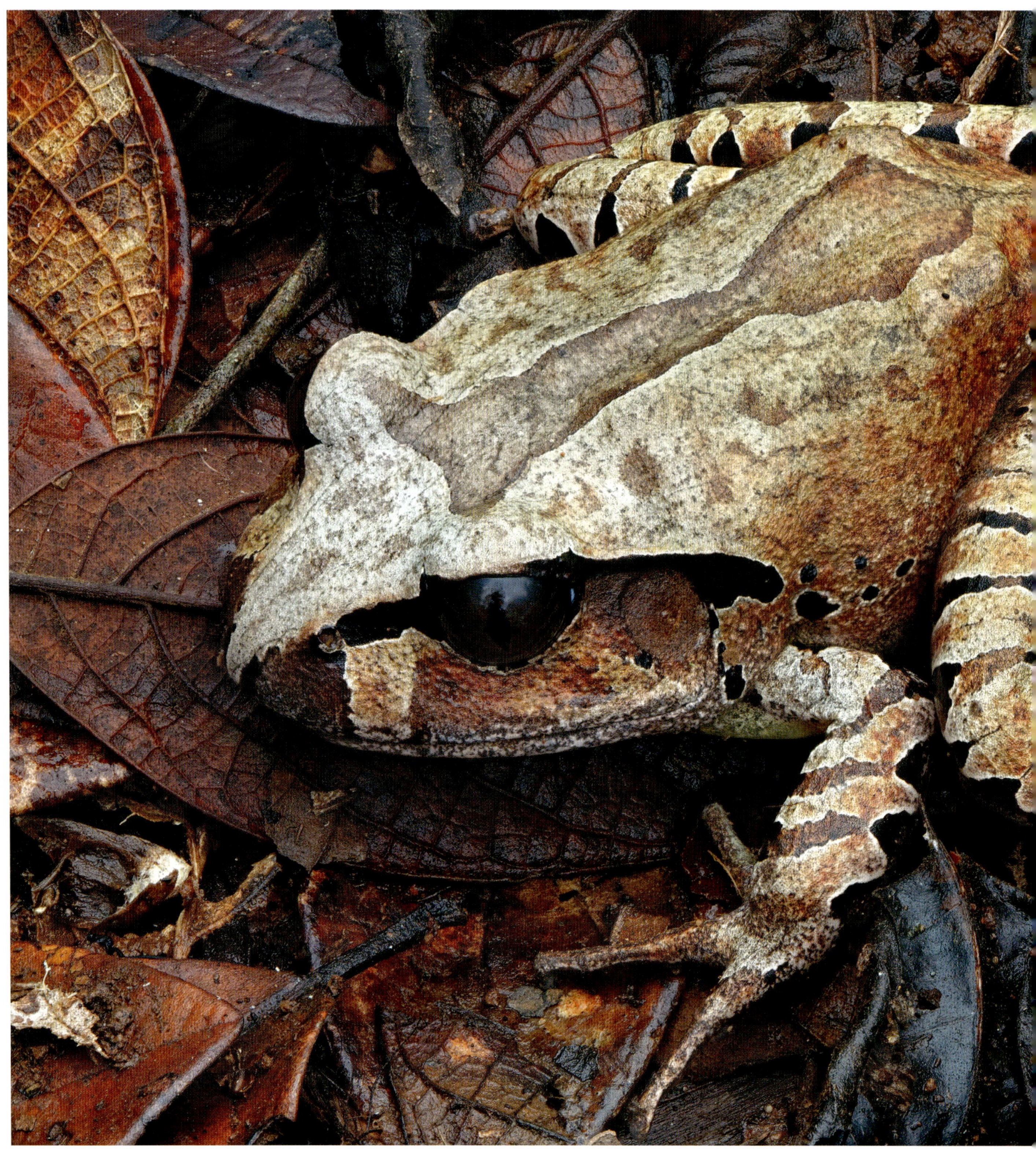

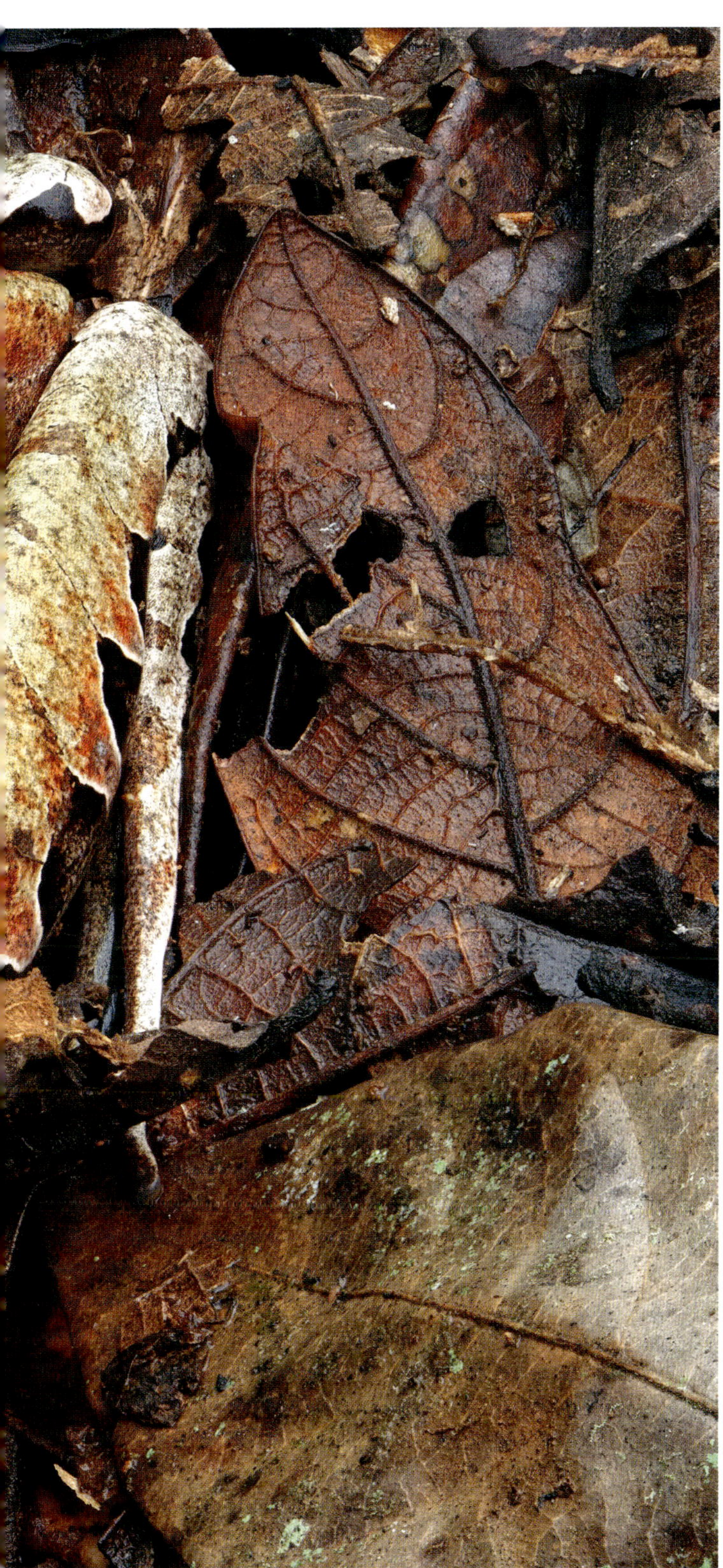

Page 94

A Striped Possum, *Dactylopsila trivirgata*, emerges from its den in a hollow branch in the tropical rainforest.

Page 95

Up to now you may have been watched over by a Tawny Frogmouth (see pages 28–29) in your pursuit of nature's miniatures. But here in the tropical rainforest another, larger, species could be keeping an eye on you. This is the red-eyed Papuan Frogmouth, *Podargus papuensis*.

Left

At dawn the cryptically patterned Northern Barred Frog, *Mixophyes schevilli*, buries itself into the soil beneath the leaflitter and disappears from view.

Page 98

When the morning sun infiltrates the rainforest, butterflies settle on leaves in patches of sunlight. A female Cruiser, *Vindula arsinoe*, has spread her wings to soak up the early warmth.

Page 99

Small, fast-flying and with a preference for the treetops, the Peacock Jewel, *Hypochrysops pythias*, is rarely seen. This one may have come down to lower levels after a narrow escape from a predator – probably a small bird who took a bite out of the butterfly's hind wings. ☙

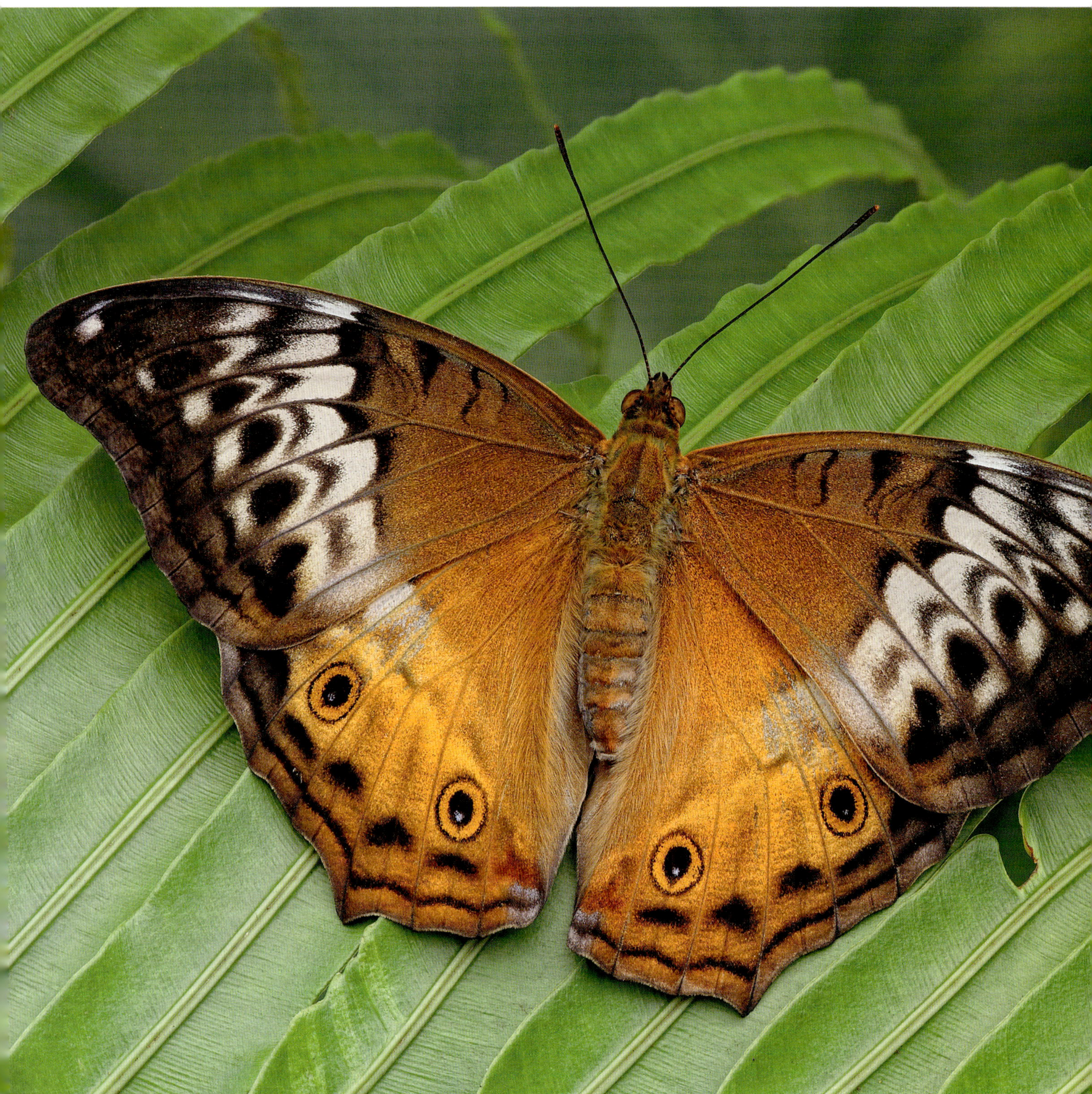

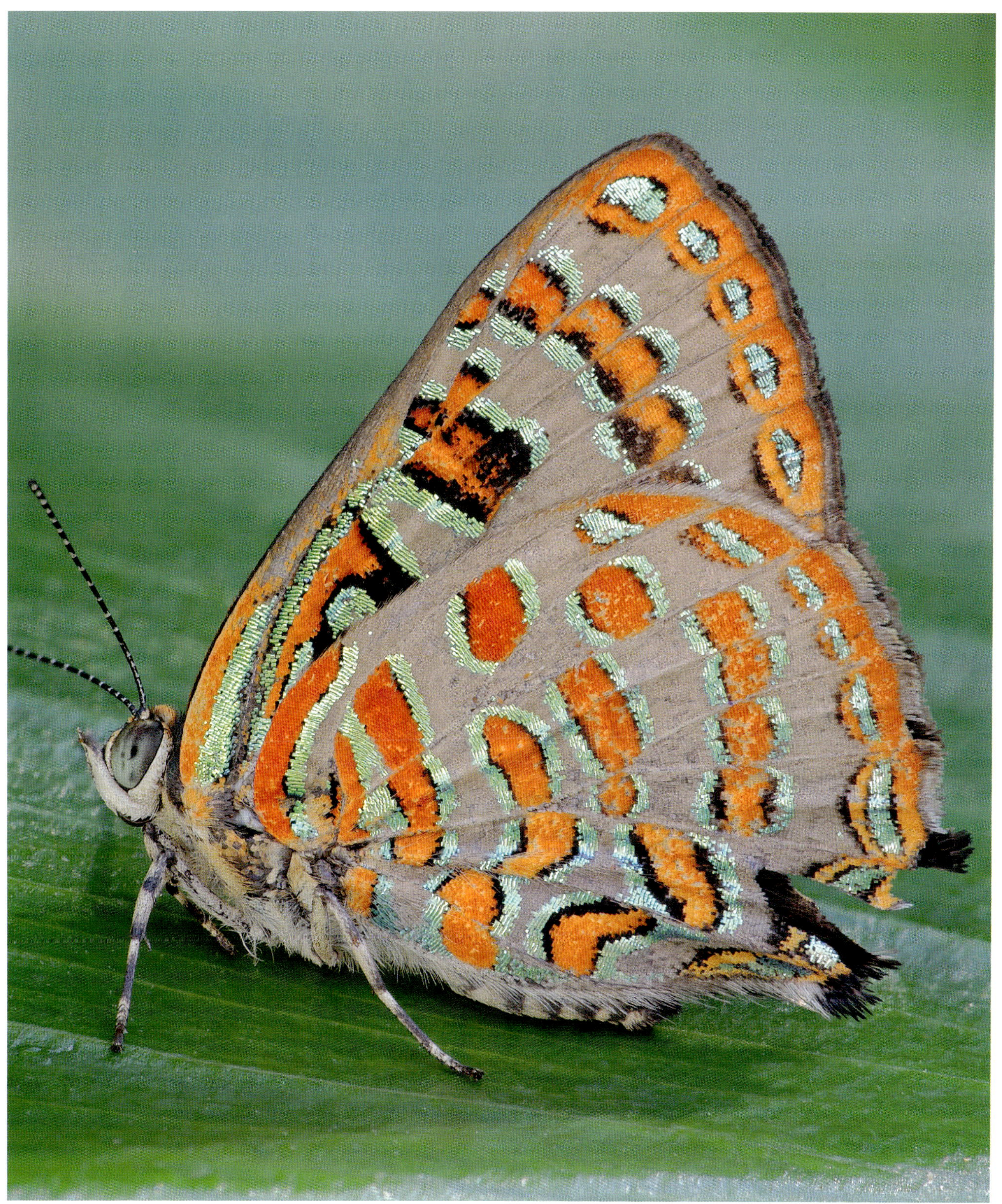

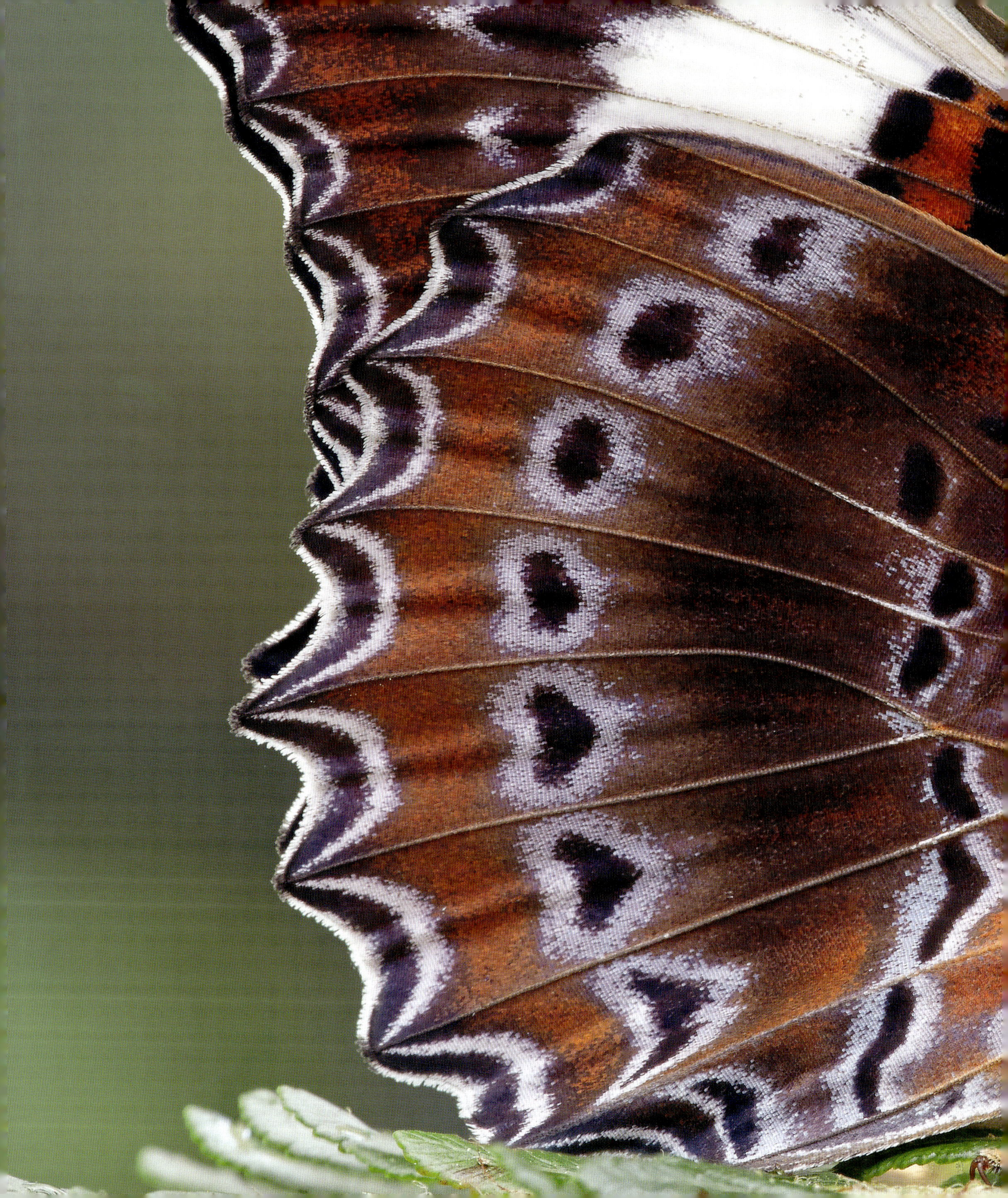

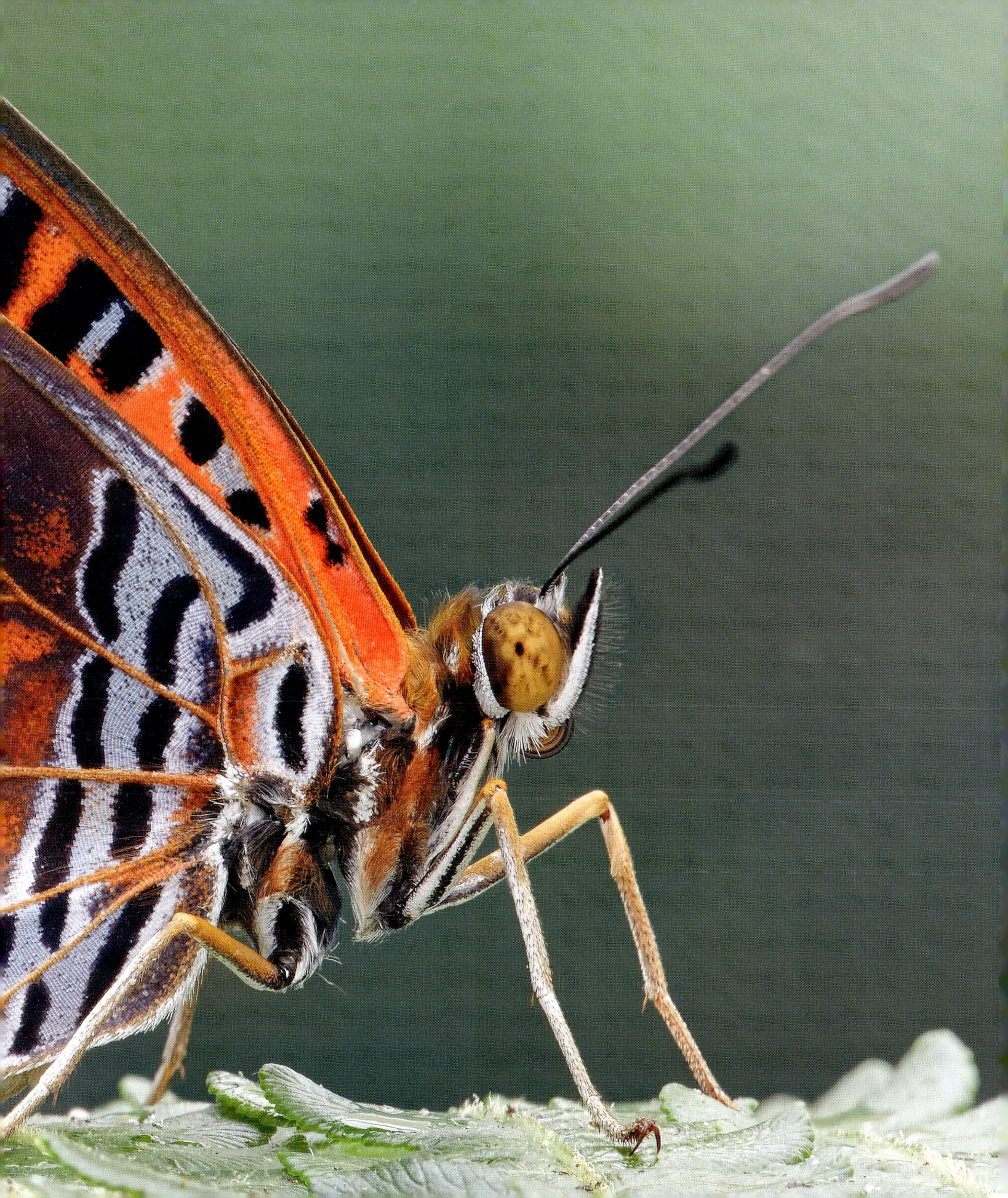

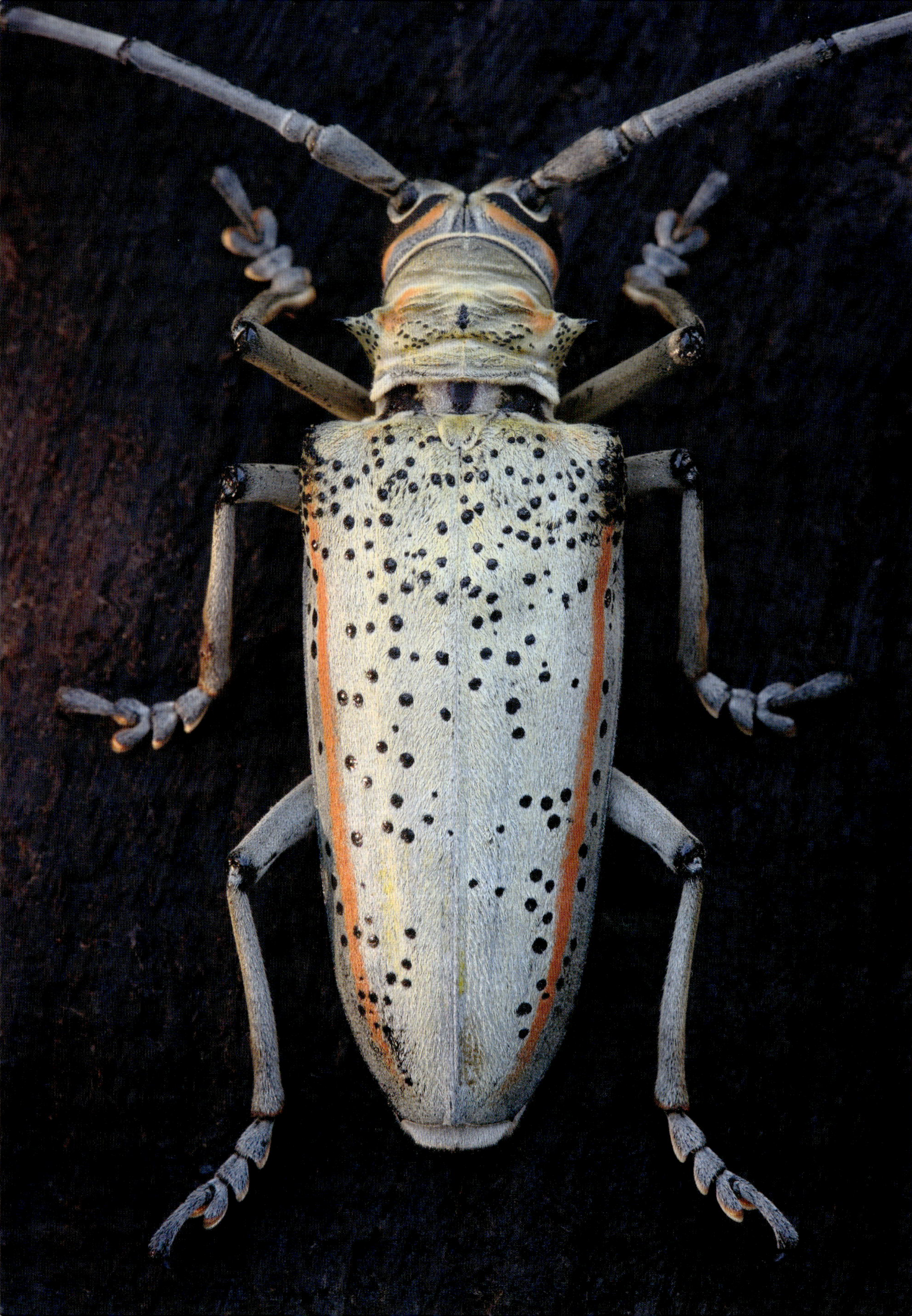

Preceding pages

Once thoroughly warmed, the butterflies sail through the forest in slow, gliding wing beats before settling in the shade with wings folded – like this Red Lacewing, *Cethosia cydippe*.

Opposite and below

Like all other insects and spiders, beetles have an exoskeleton, their 'skin' (see page 71). It is made of a substance called chitin. In beetles this is hard, sometimes very hard. The chitin may be coloured with pigments such as the red and yellow in ladybird beetles. In other species the chitin can be overlain by coloured powder and fine hairs. Through the wear and tear of everyday life both powder and hairs gradually rub off. Many insects, but especially beetles, have structural colours. These are not pigments but are created by refractions of light falling on thin layers of chitin.

The structural colours of the Rainforest Christmas Beetle, *Anoplognathus aeneus* (below), appear green or golden, depending on the direction of the light. The longicorn beetle *Rosenbergia megalocephala* (left) gets its colour from an orange powder and pale grey hairs. Newly emerged from its pupa in rotting wood, it still has all its colour.

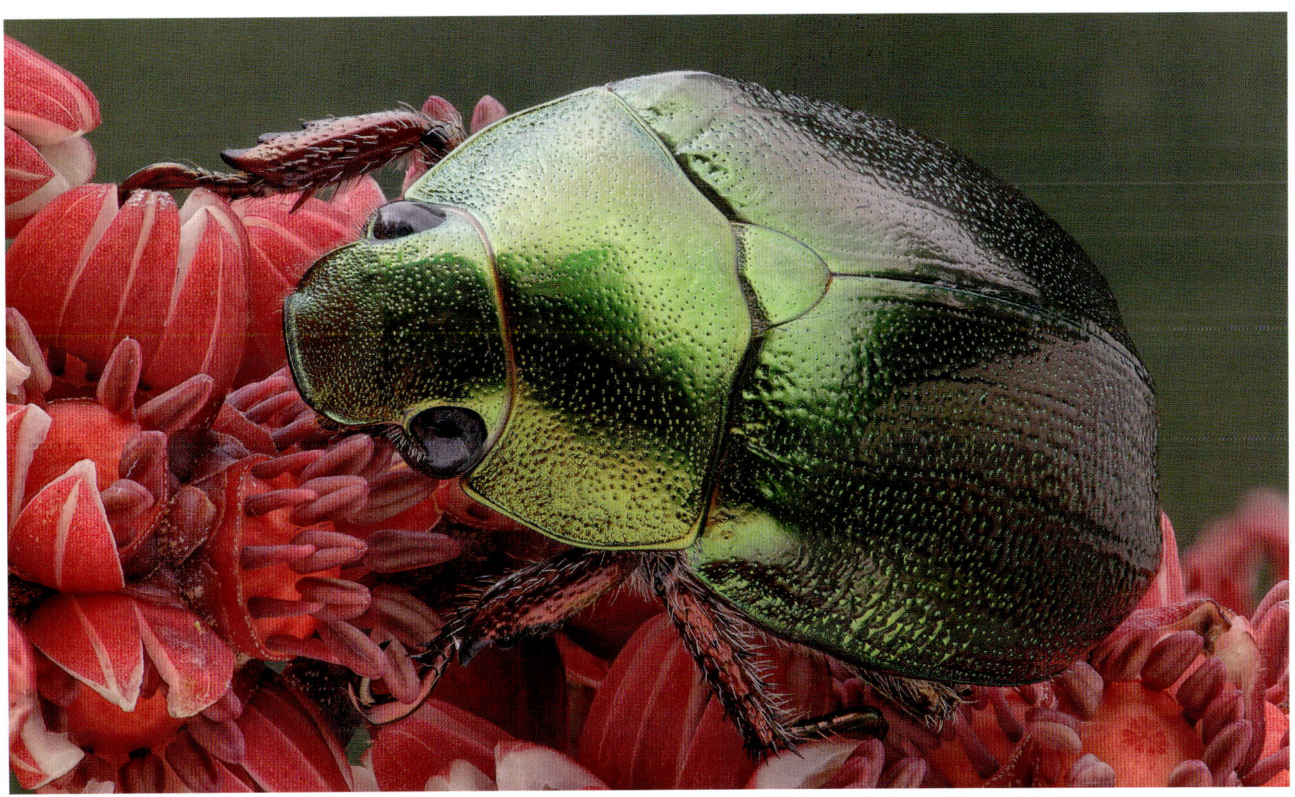

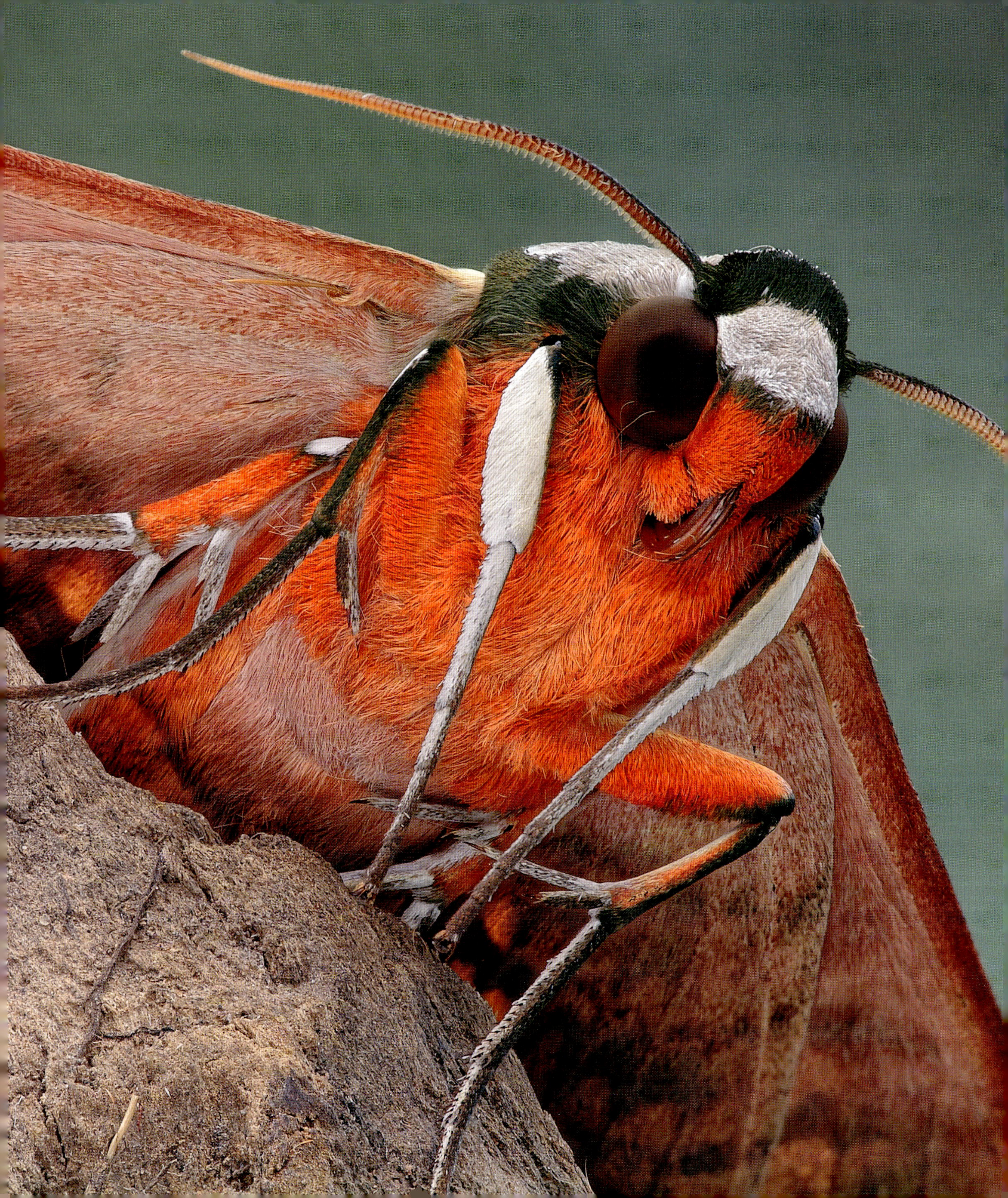

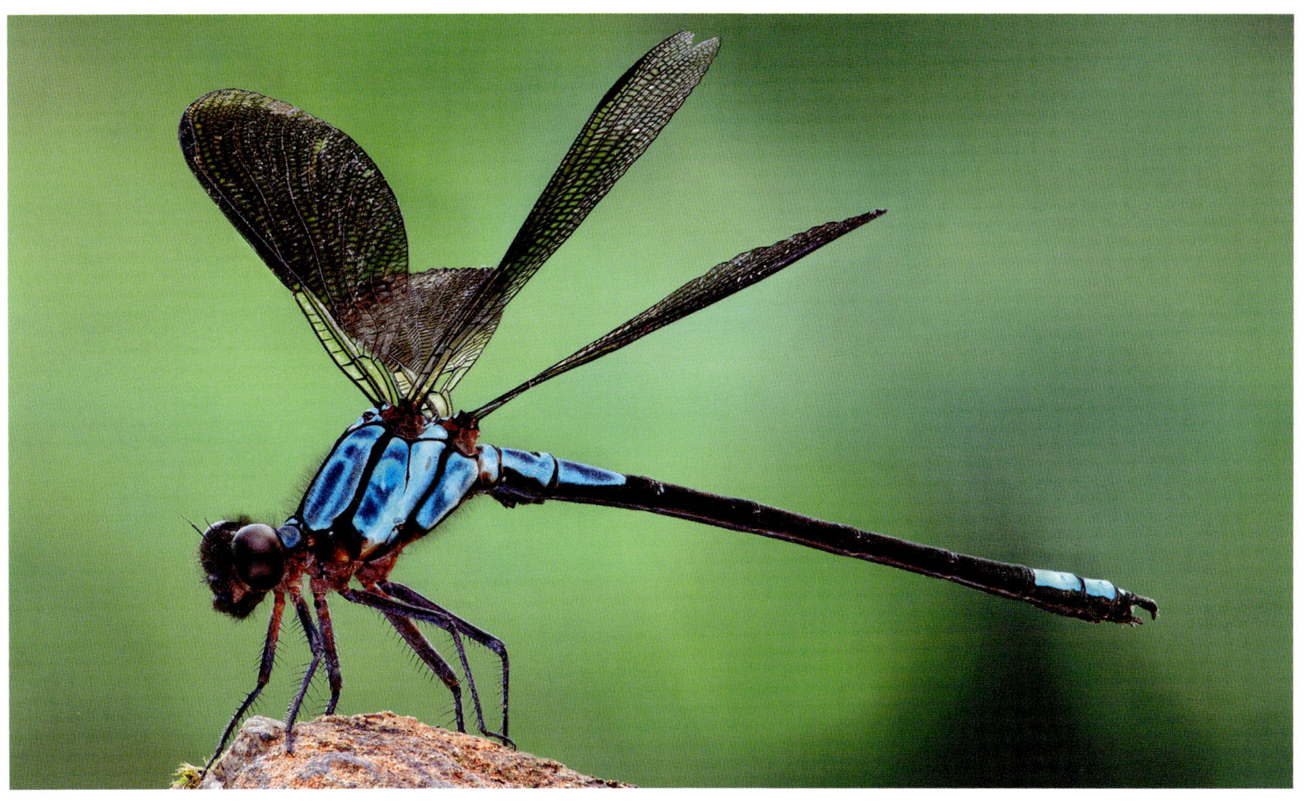

Left

The hawkmoth *Ambulyx dohertyi* seems to be patterned and coloured for a double life. Its upper side is in subdued colours, mostly browns, and blends with the tree trunks on which it rests. But what of the flamboyance of its underside?

Above

A Blue Damselfly, *Diphlebia euphaeoides*, rests between fast-flying sorties after mosquitoes and other tiny insect prey. The damselfly lives around forest pools.

Page 106

A diminutive jumping spider on a flower spike of the Australian Turmeric, *Curcuma australasica*.

Page 107

Orange-eyed Tree Frog, *Litoria xanthomera*, on a wet afternoon.

Pages 108–109

We entered the world of miniatures in the southwest corner of the continent, among eucalypts and wildflowers in a dry climate (see pages 18–19). We emerge in the diagonally opposite corner among tall trees in dense forests in a wet climate. It has been a journey into a little-known world, one of surprising colour and texture and, we hope, one that stimulates the imagination.

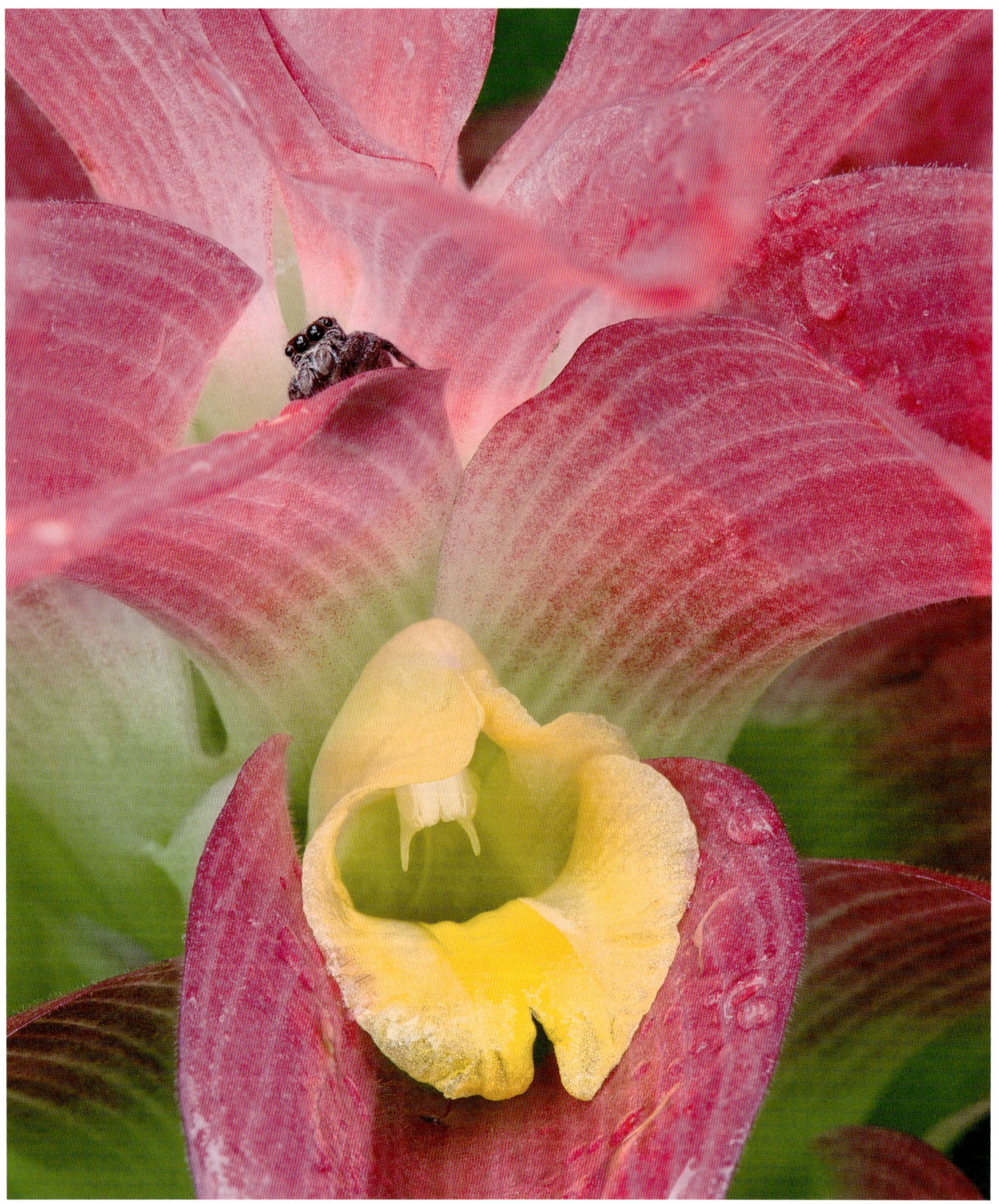

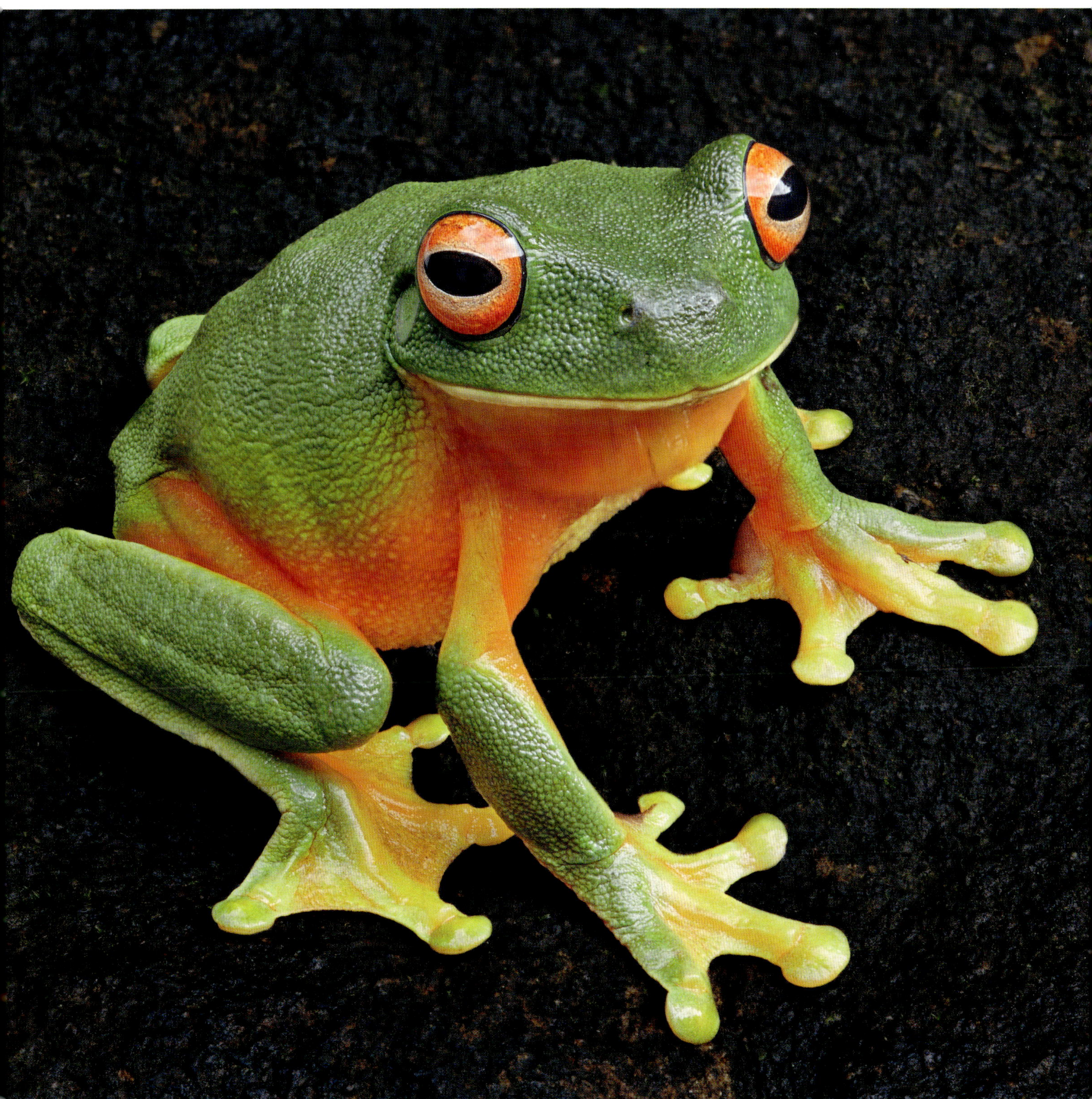

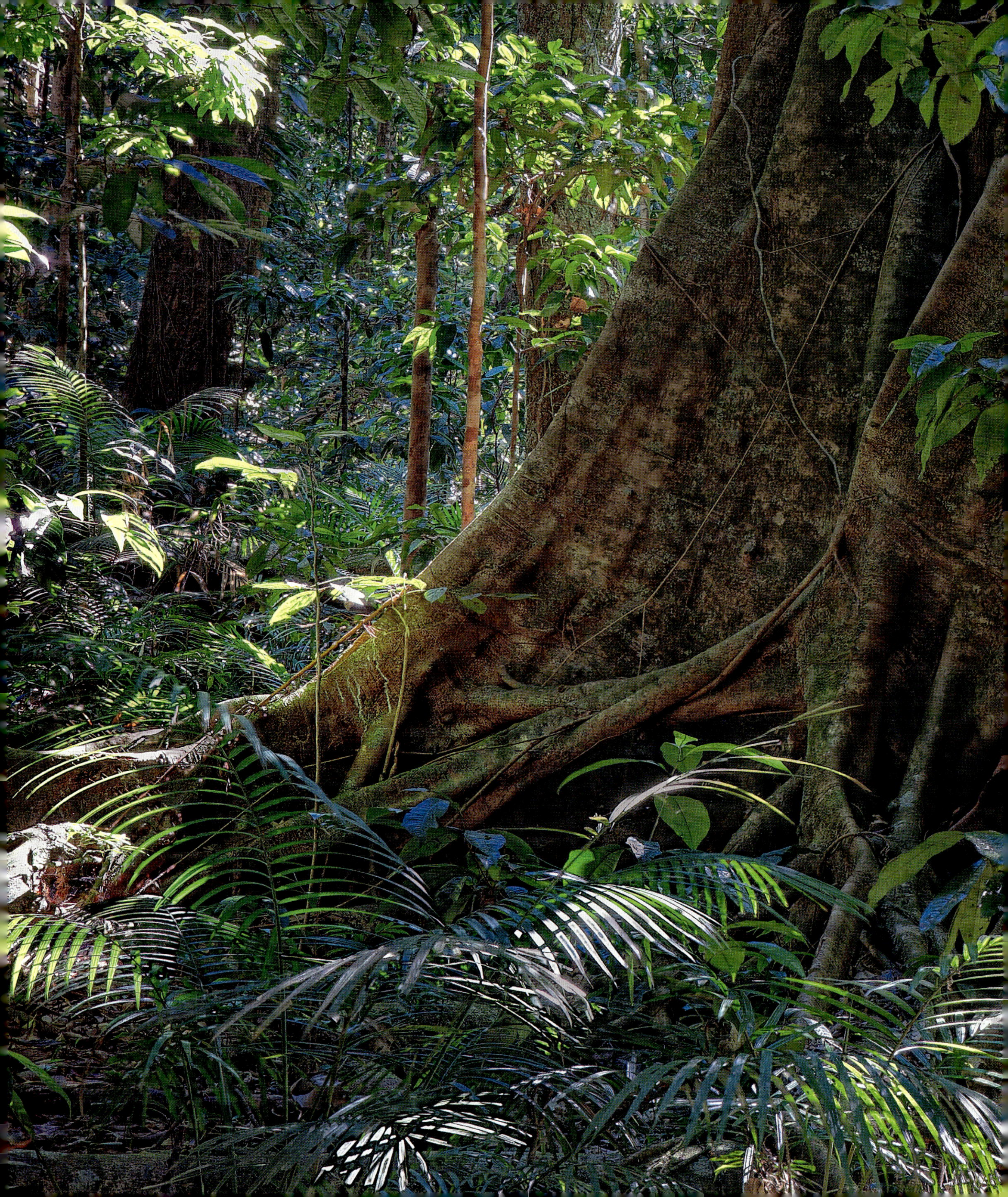

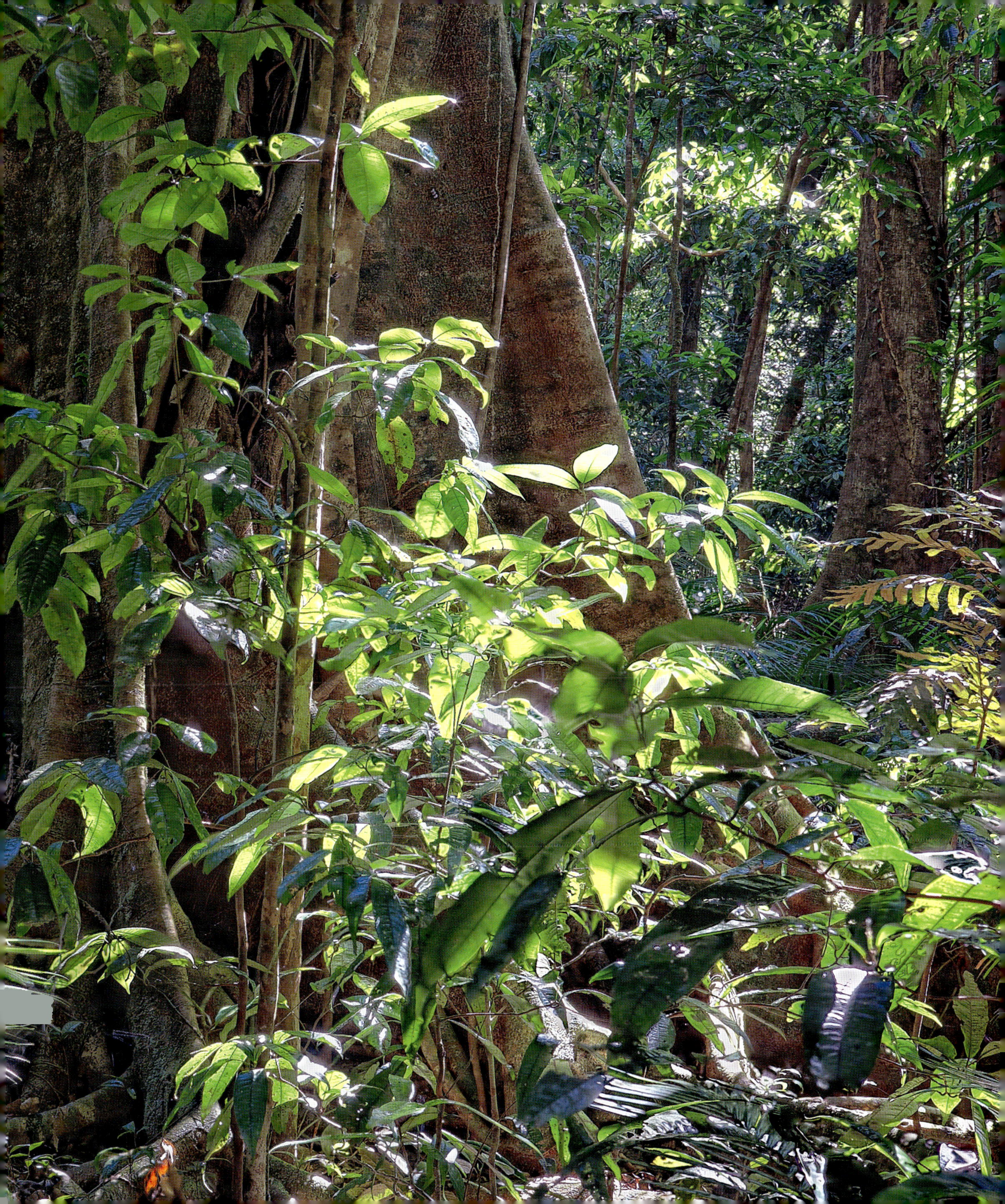

Selected subjects at life-size

Most of the photographs in this book are not single exposures. Rather they are crafted from multiple photographs taken at different focal points, to expand the depth of field. This process is called focus stacking. It can take anywhere from 5 to 30 or more exposures to get enough depth for such tiny subjects. Here are some examples, shown at life-size for comparison.

PAGES 8–9 ☙ Giant Shield Bug: 9-exposure focus stack.

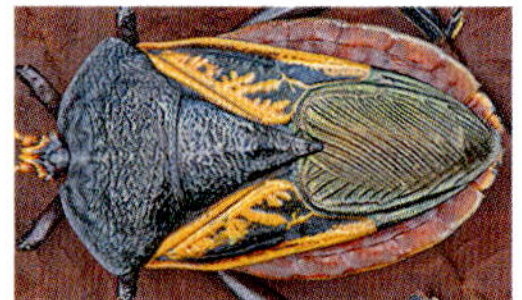

PAGE 12 ☙ Sleeping Cuckoo Wasp: 14-exposure focus stack.

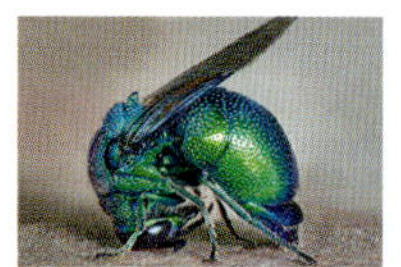

PAGE 31 ☙ Pink-faced Emerald: 30-exposure focus stack.

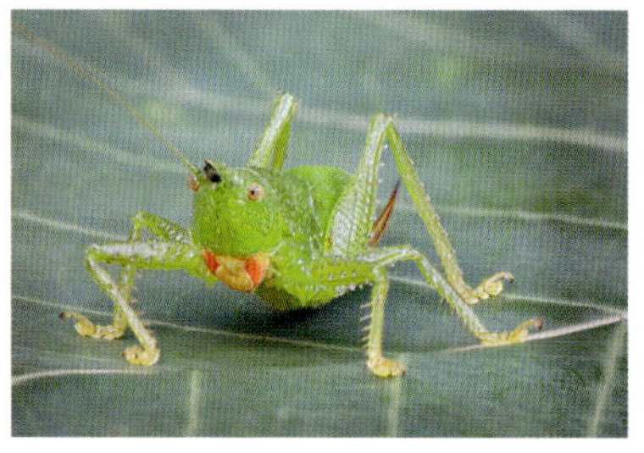

PAGE 33 ☙ Proud Moth: 20-exposure focus stack.

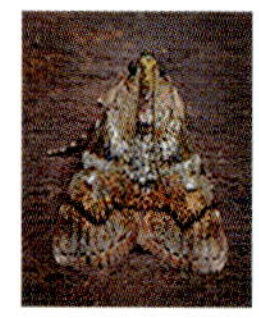

PAGE 37 ☙ Red and Purple Jewel Beetle: 8-exposure focus stack.

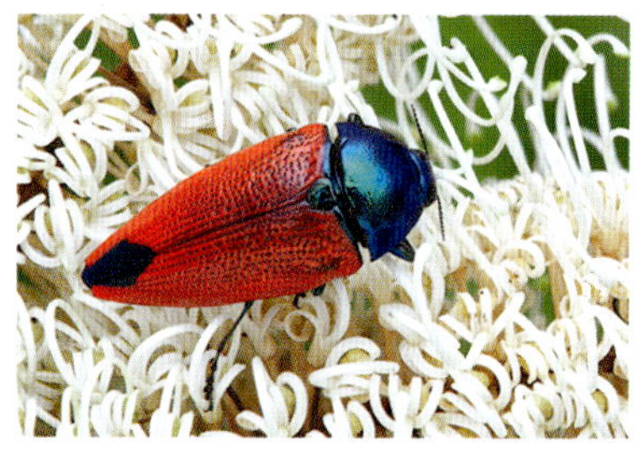

PAGE 51 ☙ Broken-stick Moth: 24-exposure focus stack.

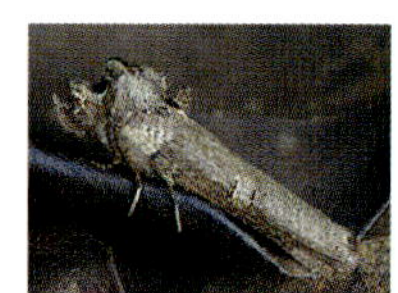

PAGE 53 ☙ Mercury Moth: 12-exposure focus stack.

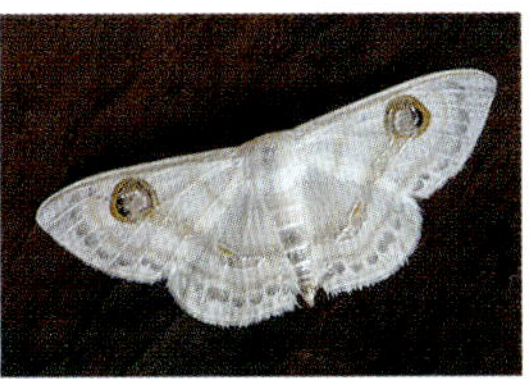

PAGES 60–61 ☙ Chafer beetle: 14-exposure focus stack.

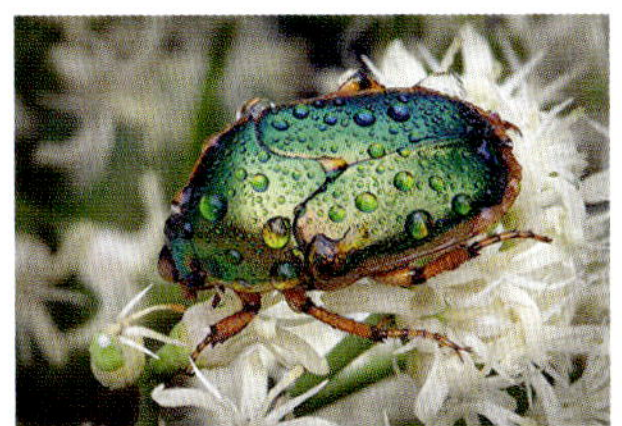

PAGE 63 ☙ Bunyip cicada: 8-exposure focus stack.

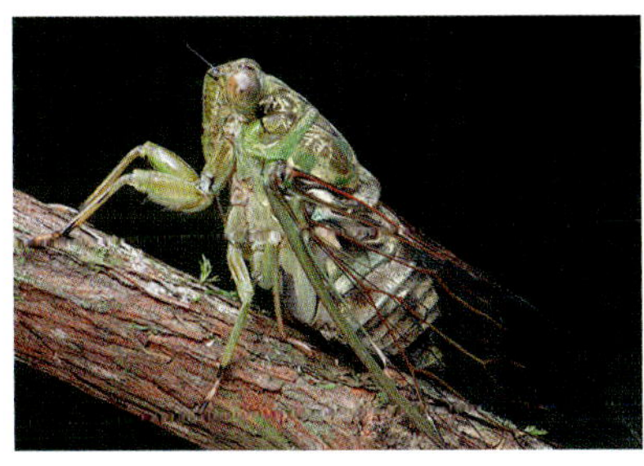

PAGE 68 ☙ Brass-button Moth: 9-exposure focus stack.

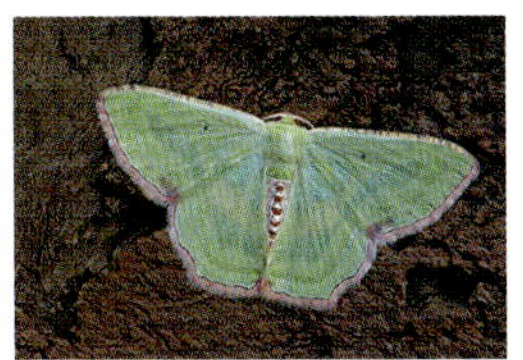

PAGE 69 ☙ Weevil: a single exposure.

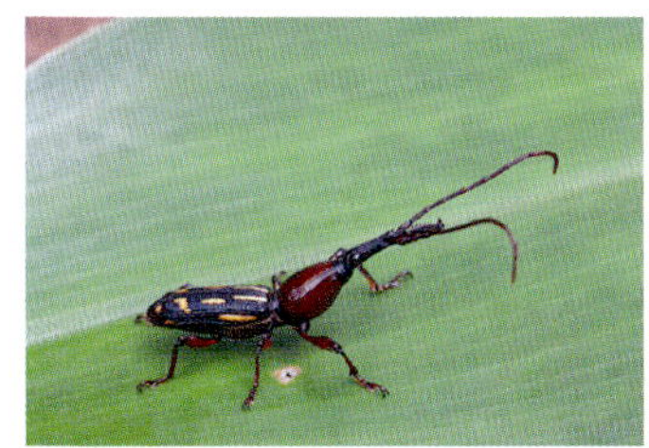

PAGES 90–91 ☙ Striped Marsh Frog: 25-exposure focus stack.

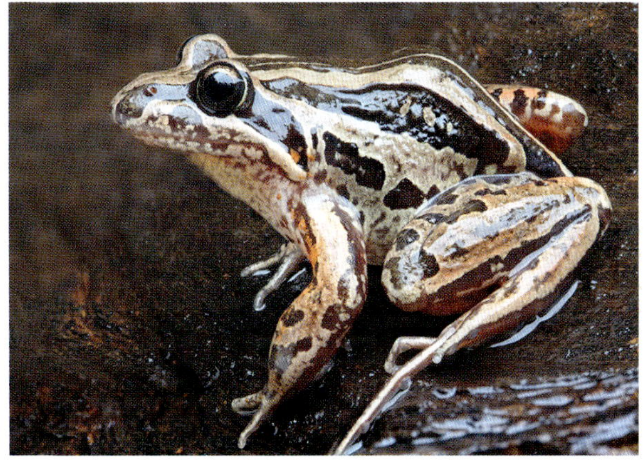

PAGE 99 ☙ Peacock Jewel butterfly: 6-exposure focus stack.

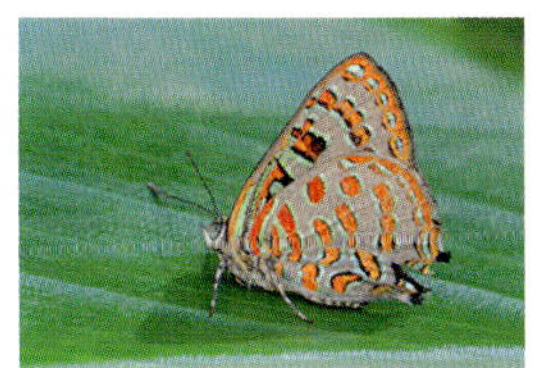

Index

Photographs are listed in bold

Birds

Papuan Frogmouth **95**, 97
Podargus papuensis **95**, 97
Podargus strigoides 17, 27, **28–9**
Rainbow Lorikeet 62, **64–5**
Tawny Frogmouth 17, 27, **28–9**
Trichoglossus haematodus 62, **64–5**

Frogs

Green-eyed Tree Frog **89**, 91
Limnodynastes peronii **90**, 91, **111**
Litoria infrafrenata **88**, 91
Litoria serrata **89**, 91
Litoria xanthomera 105, **107**
Mixophyes schevilli **96**, 97
Northern Barred Frog **96**, 97
Orange-eyed Tree Frog 105, **107**
Striped Marsh Frog **90**, 91, **111**
White-lipped Tree Frog **88**, 91

Insects

BEETLES 69, 103
- *Anoplognathus aeneus* 103, **103**
- *Batocera frenchii* **6**, 7
- Brown Stag Beetle 32, **32**
- *Cacodacnus planicollis* **42–3**, 45
- *Castiarina sagittaria* **16**, 17
- chafer beetles **60–1**, 62, **111**
- *Ectochemus decimmaculatus* 69, **69**, **111**
- Fig Borer **6**, 7
- jewel beetles **16**, 17, **24–5**, 27, **37**, 39, **110**
- longicorn beetles **42–3**, 45, **102**, 103
- *Metaxymorpha hauseri* **37**, 39, **110**
- Mueller's Stag Beetle 72, **73**
- *Mycterophallus duboulayi* **60–1**, 62, **111**
- *Phalacrognathus muelleri* 72, **73**
- *Prosopocoilus torrensis* 32, **32**
- Rainforest Christmas Beetle 103, **103**
- Red and Purple Jewel Beetle **37**, 39, **110**
- *Rosenbergia megalocephala* **102**, 103
- stag beetles 32, **32**, 72, **73**
- *Stigmodera roei* **24–5**, 27
- weevils 69, **69**, **111**

BUTTERFLIES
- *Cethosia cydippe* **100–1**, 103
- Common Jezebel 4, **5**
- Cruiser 97, **98**
- *Delias nigrina* 4, **5**
- *Hypochrysops pythias* 97, **99**, **111**
- Orchard Butterfly **44**, 45
- *Papilio aegeus* **44**, 45
- Peacock Jewel 97, **99**, **111**
- *Polyura sempronius* 17, **36**, 39
- Red Lacewing **100–1**, 103
- Tailed Emperor 17, **36**, 39
- *Vindula arsinoe* 97, **98**

CICADAS
- Bunyip 62, **63**, **111**
- *Cyclochila virens* 91, **92–3**
- Double Drummer 79, **79**
- *Macrotristria sylvara* 32, **34–5**
- Northern Cherrynose Cicada 32, **34–5**
- Northern Greengrocer 91, **92–3**
- *Tamasa* sp. 62, **63**, **111**
- *Thopha saccata* 79, **79**

KATYDIDS and CRICKETS
- *Acauloplacella hasenpuschae* **66**, 69
- Brown-faced Katydid **74**, 77
- Bush Katydid **84**, 85
- *Caedicia webberi* **84**, 85
- *Emeraldagraecia munggarifrons* **31**, 32, **110**
- *Ephippitytha kuranda* **74**, 77
- Leaf-mimicking Katydid **66**, 69
- Lichen-mimicking katydid 7, **7**, 17
- *Lichenagraecia cataphracta* 7, **7**, 17
- *Mooracra* sp. **82–3**, 85
- *Penalva flavocalceatus* 39, **40**
- *Phricta spinosa* **70**, 72
- Pink-faced Emerald **31**, 32, **110**
- Raspy Cricket **82–3**, 85
- Spiny Katydid **70**, 72
- White-kneed Cricket 39, **40**

MOTHS
- *Aglaopus gemmulosa* **52**, 53
- *Ambulyx dohertyi* **104**, 105
- Brass-button Moth **68**, 69, **111**
- Broken-stick Moth **51**, 53, **110**
- *Cleora* genus **55**, 57
- *Coscinocera hercules* 4, **10**, 11
- *Daphnis protrudens* **67**, 69
- *Eudocima fullonia* 45, **48–9**
  - caterpillar 45, **47**
- Fruit-piercing Moth 45, **48–9**
  - caterpillar 45, **47**
- Grey and Orange Hypsidia 79, **80–1**
- hawkmoths **67**, 69, **104**, 105
- Hercules Moth 4, **10**, 11
- *Hypsidia erythropsalis* **1**, 4
- *Hypsidia robinsoni* 79, **80–1**
- *Margarosticha australis* **10**, 11
- Mercury Moth 53, **53**
- *Metallochlora lineata* **68**, 69, **111**
- *Opodiphthera fervida* **50**, 53
  - caterpillar 45, **46**
- *Problepsis apollinaria* 53, **53**
- Proud Moth 32, **33**, **110**
- Redspot Hypsidia **1**, 4

OTHER INSECTS
- *Agrionoptera longitudinalis* **75**, 77
- ants 21, **22–3**, 27, **27**
- Blue Damselfly 105, **105**
- Cuckoo Wasp 11, **12**, **110**
- *Diphlebia euphaeoides* 105, **105**
- Giant Burrowing Cockroach **78**, 79
- Giant Shield Bug 7, **8–9**, **110**
- Harlequin Bug **2**, 4
- *Hierodula majuscula* **38**, 39
- *Macropanesthia rhinoceros* **78**, 79
- *Oncomeris flavicornis* 7, **8–9**, **110**
- plant lice **30**, 32
- *Stilbum cyanurum* 11, **12**, **110**
- Striped Swamp Dragonfly **75**, 77
- *Tectocoris diophthalmus* **2**, 4

Plants

Australian Turmeric 105, **106**
Banksia praemorsa 27, **27**
Black Palm **30**, 32
Coastal Blackbutt **18–19**, 21
Curcuma australasica 105, **106**
Cut-leaf Banksia 27, **27**
Drosera stolonifera **26**, 27
Eucalyptus macrocarpa 21, **22–3**
Eucalyptus todtiana **18–19**, 21
Lambswool **16**, 17
Leafy Sundew **26**, 27
Mottlecah 21, **22–3**
Normanbya normanbyi **30**, 32
Powderpuff Satinash **84**, 85
Syzygium wilsonii **84**, 85
Verticordia eriocephala **16**, 17
wildflowers **20**, 21

Possums

Cercartetus caudatus 14, **15**
Dactylopsila trivirgata **94**, 97
Long-tailed Pygmy Possum 14, **15**
Striped Possum **94**, 97

Reptiles

Boyd's Rainforest Dragon **56**, 57
Carpet Python 85, **86–7**
Concinnia tigrina 57, **57**
Hypsilurus boydii **56**, 57
Leaf-tailed Gecko 39, **41**
Morelia spilota 85, **86–7**
Pilbara Barking Gecko 17, **76**, 77
Pine-cone Lizard 17, 57, **58–9**
Pseudechis porphyriacus **54**, 57
Red-bellied Black Snake **54**, 57
Saltuarius cornutus 39, **41**
Shingleback Lizard 17, 57, **58–9**
Tiger Skink 57, **57**
Trachydosaurus rugosus 17, 57, **58–9**
Underwoodisaurus seorsus 17, **76**, 77

Spiders and other arachnids

Arcys sp. 62, **62**
huntsman spider **71**, 72
jumping spider 105, **106**
mites **6**, 7
Triangle Spider 62, **62**

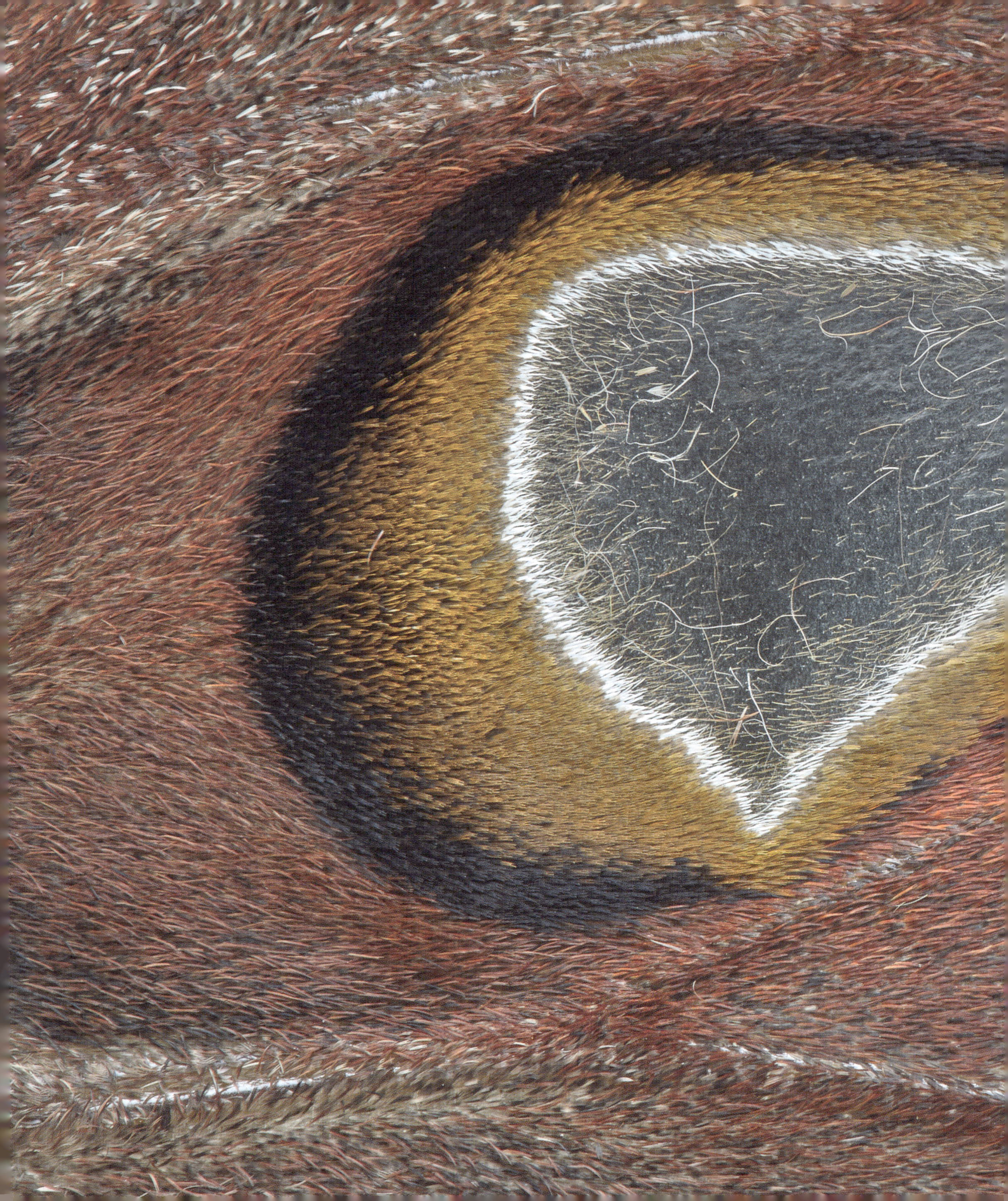